Playing Catch with My Mother

Playing Catch
with
My Mother

■ ▮ ■

COMING TO MANHOOD

WHEN ALL THE RULES

HAVE CHANGED

■ ▮ ■

Greg Lichtenberg

Bantam Books
NEW YORK   TORONTO   LONDON   SYDNEY   AUCKLAND

PLAYING CATCH WITH MY MOTHER
A Bantam Book / April 1999

A portion of "Scrimmage" originally
appeared in *The New York Times Magazine.*

Library of Congress Cataloging-in-Publication Data
Lichtenberg, Greg.
Playing catch with my mother: coming to manhood
when all the rules have changed / Greg Lichtenberg.
p.   cm.
ISBN 0-553-09982-5
1. Sex role—United States.   2. Gender identity—United States.
3. Men—United States.   4. Family—United States.
5. Family violence—United States.   6. Work and family—United States.
I. Title.
HQ1075.5.U6L53   1999
305.3—dc21   98-42355
CIP

Published simultaneously in the United States and Canada

Bantam Books are published by Bantam Books, a division of Random House, Inc.
Its trademark, consisting of the words "Bantam Books" and the portrayal of a
rooster, is Registered in U.S. Patent and Trademark Office and in other countries.
Marca Registrada. Bantam Books, 1540 Broadway, New York, New York 10036.

PRINTED IN THE UNITED STATES OF AMERICA

BVG   10   9   8   7   6   5   4   3   2   1

for Mer

and

for Amanda

Contents

Playing Catch with My Mother

Prologue:
New Year's Eve

■ ▮ ■

I F THIS IS obsession—obsession, one could say, right
down to the words, *boy, man, girl, woman*—then I've had
it since I could speak. I've breathed it, no more conscious of
it than of the bite of pollution in the New York City air. I went
about my business like any other boy until someone brought it
to my attention, as when my tall father bent down the branch
of a young maple on our street in Greenwich Village, to show
me the brown-edged holes in the green leaves. Invisible acid in
the air had burned holes just big enough to peer through.
When I looked, I saw my long-haired father, my cobblestone
street, my upthrust city darkly framed as by a pinhole camera.

On the first New Year's Eve I remember, when my parents
brought my toddler sister and me to celebrate with family
friends, I was not thinking that the air between men and
women burned with angry confusion. I knew that my struggling parents had been fighting more, and more publicly, than
before, but their fights were beyond me, facts of nature, forest
fires. On the way to Princeton, I remember thinking of my

1

good luck—we'd gotten to ride not just the subway but two real trains, the impressively long Trenton local and now, from the junction, the little "dinky," with its deep-voiced conductor and its door excitingly open to the air.

When I tired of the train, I thought about the toy airplane in our overnight bag. I'd made it in my kindergarten's first-ever turn in wood shop, with a scrap of two-by-two for a body, and for wings a flat narrow board the shop teacher held while I painstakingly hammered. The wheels were wooden buttons that really spun, and across the wings and to each side of the nose, where model planes showed military insignia, I'd inked the numbers of the coming year with indelible purple Magic Marker: 1972!

We got to our friends' house as the evening sky deepened. The trees beyond their living room windows had turned black. Peter's mother lit candles by the stereo, on the side tables, and in the dining room. Firelight flickered off glass tabletops and chrome tubing and bright black leather. The whole downstairs filled with a fireplace glow, cozy and unreal.

Soon the dads, long-haired and bearded, were sitting on the couch, talking in important-sounding dad sentences, and the moms were standing in the kitchen, chopping salad vegetables on wooden boards. The kitchen had doorways but no doors, so what the moms said could be heard in the living room even over the music: sharp laughter, criticisms long pent up.

My friend Peter and I went upstairs to his room, to push toy cars and trucks and to play-fly my New Year's plane. The comforter on his bed was good to sit on, but bumpy for Matchbox vehicles and wooden wheels. In time, Peter's sister came to the door, and a familiar dispute began. Peter argued from strict principle—older brothers with older brothers, younger sisters with younger sisters—and his sister countered with a plea for reason and flexibility: Amanda downstairs, just two, was too young for games. Peter relented. The three of us were playing together when I felt the tremor of my parents' argument on the stairs.

My father's step was heavy, his voice distorted; it was hard to recognize him. My mother's voice made a flat, distancing drone, a sound that said *not you, not what you say, never, nothing, no.* This was a bad one. I felt I should step into the hallway and show myself, to remind them where we were, that this was supposed to be a holiday.

Peter was driving a dump truck up the side of his bed, and his sister was asking how it kept from crashing when the mountain was so steep; to them, adult voices on the stairs were nothing to notice. I wished then that I didn't have this ear always listening for out-of-tune conversations.

My father's voice rose and my mother's followed. She yelled his name, and something thumped dully down the stairs. Peter and Amy looked up. My father's fast steps pounded toward us, shaking the floor, then veered into Amy's room, one wall away. We heard a crack, and rapid distant tinkling—wind chimes in a gale. Then came a sound I'd never heard before, like the ripping of heavy fabric, but deeper. We heard my father cross the hall again, then the slam of a door and the snap of the bathroom lock.

In the silence, I pulled open Peter's door, and all three of us edged out into the hall. At first we saw no one, only the stairway railing and the shelf of books built into the wall. The air was strangely cold. Downstairs, I could hear my sister crying and Peter's father asking my mother if she was all right.

We leaned into the room where the strange noises had come from, saw the holes my father had punched in the glass window and the wall. Until then I hadn't thought of the wall of a house as something a man's fist could break. Night air, cold and oily, snaked past the shards of the broken windowpane.

Peter's mother ran up the stairs to shepherd us into the safety of her office, a room with midnight blue walls where we weren't usually allowed. In that grown-up place there was nothing to do but listen. We heard her knock on the locked bathroom door and speak soothingly to my father, as though to a child who had been ill and now would be put to bed. He unlocked the door and went downstairs.

No one seemed to know what had happened or what to do

about it. In time I think we were led to the dinner table for spaghetti. I don't remember if we ate. My mother lay stretched out on the couch, wincing at the pain in her ribs. My father sat apart, staring out the darkened windows. Peter's mother spoke to him again.

"I'd like you to leave," she said.

Peter's father stood up and moved beside his wife, his jaw set hard beneath the thick red-brown of his beard. My father had barely spoken since he'd come downstairs.

"I want you out of my house," she said. She spoke in a controlled, formal voice put on for the occasion. I didn't recognize her in it, as I hadn't recognized my father in his screaming.

My mother lay wounded on the couch while my father—suddenly, now, my not-kind, not-brave, not-right father—collected his things in a brown paper shopping bag. Everyone was quiet, waiting for him to leave.

With just quick kisses on the head for my sister and me, and an awful jerky nod to my mother, he followed Peter's father out the door. I watched from the window seat, kneeling by little panes closing up with frost as he walked past the porch light into the darkness. A slow draft crept up from around my knees, and I tilted my head so my breath on the glass wouldn't fog my view of him. I could see him in the passenger seat with his paper bag on his lap, staring at nothing.

As the car's red taillights dwindled down the driveway, my sister ran stiff-legged to my mother on the couch. She clung tight and burrowed her head into my mother's uninjured side. Peter's mother joined them, and over my shoulder I watched hungrily, imagining how good Amanda must feel in that gathering of reassurance and warmth. My mother held out an arm to me, offering a hug and a sad smile. I wanted to run to her, to be comforted and to let her know I was with her, but I hesitated. Peter and Amy had been sent upstairs; I was the only boy in the room now.

I stood alone, learning to feel like a traitor. It was as though something dug into me then, setting barbs, never meaning to let me go. Knotted to those barbs were ropes, one tied to my mother's outstretched hand, one pulling from the fender of my father's retreating car. It's hard for me to say how long I waited by that window. Perhaps it was fifteen years.

THE NEXT DAY in our little apartment, my mother talked to me on the brown corduroy couch. I sat with my back against a cushion, my legs sticking straight out in front, wishing I'd distracted my parents before the fight got so bad. I kept my eyes on the floor, away from the bare wooden beams of their empty loft bed rising up near the ceiling.

My mother told me that my father would not be coming back unless he learned to control himself and to treat us right. She would call a locksmith to change the locks, she explained, and then we would be safe. On this unthinkable day, she knew what had to be done. I felt gratitude, so much gratitude it knocked the wind out of me.

She told me that sometimes when parents have fights, kids think it's their fault. I stared up at her, amazed at what she knew—just hearing her say so made me feel a little better. I pulled my legs in close where I could hug them, and I looked at her, the sincerity in her dark brown eyes, the upbeat gestures she made when she gave explanations.

She said that in the past, when my father had screamed and hit, she'd thought it was her fault. She'd thought she made him angry by being a bad wife. But now, thanks to her women's group, she understood that he had a problem. His screaming and hitting and smashing were wrong, she said. It was very important that she realize, and I realize, and even baby Amanda realize that he had this problem. It was his problem. His alone.

When she glanced down to see if I understood, I studied the blue valleys on the denim-patched tops of my knees. I knew she was waiting for me to say something, but I sat silent, lost. In my silence, she repeated her idea slowly and carefully, as if it was hard to understand. It was not. Nearly every day in school, kids pushed other kids. They punched and wrestled and screamed and smacked until a teacher stopped them. Mostly, those kids were boys. Boys broke things that didn't even belong to them. Boys gave scratches and bloody noses. Boys made other kids cry. I'd done these things myself sometimes. Everyone knew it was bad.

My mother didn't try to explain to her five-year-old all she had learned in her women's group, but I got the message. My father had a problem. His problem was being a boy.

A House Explodes

■ ▌ ■

W HEN WE BROUGHT my mother home from the hospital in 1969, the only change we expected was the new baby in her arms. I was three and a half, new to almost everything, yet barely less aware than my parents of what was to come. I rode with my father in the taxi, dazzled by the rush and sparkle of the Manhattan evening, the bright November air pulsing with lights.

Back in Greenwich Village, my father helped my tired, smiling mother out of the cab. We herded her into our high-rise apartment building, eager as sheepdogs, as though afraid she'd forgotten the way. In the living room, with the chill still on our cheeks, my mother again presented my new sister, unwrapping Amanda from a fringed blanket the colors of cream and caramel. The baby had a dimply moon face, and shiny eyes that wandered everywhere. Her miniature fingers and toes had tiny fingernails, delicate as insect shells, bright as seeds. I was amazed at the baby's feather-soft hair, at the strength of her grip, at the silken wrinkles on her knuckles. She knew so many things already: to blink, to burble, to gaze, to cry, to hold on.

My mother had made the baby at the hospital, as I understood it, while my father held her hand. Now finally my mother was returned to us, holding the baby up for me to touch, looking sleepy but proud, moving gingerly.

Back in my bright yellow room, too excited to put on my pajamas, I looked over my Magic Markers and my drawing paper, my fingerpaints and Play-Doh. Just as I went to nursery school to make pictures and fingerpaintings and clay sculptures, my mother had gone to the hospital to make a baby—all the tiny, complicated parts. She was better at making things than I'd realized. I'd certainly never seen my father make anything like a baby.

The next afternoon, I sat with my mother in the sun-brightened kitchen, drinking chocolate Ovaltine from a blue enamel mug. She wore a bathrobe, and held baby Amanda in her arms. Her brown hair, usually so even and straight, lay jumbled. Her voice was raggedy, her movements slow, but her fatigue seemed a pleasure, like staying in bed for the smoothness of the sheets. She smiled her enormous new smile.

Before Amanda was born, when my mother was home with me, she'd often said she was tired, but there was no pleasure in her voice then. Her eyes emptied, and her touch turned rubbery cold. Sometimes I put my small hand on her cheek, and asked if she was sad. She stuck a close-mouthed smile on her face like a disguise; the giveaway was her tight, pale lips. She sighed, and it seemed she had disappeared. In her hands then, if she touched me at all, I was only a plate she soaped. My little desk and chair made a dish rack, my bed a cupboard. She might accept a stuffed animal or a drawing from me, but she'd forgotten those things were fun. As the afternoon wore on, my hands held themselves, one thumb worrying the other palm. I was not Gigantor, not Spider-Man. My cleverness was a distracting glint on the ground, a bit of foil. I was no use to her.

I would wait for my father to come home, hoping for jokes and stories to cheer us up. Many nights, his work didn't let him come home until I was asleep. Besides fleeting kisses, smooth and after-shave sharp in the mornings, smoky and rough-faced at night, I got nothing of him. Other nights he brought home only frightening silences and explosions of sharp words. From my bedroom I heard smacking sounds, and in the spaces between his screams my mother pleading with him to stop.

My mother's disappearances were a mystery to me, like my father's explosions, which her vanishing sometimes followed. But I could not yet make that connection. She was the one who began to make herself a story. At the white Formica tabletop in the sunlit kitchen, she told me about the doctors, male doctors, bad men, who had held her back when she was a girl. They had told her that because her heart was so big, a third again the size of the normal human heart, she must live within strict limits. The doctors weren't even sure her big heart made her sick, but still she was forbidden to dive, to play hard, to think of herself as anything but fragile and weak. Maybe, she said, the doctors thought that was okay for a girl.

Pregnant with me in Italy, she wanted to have natural childbirth, but the doctors there, men again, put her to sleep and barred my father from the room. With Amanda, though, she insisted. She took lessons to help her stay awake and undrugged through the birth. Through the whole pregnancy, she told me, she felt fit as a fiddle. Giving birth, she was strong as an ox.

My mother told a rousing story. I particularly liked the part about the ox. As I listened to my mother, I raged inwardly at the doctors who had stolen so much of her freedom. This was a story my mother made to share with me, and hearing it, I felt I was meeting her as I'd just met Amanda, for the first time. I thrilled as she thwarted the bad men. I felt proud to have a mother strong as an ox.

MY FATHER SEEMED as happy as my mother about the new baby. Now when he came home in his three-piece suit, his

9

pleasure warmed the apartment. He lifted me high in the air, and the green plants and brown furniture and the paintings went kaleidoscope. He hugged me to him, and I breathed wool and smoke and winter wind, and underneath a hint of something deeper, a zoo smell. Horse? Bear? I was never certain.

He kissed us all, hugged us all, then he rushed to the record player. His job, I knew, was to help sell movies, mostly movies he wouldn't watch again if you paid him. What he loved was rock and roll. He stood over the record player and me, thinking out loud about what to put on first, wondering what would be what he called ear candy. He threw his suit jacket over the couch arm, unbuttoned his vest, yanked loose his shirttails and his tie, pulled off his shoes. Then he sat down on the rug with me, riffling through record albums until my mother called us to dinner.

When he sat, I saw the swell of his belly on his skinny frame, as though like my mother he could hold someone else inside him. Sometimes she teased him about his baby—she called it Pauncho Villa. Even sitting down, my father was taller than I was standing. He tickled, he wrestled, he hugged, he asked me what I thought of the music he played—he was how I imagined a big brother would be, if big brothers came big as giraffes. I liked to study his hair: black hair that swirled down his forehead to his eyebrows, long furry sideburns, a mustache that stretched beyond the corners of his mouth. Set in the middle of it all were the tiny circles of his eyeglasses. I'd found a face like his on an album cover: John Lennon in the front row on *Sgt. Pepper's Lonely Hearts Club Band*. When he called me "lad," I was a lad from Liverpool, too.

I had mastered the hi-fi controls before I was three, but I still liked to watch my father start a record. He poured the black disk from its paper sleeve to his wide, waiting hand, then settled it to wobble on the spindle. I liked the small knock as he cocked the start control, and the surprising fall as the record slid like a fireman down the tiny pole. The tonearm jerked up stiffly, its angled head shell earnest-looking, then it swung sideways, dragging the stylus across the black hairs of the dust-cleaner. The sound from the speakers was like a man clearing his throat. Finally the tonearm settled the stylus on the wide, shiny edge of the twirling disc. I loved this jerky precision, this magic, furniture coming to life. I followed it with such single-minded interest that sometimes the start of the record took me by surprise.

I leaned against the woolly face of the speaker. Through my back and neck came Bob Dylan, Jefferson Airplane, Janis Joplin—songs of love and revolution, thrumming in my ribs. My father described for me the light shows he watched at the Fillmore East, the bands he discovered at Max's Kansas City. His name for the songs we listened to was "New Culture music." He wrote about this music, and showed me the skinny newspapers with funny names where his reviews and other pieces were printed—*The East Village Other*, *Cheetah*. Once he'd put me in an article he wrote, telling how we'd gone to the beach on Cape Cod. We'd heard bombers taking target practice offshore, so the men in the planes could kill better in Vietnam. He wrote how he'd had to explain to me that the sound we heard wasn't thunder.

Other nights, when he came home, he put on finger-picked blues guitar. I didn't know the names of all the musicians, but I knew their sounds, the plunking strings, the honest voices. My father could play some of these songs on his own steel-string guitar:

> *"Cocaine's for horses,*
> *not for men."*
> *They say it'll kill you*
> *but they don't say when.*

Cocaine was a shot they gave racehorses to make them run faster, my father said, but some people tried it, too, even though it wasn't allowed. The singer was doing something forbidden, and I liked him for it. At nursery school there was a teacher who didn't want us to say "hey." She said you could say "hello" or "hi," but if you said "hey," she'd respond, "Hay is for horses." Then she'd pretend she didn't know you were there. But my father said "hey," and he said the teacher was a square and a heavy. Sometimes at school I sang under my breath:

> " 'Hey' is for horses,
> not for men."
> They say it'll kill you
> but they don't say when.

The songs pulsed in my small body and whispered over my skin. With music playing and my father smiling, I was not afraid. It seemed I sat on a good rug in a good house, with a good song inside me.

MY FATHER SURPRISED us one evening with an old record I didn't know. The unfamiliar backbeat and bluesy wail made him gyrate his hips and flop his mop of hair. My mother came out of the kitchen with the baby, and he held out his hand, coaxing her to dance. I thought she wouldn't, thought the music was *too rambunctious*, like me sometimes, but she put Amanda down beside me and gave him her hand. Maybe he'd felt the change in her, too, how she was here these days, with us.

As the breathless music thumped, my enormous parents walked the living room, my mother tall in my eyes but my father a giant—the top of her head barely reached the bottom of his chin. Then, as though it was common and unremarkable, they began to move together. My mother twirled, beaming, her hair fanning out around her head. From where I sat on the rug below, her hair made a disc, shiny and dark. My father's arm slanted down to her like the tonearm of the stereo—some magic let her twirl yet stay connected to him.

The dance seemed fantastic, as extravagant as my father's claim that the tip of the tonearm was a diamond. The diamond somehow lifted the song out of the grooves and sent it coursing along hair-thin wires to the speakers. I could not have explained (though I often asked) how music could live in a black plastic plate, or how it could slide through wires. Yet I felt I was wired, too. I sensed my parents' vibrations and amplified them, until my heart thumped like the woofer in a stereo speaker.

MY FAVORITE BOOK that year was *Fireman Small*. A little girl and her cat are trapped in a burning building. Fireman Small calls up to the girl to climb out her window and stand on the ledge. Black smoke billows from nearby windows. Sirens fill the air. The girl stands with her kitty in her arms, looking down at the street below, very frightened. The little fireman tells the girl to hold still. He promises to save her.

Even though I might have heard the same story at the same time the day before, every time my mother read it, I felt fear. Every time the helpless girl stepped out on the ledge, I clenched my hands. Every time the fireman rescued her, I cheered.

After the story, my mother might talk about raising a daughter. What stories would she read my sister? Would any books let a girl be a rescuer, or would all the girls be told to hold still and wait?

My mother's questions were new to me. They were even new to her. I wasn't sure why she asked them. I did understand, though, about wanting to be the fireman. I had always wanted to be the fireman. And when my mother brought it up, I agreed it would be wrong to make Amanda always the girl on the ledge. It didn't seem right; for one thing, I had always pictured the girl as my mother.

AFTER MY MOTHER made a baby, she kept on making things. One day, when she brought me back from nursery school, she told me she had made a poem. She had written it out on a long yellow pad while Amanda slept. I had never heard of her making a poem, and I couldn't read it, but there it was, pages and pages of patient work on the yellow loom of her legal pad, blue cursive woven into the horizontal lines. Her voice as she described her work was low, and though I didn't understand much of what she said, I liked the sound of it. It sounded like another story, like setting off on an adventure.

She did not tell me then, would not tell me for twenty years, that when she married my father she had given up her writing, her graduate school fellowship, and all outside work, as her own mother had given up her beloved career in theater when she had married. She did not yet tell stories about years of predawn writing hidden from my father, and stubborn sleeplessness, and trips to doctors for mystery ailments with no clear physical cause.

She did not share her fear that in response to what she had just done, making this poem, my father might strike her, demand a divorce on the spot—nor did she say she had resolved to leave him and raise her children alone, if it came to that.

But that afternoon, as she would tell me later, she telephoned my father at work. From this safe distance, she told him she was writing poetry again, and that she wasn't going to stop. Then she held her breath and waited for the onslaught.

My father surprised her. He didn't rage and give orders, didn't forbid her to write. He said he could understand that she was unhappy in her housewife life. He was unhappy in his corporate one. Now that President Nixon had asked the big record and movie companies to stop advertising in the anti-war, underground press, one small paper after another was going bankrupt, and my father felt like a collaborator. They had a three-bedroom apartment, a Thunderbird, a maid, a son in a famous nursery school, more money than they knew what to do with—and they were both unhappy. Maybe, he said, they had the wrong things. Maybe, he told her, they had the wrong life.

THE DAY THE house exploded was a drizzly March afternoon soon after my parents began to plan our new life. The phone rang, and I heard in my mother's voice that it was my father. I ran to the living room to ask if he would be home soon. My mother shook her head no. She talked to him, and I looked up out the window. The cloudy sky was turning black.

"Wait a sec," my mother said into the phone. "Something's going on. Everything is completely misty."

I pulled myself up onto the cold windowsill. Gray dust and billowing black smoke were filling up the sky. We heard sirens, police cars and ambulances and fire trucks.

It seemed that an ugly, early night had fallen, and perhaps because I saw it come when my father called my mother, I grew afraid that he would get caught in the fire or that he'd made the fire. I worked myself into a panic, watching the sky and rubbing my hands and pulling away from my mother, whose reassurances only seemed to confirm that she didn't see the danger.

Until the Weather Underground's bombs went off, destroying the townhouse down the street from us, I'd showed little interest in the outside world, the one beyond my home and school and grandmothers. But in the weeks after, when my father took me for a walk, I led him to the place where the house had exploded. First we saw the charred and steaming ruin, crumpled like a man in defeat. We saw the wrecking crew that knocked the building down and carted the rubble away, to prevent a safety hazard, my father said, and to hide a political symbol. Then the building was gone, though the burn marks still streaked up the neighboring walls. In the spring, the cleared lot filled with weeds.

On all of these visits, I asked my father the same questions. He told me that the house blew up because of the war. He said the Weathermen were right to want to stop the war, but that they were doing it the wrong way. He reminded me how I'd ridden on his shoulders as we marched to the United Nations, making the peace sign and smiling. I couldn't understand most of what he said about the war, but I did know the Dylan song that gave the Weathermen their name: "You don't need a weatherman to know which way the wind blows."

Slowly, as I kept asking, he came to give me what I wanted, simple answers to specific questions.

The house was gone because of an explosion.

The explosion came from a bomb.

The bomb was built by protesters.

The protesters made mistakes.

What would happen now? Now someone would have to clean up all the mess and build a new house.

These answers quieted me. We could go on to Washington Square Park, or to the playground by Grandmother Jane's apartment building. But on the next walk, I'd want to stop again where the house burned down. I'd stand at the ragged hole and ask my questions, as though the explosion was new that day.

Our New Life

■ ▌ ■

I FIRST NOTICED THE stares when our plane stopped in Prague. We passengers were invited to stretch our legs in the terminal, but only as a supervised group. It took my parents too long to wake me and Amanda, to pick up our toys and pull on our sweaters. When we got down the aisle to the door of the plane, the police had already led the other passengers away.

My father asked a stewardess in a pillbox hat if we could stand out on the rolling stairs to get some air. She smiled and opened the door for us. Below the heavy gray sky squatted the low airline terminal. The roof was full of people waiting and watching. The Czechs must have seen my father with his new, full beard, his now shoulder-length hair roped in with a beaded headband, his turtleneck, and his bib-front overalls. They must have seen my mother in her fuzzy sweater, bell-bottoms, and tennis shoes, with a wavy-haired little boy at her side and an infant in her arms.

The people on the roof started waving to us and flashing

peace signs. I knew how to make the peace sign, too. As we waved, they pressed forward to the guardrail. Some men started to yell. "Hello, America!" they cried. "America! Hello!"

The stewardess stuck her head out the plane door, visibly frightened. The police had radioed the captain, she said. Would we come back inside, please? Right now, please?

On the Italian island of Panarea, as my sunburn-red father walked by in his bikini, the peasant women gardening in their long black dresses called out to the Madonna and made the sign of the cross. At a villa owned by movie-business friends, the sounds of the servants whispering about us was as constant and unnerving as the buzzing of a wasp nest. In London, I saw a little boy slapped across the head, and this time I was the one who stared, feeling sorry for him, until I realized he'd been hit for staring at us.

Only rarely were words exchanged—my father would call a stranger a motherfucker or a fascist—but just by standing in his hippie threads, he picked a fight with the world. Did they have a problem? Did they think something was wrong?

He told me he dug shaking up the bourgeois types, that the straight world needed people like us to loosen up their heads. That may have been true, but I wished that the starers would talk to us. The look in their eyes said they knew what we were, and sometimes I pretended that even if they didn't want us around, they might know where we belonged. My parents hadn't found our new life in any of the countries we'd visited, and I could feel disappointment hardening in them.

It was a relief to come to California. In San Francisco, hippies with cars stopped to offer us rides, so we didn't have to pay for the bus. They had stories to share, advice to give, grass to sell my father, and sometimes a potato sack or cardboard box full of puppies for Amanda and me to play with. My parents told me that new communities were starting up in hills to the north; one would be right for us. My father had a friend from Harvard who was building his own house himself, on his own land. We would visit him and see a new life in action.

We stayed at first with Granny Fran, my father's mother,

who wore wide, floppy hats, and greeted me with jelly beans in her purse and the news that her cats had brought a live snake into the house. She'd saved it in a wine jug for me to play with. She had a temper like my father's, sudden and frightening, but when it passed she was again all winks and treats and pleasure in her family.

One day Granny Fran came driving up her hill in a car her neighbor was looking to sell. My father and I went running to see it.

"It's a '55 Chevy," he said. "A Bel Air!"

He circled the pink-and-white car, leaning down to look in the windows. He stroked a fin with his hand.

"It's a good car?" I asked. "Is it fast?"

"Is it a *good car*. . . ." he repeated. "Well, it's not the fastest, or as cool as a coupe convertible. . . . But a '55 Bel Air!"

He pointed out the big numbers on the speedometer—sixty! eighty! one hundred!—and the high unsloping windshield. The headlights were round like cartoon eyes, and the front fender curved up at the ends, like the beginning of a smile. My father made a voice for it.

"Hullo," said the car. "I'm your car. I'll be taking you to your new life."

In the Chevy's big trunk my parents loaded coolers for picnic food, bottles of Martinelli apple juice, boxes of Pampers. They drove us up Route 101, winding north along the coast. My parents said we'd know the place we needed when we saw it. We'd come over a rise and see a pleasant valley, with a little house nestled by a river. We'd know our spot by the flowers blooming, the green grass growing, the rich land to clear for an organic garden. We were pioneers, they told me, with a Chevy Bel Air for a covered wagon. My mother would write her poetry and my father his rock criticism. When East Coast types came to visit, my father said, or even when they saw our address on an envelope, they would all die of envy.

Usually my father drove and my mother was navigator, with maps in her lap and a flashlight at her feet for when it got dark. I rode in back, beside Amanda in her safety seat. My mother traced with her finger how far on the map we'd come, and though I couldn't read the names, I liked to hear her say them—Ukiah, Longvale, Bell Springs. There was lots of time in the car to talk.

My mother said we were so lucky we were all on this trip together. Her parents, she said, went off to Cuba and Mexico and all over Europe, but they always left her and her brother at home. They'd come back with presents of matching "native" costumes. For the last photographs of the trip, they dressed the kids up like dolls.

It was true, my father said. Kids back then were treated like toys or pets. They were ordered around for no reason, told what to do and what they were going to feel about it. On the day my father left for college, his parents threw away his baseball card collection and his BB guns, because he was too old to care about childhood things.

My mother told how she'd only been allowed to call her mother one thing, "Mother." She said it felt back then like families weren't made up of people, only of roles, like acting in a play. That was why now it was *perfectly okay* for me to call my parents Margaret and Jimmy.

My father said his family had been stuck in roles, too. My grandfather had referred to him and his sister as "the children," even if they were sitting right next to him. "The children should have been in bed by now." "The children are making too much noise." He came home late and didn't want to talk; kids were the mother's department. My father said that for his whole life, he'd wanted to be different from his father.

I was amazed that the wife in that story was the same person as Granny Fran. My mother explained that Granny Fran had started a new life, too. She'd left Washington, D.C., where she could only ever be the doctor's widow, and come to California. With the design skills from her theater days before she got married, she had helped her architect think up her house: the bedroom that overlooked the living room like a theater box, and the long, curving staircase for dramatic entrances. Now she worked with people so hurt or sick they'd gone dumb. She taught them to talk again.

As we rode in the bumpy Chevy, and at night in our motel rooms, I asked my parents to tell and retell these stories, until I almost felt I'd lived them myself. They asked how I felt about staying in California, and what I thought of the country folk and the scraggly hippies we met. It was not that I had a vote— everyone knew I was too little for that—but that their decisions were going to matter to me, too, so they wanted my opinions. I loved being in on the conversation.

IN HUMBOLDT COUNTY, not far from my father's house-building friend, we rented a motel cabin to be our base while we explored. The cabin was in the middle of a redwood grove. Shafts of golden light slanted through the high trees, shimmering in the evergreens, dappling the ground. There was red in the brown tree trunks, and red in the brown dirt, like in storybooks; in New York City, dirt was gray. Here, the trees laid down pine-needle carpets, and the air had a taste, cool and sharp, with a good bite of pine oil and sea salt, and the tang of moist earth. The redwoods were too high to climb, and even the scrub oaks had too few handholds, but I found a playground of fallen jungle-gym trees and climbing rocks. After a rain shower, the huge trees steamed.

We hiked almost every day. My mother, once a passionate summer camper, taught me to follow the blazes of trails. With the red-and-white-striped beach bag swinging from her shoulder, she pointed out edible clover and grasses, and made me laugh by posing as a tree, her arm-limbs waving gently in the wind. Sometimes we hiked along the summer-low Eel River, walking on its bed of smooth, silvery pebbles.

I saw more of my father in one of those days than in a week of our old life. He was there to be coach and safety net during tree-climbing, and to help me keep an eye out for Bigfoot. When he was happy, picnicking was a game. He cracked hard-boiled eggs against his forehead, poured drinks from high above the target cups, and made telephone calls on bananas. If he called you, and you answered, he was very sorry but he couldn't hear you. He had a banana in his ear. He liked to roughhouse and goof around. Kneeling, he was a horse, his long hair a mane. Rearing up, he was a monster to play-fight. When he took me by the arms and twirled me through the air, he was a carnival ride.

When he turned quiet and sad, there were always the trees. We would stop for a break or a meal, and as soon as Amanda was off his back and on the picnic blanket, he was up a scrub oak, lost in thought. I don't remember his temper exploding in California. He told me he was always okay up a tree.

My father cut salami for sandwiches, poured our juice, helped my mother clean up when the meal was finished. I'd never seen him do these food things before. He also changed Amanda's diapers. With me for an audience, he held the soiled diaper at arm's length with one hand, clothespinning his nose with the other.

"Pee-yew!" he'd yodel to my mother. "You have got one smelly daughter!"

As I laughed, he hammed it up even more, staggering as though overcome by the smell. When the diaper was finally wrapped and thrown away, he waved his hands toward his face, gasping fresh air.

"Is that so," my mother answered, playing at hiding her amusement. "So all of a sudden she's only *my* daughter, is that it?"

In the afternoons, when Amanda and I had nap or quiet time, he and my mother sat writing, side by side at the same table. This was another thing I'd never seen before. They were keeping a trip journal together, not a diary of what happened every day, but notes on the life they were finding, and what they thought about it. My mother was making poems, and my father was writing profiles of the people and trends in rock music, one a month for *Cue* magazine. It was a straight magazine, as he liked to explain, but he was using it for guerilla warfare, doing the work of the underground press behind enemy lines, spreading the New Culture.

The cabin was quiet when they wrote. You could hear their pens whispering across paper, and the blue jays squabbling outside.

MY FATHER'S FRIEND Allen had been renowned at Harvard for sleeping sixteen hours a day, my father said, but when our Chevy bumped to the end of the rutted dirt road, he was awake and pushing a wheelbarrow. He was laying the foundation for a house, pouring soupy gray concrete into a pit lined with wooden boards. My father followed him as he worked, listening attentively, asking questions. When the foundation was finished, they went off together, talking about carpentry and plumbing and electrical wiring.

It seemed as though every hippie man in California was working with his hands. They filled the air with the sounds of sawing and drilling, with clanking and banging. Sawdust frosted their long hair and beards; wood stain browned their old blue jeans and their newly muscular hands. They made an extraordinary mess, and when they stopped for a drink they guzzled and slurped and moaned. I could feel their satisfaction.

Allen's wife, Susan, was dark-haired and serious. She'd had a baby just a few days before, and she was carrying her as she led my mother and Amanda and me to their home. Their real house wasn't built yet, of course. For now, they slept in the goat barn. It was a weathered gray building with white doors that didn't match. A refrigerator stood on the small porch, with gleaming steel garbage cans chained shut against raccoons and bears. Around it on the parched grass lay stacks of lumber wrapped in plastic, a gas can, a bathtub, a sawhorse and a toy plastic duck. Off by the chicken coop I saw a child's upended go-cart, homemade from a wooden crate-top and four red wheels. I was amazed. Even in the woods, I had to put my toys away.

Inside the goat barn, Susan was showing my mother her wood-burning stove. The barn had a funny smell, foodlike but not Susan's cooking. She dished up stringy mixtures, greenish or earth-toned. As she served, she instructed my mother in the preparation of vegetables I'd never heard of: Swiss chard and rutabaga and kale.

"That's cool," my mother said, all politeness and good behavior. "I didn't *know* that!" Susan went on a long time. "Well!" my mother said. "It certainly sounds like a process!"

With the people all living in the goat barn, I asked, where were the goats? I was only making a joke, trying to get the talk away from cooking and babies, but when I asked, Susan pointed me out back. The she-goat was black, with pendulous pink udders and a thick rope leash around her neck. She gave off the smell I had noticed, a smell I imagined a dog might bring home if it spent a day rolling in cheese. Her knobby skeleton was covered by thin fur, and her yellow eyes glittered in her boxy head. I reached out to pet her flank and she turned to look at my hand. Her glance was not curious but shrewd, as though judging if I was edible.

After lunch, we all walked down to the swimming hole, the moms carrying the infants. It was a small pond, cauldron-shaped, warm and green at the surface, cold and black below. My mother stayed dry with the babies. I got my hands on a black watersnake undulating through the algae, but when it showed its white fangs I let it go. I splashed toward my father and Allen, who stood naked, thigh-high in the water, too far out for me.

Beyond them, up the mountain above us, a dark haze was rising. I called to the men to look. Coming in, we'd heard the reports of forest fires on the car radio. Allen said the wind had shifted, that the blaze was blowing our way again.

I asked what would happen if the fire came. Allen said we would wet down the top of the goat barn and go inside for protection.

"Water puts out fire, Gregory," he added.

"I know that," I said, but the men had turned away.

"What about the goat?" I called. "Would the goat stay in the barn with us?"

"Why would you want to live with a goat?" my father joked, dismissing me.

I slogged through the thick, resistant water back toward my mother, who was sitting on a towel with the babies, looking down at the ground.

"There's not enough water," I said.

She didn't answer. In her brown eyes there were only circles and flickers. No one was home.

"There's not enough water for the fire," I said, "but Allen says we have to stay in the goat barn."

"What fire?" my mother asked.

I pointed. She stood up. For a long time she gazed at the darkening sky.

"We're not staying with any goats," she said.

In the car on the way back to our cabin, Amanda was wracked with fits of tears, and my mother had to hold her for most of the ride. My father tuned in weather reports on the buzzing car radio. In time we heard that the wind had changed direction. The fire blew away from our friends, toward someone else.

"Are we going to find our new house tomorrow?" I asked.

"I don't know," my mother said. "We might. That's part of the adventure, not knowing."

We'd been over this many times before, and this round of the chorus lacked feeling.

"Is tomorrow going to be a long car day?" I asked.

"I'm afraid it might be a little long," my mother said.

"It will? You know for sure?"

My mother nodded, shaking the curtain of her thick brown hair.

"But if you know, then it's not an adventure!" I said.

My father laughed, one sharp bark, but the laughter didn't catch and spread around the car. We were silent again, except

PLAYING CATCH WITH MY MOTHER

for Amanda grumping to herself, and the silence was worse than before.

I COULD HAVE started crying, right then or at my sister's next outburst. I could have made myself slow, obscure, frustrating. I knew how to talk back, to scream, to go stiff as a board, to quit playing the oh-so-grown-up little boy right when my parents were counting on me. I could embarrass them in front of waitresses and shop owners, spoil their hikes with major fussing, yank them panicky out of fitful motel sleep. I knew, too, that they relied on me to keep an eye on my sister. In the backseat with her, I saw first when she needed attention or a change. And just by ignoring her, by failing to notice the gift of a pebble or a curious touch, I could play on her feelings until the car was an echo chamber for her screams.

But I took no revenge. I didn't want to go back to the days of sad absence before my sister was born, didn't want to be the reason we gave up. I sat in the backseat and I asked my questions, and when my parents turned quiet I sang songs and made up stories in my head. At the end of a long day of driving, I reminded my parents if we'd forgotten to eat dinner, or that I needed a cot or some other place to sleep. At the general store, I carried my own shopping basket, steering around the hippies who fell asleep standing in the aisles. They were tired, I knew, from their acid trips. I stepped quietly past them, and filled my basket with pretend groceries.

MY PARENTS DISCOVERED a wooden house for sale up a graded, unpaved road, more or less as they'd imagined. The owners were eager to sell, though they worried my father didn't have time to chop all the wood we'd need to heat the house through the winter. My parents said this was the place for us, but still put off the purchase. They visited the local nursery school; they researched fitting the house with oil heat. They had Granny Fran up to see the place. They even made some friends in the area. Sandy was a squinty-eyed man who wrote about rock music. His wife, Jeanie, wore long homemade dresses and kept an organic garden. They had a son, too young for me, but by then even the idea of a playmate was exciting.

Amanda's first birthday was in November, and my parents gave her a set of wooden nesting bowls and spoons. She would sit outside on a blanket or on the kitchen floor, and lift the smaller bowls out of the larger ones. Then she would stack them together again, placing each unsteadily in the next with her thick-fingered little hands. She looked intent, absorbed, happy. A girl working seriously at being a one-year-old.

"Look at Pand," my father would say. "Look at Pand." My mother would turn from her book or her cooking, and gaze down on her contented daughter.

But I was too old for nesting bowls. I missed my nursery school and the games I didn't have to invent and play by myself. I missed building skyscrapers, whole precarious downtowns out of wooden blocks, and then arguing with the other boys about who had knocked them down. I missed water play, where we raised tidal waves and sank plastic-bottle ships in big tubs. True, my mother could fill our cabin's sink with suds, and stand me on a chair with some toys, but it wasn't the same game alone, and she didn't like it. The sight of me smiling over the sink like a housewife in a dish soap ad made her grumbly.

"Water play again?" she'd ask. "This is fun? You *like* this?"

Some nights there were parties—to me, at least, they seemed parties, though perhaps they were only get-togethers at our new friends' house. Rugs and cushions lined the floor, and pungent smoke hung in the air. My parents told stories that made me out to be quite the hip kid: how at Buckingham Palace I'd wanted the guards to be allowed to show their feelings; how I'd asked if the Queen did her own grocery shopping. I stretched and the moms crowed over how limber I was. I giggled and the dads complimented my contact high. For the first half hour at these parties, I was like a star to them, and as they praised me and played with me, I felt safe from the unhappy childhood of my parents' stories.

But soon the conversation moved beyond me, to Nixon's fading prospects after the midterm elections, and to fine points of doctrine. Were this neighbor's clothes fully organic? Was that musician truly hip? I went crazy for something to do. Jeanie would lead me into her pantry, where she explained how to turn the grinder handle to grind a whole grain to flour. She had shown me before, and I hadn't forgotten, but each time I let her play teacher. I turned the handle slowly and evenly as she said, to keep a gold fall of corn flour piling steadily in the basin at my feet. It was not an especially good game, but the growing pile gave me a feeling of accomplishment.

One night the party went very late, and I was feeling sorry for myself. My parents had decided not to enroll me in the local nursery school after all. My mother had gone back to visit a second time, and heard a story about the school's Halloween party. Someone had put tabs of acid in the punch, and the whole nursery school had bad trips. "It was a freak show," she told me. "An absolute freak show."

That night I finished grinding the entire bin of cornmeal. I kept myself awake so I could show Jeanie. She came in on tiptoes.

"What did you go and grind all that for?" she cried, when she saw what I'd done. "How am I going to use that before it goes stale?"

NOW, EACH MORNING when I woke, I hurried to the window, to see what the day had brought. More and more, it brought rain trailing down the steamed windowpane. The ground outside, recently my friend, turned traitor. Branches and cobwebs wetted me down, and all our hikes were washed to muddy sameness. The air in the cabin grew thick and close, smoky from the wood fire and faintly sour with mildew. When I complained to my father, he said, "I guess that's why they call it the rainy season," joking—but then, like the rain, it soaked in.

With the rainy season, my memory dims. I don't recall our visits to the wooden house in the valley, or whether I managed any fun with Sandy and Jeanie's little boy. Apparently I didn't complain, didn't fight, didn't ask why we had to stay in California, but gradually my parents saw me fade. In photographs, as the autumn deepens, my face turns pale, and dark bags swell under my eyes. My cheeks pinch, my smile for the camera cracks mournfully. The pictures are like a time-lapse series of a plant withering; by December the sight and silence of me so frightened my parents that I became their clear reason to go home.

BACK IN GREENWICH Village, while my parents looked for an apartment we could still afford, we lived in a single-room-occupancy hotel. It was only a few blocks from our old apartment, but across one of the invisible lines that cleave neighborhoods in New York City. Sometimes in our hall in the mornings I saw the prostitutes coming in, gauntly pretty men in miniskirts, their mascara-smudged eyes big and vulnerable, their wigs crooked, holes in the nets of their stockings. My father said their beautiful, luminous skin was from the heroin. They stepped hesitantly under the bare hallway lightbulbs, embarrassed at the noise of their heels.

In the lobby, thick-necked pimps and wild-eyed junkies shouted at my mother and me, to make us jump. My mother gripped my hand until it hurt, and hurried past their laughter to our room, where she could bolt the door with a wooden beam and catch her breath. Safely inside, she told me that our neighbors were barely human. They were so lost and unlike us, she said, they were beyond understanding. She talked away her fright, and I welcomed the reassuring sound of her voice.

My father had been asked to write rock criticism for *The New York Times,* and his excitement was infectious. There was no desk in our room, but the bathroom, as he had showed me, offered good light and a door to close. He could unzip his portable typewriter on the toilet seat and cross his long legs beneath the bowl while he worked.

We had Christmas at the hotel, propping our small tree atop the radiator. I got a child's easel with a shelf for brushes and five plastic pots of paint. I loved the easel like a friend, working with it for hours by the window. Afterward, one of my parents loosened the wing nuts and folded the easel up, to make room to get to my cot.

Often at night we heard scratching at the lock and clumsy bumping against the door—a junkie digging for hawkable treasures in the room of the hippie family. My father went to the door to check the long wooden bolt, then he let himself go. He thundered in his angriest voice, promising to call the manager, the police, the vice squad, the mental hospital. His face scorched red, and black eyebrow hairs protruded like burned-out wires. His first reverberating words and the smack of his broad hand against the door usually startled the thief into retreat, but even the most determined or desperate shuffled down the hall before long. Still my father yelled on. He cursed and hurled insults, reminding the would-be thief how worthless and pathetic he was, how much a freak.

This tactic never failed, but I hated it more than anything I knew. My father's explosions knocked the wind out of me, and the hope. He became another person—one of the men in the lobby who barked at my mother and me, laughing as we bumped helplessly together, relishing the sight of people in animal panic.

I'd kept faith with my parents' new life through seven disappointing months of wandering, but when my father raged through the bolted door, I learned to doubt. Maybe, I let myself suspect, we were not the pioneers my parents described. Maybe we were only a new strain of freak, the latest lost newcomers to the freak show hotel.

I knew this thought led nowhere good, and I hardened my young will against it with all I had learned of courage and denial. Often the scratching at the lock came after bedtime, when my mother was behind the green plywood room divider, and my father typing in the echoey bathroom. I didn't call for my parents. By the glow of my night-light and the sliver of yellow beneath his door, I walked toward the scratching. In my best guess at an adult voice, insistent but not unkind, I called, "You have to go away now. You have to go away now." I listened for a grunt, or the smack and scatter of a dropped screwdriver, and footflaps in retreat. Then I walked through the semidarkness to my cot and tried to sleep.

Living on
Rock and Roll

■ ▮ ■

O N   A   B R I G H T   February afternoon, I walked with my
father to see our new home. We angled down narrow
streets almost as far west as we could go, until the dark asphalt
street changed to old cobblestone. Beyond the elevated highway at the end of the block, the sun flashed off the gray-green
Hudson River.

My father stopped in front of an old brick town house with a
brownstone stoop. He pointed out what would be our two little windows.

"We're very lucky," he said.

"We are?"

"Most people in cities live on streets that only have numbers. Ours has a name: Horatio."

I had no idea why this made us so lucky, but he delivered the
news with such fatherly, secret-confiding earnestness that I
took his word for it. This mysterious fact seemed a treasure to
store away until I was old enough to understand it—and not

what it must have been, a kind of prayer. That we had at last found what we needed.

The apartment was cramped, and the old wooden floors treacherous with splinters. Amanda and I shared a bunk bed in a narrow room, with the street lamp out our window for a night-light. My parents slept on a loft bed in what we called the living room; the loft had a desk and chair and file cabinet beneath it—the office. Downstairs was a nursery school. It had no space for me, but when the students were gone we could slide open the office window, climb out on the fire escape, and then down the iron staircase to the backyard playground. There were monkey bars and a jungle gym and tall, old maple trees; I couldn't believe my luck.

I went to a Montessori nursery school nearby, where kids asked why I'd shown up in the middle of the year. When I tried to answer, they went silent or changed the subject. But these weren't snubs. It was like when a grown-up said something about politics or business, and I waited a beat and announced that I had a Tonka truck with real doors that opened. At school, though, I was the one using grown-up words—California, counterculture, SRO hotel—but I learned to stop, and to talk instead about dinosaurs and baseball and who could tie a slip knot, the knowledge expected of upright, respectable five-year-olds.

Some days, my father brought me home from school. We climbed the steep, creaky staircase up to our landing. In the dim light, leaning in against the wooden rail, were square brown packages of record albums. They were sent by record companies for my father to write about. The packages seemed like presents, and he made them mine to open, springing the staples with a screwdriver so I could tear off the corrugated cardboard. As I pulled out the bright, shrink-wrapped album covers, he said the words of an old deejay: "Is it a hit (bong!) or a miss (thud . . .)?"

Possible winners joined one pile, and children's albums and covers I really liked joined a smaller pile for me. The biggest pile was to sell at Max's. On Saturdays, my father took down the laundry cart from its hooks in the hallway, and piled in the shrink-wrapped rejects and the albums he'd heard but decided not to keep. As he pulled the heavy cart, it thumped down the stairs from step to step like a kid jumping.

Max's was dusty from thousands of albums, and smoky from Max's cigars. He stood on a raised platform by the old cash register, overlooking his customers and his treasures. Between cigars, he hawked phlegm in his throat.

My father unloaded the albums onto the worn wooden counter by the register. Max bit his cigar between his teeth and went to work. He stood a handspan of records on their edges and flipped through them. In his broad hands the albums flew with the speed of a deck of cards. When I could catch his eye, I grinned, but he only grunted.

Max paid a dollar for sealed, unmarked albums, fifty cents for open ones and ones stamped or hole-punched as demonstration copies. He counted out cash into my father's open palm, and we took the money to do our Saturday errands. This was my favorite part. We walked around the Village, my father letting me drive the empty shopping cart and ask him endless questions. I was very big on dinosaurs, so one day he made me a version of evolution, going from the tiny invisible creatures that lived in the ancient goo on up to my favorite dinosaur, triceratops, and eventually to us, walking the shopping cart up Bleecker Street, waiting to cross Seventh Avenue. He told me about the Big Bang, how the universe started in a giant explosion that was still going on, though we couldn't feel it. I came back to these stories again and again, until the walks and the stories got mixed together, and the Big Bang became an eruption of suns and meteors and comets flying, with cabs and motorcycles and laundry carts weaving through the exploding heavens.

My father also told me about the city and how it was changing. He said this was a special time, that eyes were opening up, people learning to think for themselves. Even when he went uptown now nobody did a number on him for wearing long hair and blue jeans. He didn't think of his writing as guerilla warfare anymore, as fighting behind enemy lines, because he didn't think there *was* an enemy. People were only establishment, he said, because they didn't know what else they could be, and because they were afraid to change. But the New Culture was giving them new tools, songs and pictures and ideas. The real gas for him, he said, was to use the *Times*, the establishment's own paper, to help people loosen up their heads, so they could get aware and concerned and active.

Our last errand was always grocery shopping at D'Agostino. We followed the list my mother had made up, the meals planned out in advance. I knew my father didn't really like it—there was too much following of instructions, too much waiting on line. But his mood was good anyway. We were living on rock and roll.

EVERY OTHER NIGHT, by agreement with my mother, my father did the dishes. Before he started, he plugged in his headphones and put a record on the hi-fi. Then he strung the black curlicue headphone cord up over the brown couch and into the closet that had been made our kitchen. He stood over the little steel sink, wearing yellow rubber gloves almost to his elbows, so he could run the water hot. My mother said the heat killed germs.

As the music played in his ears, he washed and sang, danced and dried. He shook his head and seesawed his shoulders to the beat. As he moved, the headphone cord jumped on the furniture. Our new cat, a gray, tiger-stripe tom, came to investigate.

Pepperwood was a smart animal, with quick green eyes. He stood below the waggling headphone cord, rose up briefly on his back legs, and caught it in his paws, fighting the electric snake to the floor. The cat's weight on the cord tugged my father's headphones, and the right earpiece slid down his neck. This was what Amanda and I were waiting for.

My father, lost in the music, pulled the headphones back in place, and the cord jumped off the floor again, taunting the cat anew. The cat leapt, my father yanked and soaped and rinsed. Amanda and I stared, giggling, and I covered both of our mouths so our laughter wouldn't give us away.

Years later my father told me he had been waiting, back then, for me to object. He imagined I would march in one day and cry, "This is all wrong! Why are you in the kitchen? Why isn't Mommy doing this?" Yet I never did. And he murmured no barbed jokes to me under his breath, cast no ironic looks, or few enough. He let these new ways seem unremarkable, natural. If I came to talk to him while he was finishing up, the clean dishes might answer for him, forks arguing with serving spoons, two pot lids speaking as a talking clam. When the dishes were done, he hung the yellow gloves over the sink rim to dry, and helped put Amanda to bed.

ON SUNDAYS WE brought our apple juice bottles to the volunteer recycling center on Washington Street. One day, as my parents walked away, I turned to watch a man delivering a huge garbage bag crammed with bottles.

"Wait a minute!" I yelled ahead. "He's going to smash them!"

The center volunteer, a curly-haired woman with a cigarette voice, asked, "Are you talking to your father?"

I nodded, turning back to the man with the bottles.

"I'm telling you," the volunteer said. "If I'd ever yelled 'wait a minute!' to *my* father. . . ." She whistled.

On the walk home, my mother said it meant the woman would have gotten hit. That calling "wait a minute" was disrespectful.

"But what if she needed him to wait a minute?" I asked. "*He* probably asked *her* to wait, sometimes."

My mother said, "I think he'd have expected her to say it in a way that reminded everyone who was the daddy."

"Why?" I asked. "Was he going to forget?"

They both laughed. It was pretty easy, I'd found, to get laughs in talks like this. But the questions still bothered me.

"Really," I asked, "why couldn't she tell her father to wait?" I looked at my mother, who looked at my father.

"Don't ask *me*," he said, hard and fast, face turning red above his beard. We turned onto our street, and except for Amanda, singing to herself from her place on my father's shoulders, we walked the rest of the way in silence.

MY FATHER COULD do the voices of all my favorite *Sesame Street* characters, talking back to me as Ernie, and giving silly home news reports as Kermit the Frog. He sat on the floor with Amanda and me to watch the show. My mother watched too, but sometimes she looked at the little television the way she looked at strangers' dogs, to make sure they didn't get too close to her kids.

Once, before the show came on, she started asking me questions. She asked me which characters were boys, and which girls.

"The main ones?" I asked. "Or counting all the little ones?" She said the main ones.

"That's easy!" I said. "They're all boys."

She gave me a strange look, so I went over them in my head to be sure: Cookie Monster, Bert and Ernie, Kermit the Frog, Grover, Oscar the Grouch, the Count, even Snuffleupagus.

"Except Big Bird," I added. I wasn't sure about Big Bird.

"So Sesame Street is a street for boys," she said.

"Where are the girls?" I asked.

"I'd like to know that, too," she said. She told me that some of her women's-movement friends were writing articles and letters, to ask *Sesame Street* to make more room for girls. I thought it sounded pretty bad, to be kept off Sesame Street.

My mother had more questions about my new favorite book, *What Do People Do All Day?* It was a big, yellow book, and so heavy I had to read it open on the floor. On a single page there might be ten different animal characters doing different people jobs. I loved it for all the little details you saw if you kept looking, like the businessman cat flying like a flag, holding on with one paw to the back of the Busytown bus.

But my mother saw something else. Out of all the people doing things all day, she asked, what did the boys do, and what did the girls do? Well, I said, there was Father Cat, the grocer. He carried a big bag of carrots for sale and a pencil behind his ear to add up prices. His wife, Mother, wore an apron and a bonnet. Then there was Father Bear, Chief Road Engineer. He wore a hard hat and, around his neck, a bag of salt for icy roads. His wife, Mother, wore an apron and a bonnet. Rabbit Stitches was a tailor, and his wife was different. She wore a purple housedress and held a baby. Her name was Mommy.

My mother pointed out that the animals who got to do my favorite jobs were all boy animals. The girl animals had jobs like secretary, nurse, and laundress. They didn't seem to have families, and under their pictures there was no name. To get a name and a family in Busytown, a girl had to go home and be a housewife.

The feeling grew in me that something was missing from my favorite books and shows, that there were characters who weren't allowed to be seen, songs I wasn't allowed to hear, whole hours of stolen *Sesame Street*. Someone had torn pages out of all my books. I had to be careful, somehow. I had to love them less.

ONE AFTERNOON, WHEN my father was out with Amanda, my mother had the idea to make our own books. She got out gray cardboard saved from the dry cleaner's, white typing paper, scissors, a stapler, and my plastic pack of Magic Markers, and put them all on the black trunk we called the coffee table.

We sat together on the rug, and I made up a story about a family of leopards having an adventure. She copied it down on her yellow legal pad, then read it back to me, asking questions and making changes. When it was done, she folded cardboard to make a book cover, and printed my title in black block letters. Then she wrote my story on the white paper, just one or two lines to a page.

I had a lot of work to do. I needed to illustrate the cover and all the pages, showing what happened in the story. While I drew the leopards, she kept writing on her legal pad, doing her own work. For a long time we lay on the rug in our stocking feet, heads close together in serious quiet. I heard her breathing, an easy sound, and sometimes on my arm I felt the warm breeze of her breath. At one point, I stopped drawing to show her the nubbly pattern the rug pressed in red on my elbow. She touched it with her fingers. When she went back to work, I watched. Her shirt had red and blue daisies on it, and the sleeves clung all the way to her wrists. On one sleeve, she had a piece of darker red rug fuzz, and seeing it I realized that usually only my father lay all the way down on the floor with me.

Through the open back windows, as I drew and colored, I heard trucks rumbling past, and distant car horns. From above, a circling seagull called. On our long trip in Europe, we had visited old cathedrals. Inside them the world seemed calm and vast and sure. It felt that way again, while we worked together.

I WAS IN the living room when I told my mother that I wanted to talk about making love. Even though she always said we could *talk about anything*, it was still harder to ask my question than I'd expected. She asked me to sit on the couch beside her. My father was in the kitchen a few feet away, swigging cola from a glass bottle.

"Let's see," she said.

My mother spoke slowly, as she did when she thought what she was saying was important.

"When the mommy and the daddy are feeling very lovey-dovey . . ."

"Mmmmm," my father said, emerging from the kitchen. "*That* sounds nice. I think I'd like to hear this, too. Is that all right?" he asked me.

I shrugged and tried not to smile. I was already feeling a little silly, and I didn't want my father to get me giggling. My mother was ready to have a talk.

"As I was saying, when the mommy and the daddy—"

"They're *already* a mommy and a daddy?" my father asked. "I thought that part came later."

My mother gave him a sassy look. She started again.

"When the husband and the wife—"

My father interrupted again.

"*Jimmy*," she said, cutting him off, but I could tell she wasn't actually mad.

"When the husband and the wife are feeling very lovey-dovey, they get in bed and take off all their clothes—"

"You can't take off your clothes until you get in bed?" my father asked. "That sounds difficult."

"They *take off their clothes*," my mother said in a rush, "and they *get in bed*, and they hug and they kiss until they both feel very warm and good, and the man puts his penis in the woman's vagina, and in the end his sperm goes inside her."

Little brown birds were chirping on the fire escape.

"I think you explained that very nicely," my father said.

"Did that make sense?" my mother asked me.

I said that it did. I slid forward on the couch until my feet found the floor.

"*I* have a few questions," my father said.

"Oh, *do* you," my mother said. "That doesn't surprise me one bit."

I had never noticed my parents acting quite like this. It made my skin flush, and a smile that didn't feel quite mine tugged at my lips. I had heard all I needed, for now.

. . .

BETWEEN THE RECORD store and the supermarket was Horatio Street Park, an asphalt softball field with a high, chain-link fence. On a cold, not-quite-rainy spring day, I interrupted our errands to run into the park.

"We don't have a ball, lad," my father called.

I stopped and thought about that.

"Want to race?" I asked.

This was a new thing at school, challenging other kids to races.

"You're going to race against me?" he asked.

"From here to second base!" I called.

He leaned the laundry cart against the fence, and hooked his umbrella over it. I called on your mark, get set, go, and then I ran, head down, arms pumping, my sneakers slapping asphalt. I meant to win. In the corner of my eye, at two o'clock, I saw my tall father with his loping stride. He passed me easily.

I pushed myself harder, but I fell farther behind.

"No fair!" I called. "You've got your speed shoes!"

This was his name for his sneakers, and I suspected that they really did have secret powers.

He turned to face me, running backward, smiling, his hair blowing toward me. I made up the distance between us and he turned to face forward again.

I ran on, and my father matched my stride, taking short, stuttering steps, pulling ahead of me when I flagged, keeping me running flat out until he just barely beat me to the finish. I stopped, gasping, mysteriously happy.

I raised my hand to slap him five, and he slapped me five back.

"You're fast!" I said, in the space between breaths.

"You're pretty fast yourself, lad."

"I'm getting faster," I said.

"I can see that."

I couldn't have felt better. It would be a long time before

I was as fast and strong as he, it would take practice, work, but it could feel like this, like a game. We had a real home, we had a backyard and a park. We had homemade books and New Culture records, and summer was on its way. We were making it.

Vows

■ | ■

THE FALL AFTER we returned from California, I started kindergarten. My teacher, Miss Gillies, seemed the soul of welcome. Her assistant, a red-haired man whose name I forget, held my small writing hand in his big freckled one and taught me to print my name. School is most of what I remember from those months. I was not watching my parents closely, not listening carefully.

I did notice, in a day-by-day way, that the game of opening records with my father was turning less fun. The sell pile for Max's was bigger every week. The Beatles had broken up, my father reminded me, Dylan wasn't trying, the Byrds had few good songs anymore, and the Stones had turned frightening. Record companies weren't looking to help an artist grow, he said. They just wanted fast money. Often now, impatient, he took the albums from my hands and sorted them himself. "Bullshit commercial rock," he called, tossing an album on the toppling sell pile. "Bullshit commercial rock, a no, a maybe, bullshit, a maybe, bullshit, bullshit, bullshit, bullshit."

• • •

YEARS LATER I would read his columns and his reviews, trying to understand, if I could, what went wrong. Things had looked so good. He'd interviewed Jerry Garcia, the Rolling Stones, Herbie Hancock, even John and Yoko who lived down the street from us. He'd written a hundred pages of a book on Bob Dylan. Crosby, Stills and Nash wanted him to come on tour with them. That September *The New York Times* even flew him to Los Angeles, to profile the Beach Boys. The band was preparing to bring their comeback tour to Carnegie Hall.

I try to imagine how he felt sitting on that plane. That day, he was no struggling long-hair, pulling a rattling laundry cart of freebies to sell. He was a music critic for the newspaper of record, on a transcontinental business flight to the new center of the music industry, Los Angeles. He had a hotel reservation; his expenses would be paid. He had a deferential stewardess to bring him cocktails. Did he recognize himself?

The Beach Boys, he wrote, *have led a musical double life. In their early years, with a string of hits and an international following, they were a monstrously successful straight rock group.* Before we had left to find a new life, my father had worked for Columbia Pictures in Europe and then in New York—was he thinking of his own international string of hits? He'd made more money, he said, than he knew what to do with. Could he imagine success that wasn't monstrous?

When he reached L.A., and spoke to the Capitol Records people, he must have felt his old promotional skills, his establishment ways, waking in him. There he was, deep in the West Coast star-maker machinery, doing his part to revive the sales of a supergroup that had moved sixty-five million units. Could he imagine himself succeeding at this? Or was the only possible successful man a man of the old school, tough, single-minded in his work, antiartistic, hostile to women, neglectful of children—the very things my father loathed?

Starting in 1965, he wrote, *the Beach Boys changed into one of the most complex, misunderstood forces in New Culture rock. That year Brian Wilson created a work of pure inspiration, their grandly original pop album* Pet Sounds. *It was for the times a complex, introspective studio master-piece, and even the Beatles were among the throng inspired and guided by it.*

In spite of a hit single, Capitol essentially refused to pro-mote this brilliant new music. Instead they initiated a hyped and insensitive series of surfing music rereleases. The band was exiled to a life of creative obscurity.

I imagine my father, exiled to his own creative obscurity in what had not yet even been named the Far West Village, wait-ing for the music that would justify his rebellious gambles and his faith, and reunite his divided life. But the Beach Boys' new album, *Surf's Up,* did not herald the resurgence of the New Culture.

In his profile of the band, my father chose to ignore the new album, and to describe instead Carl Wilson's experience as a conscientious objector to the war. In their interview, Carl had made an analogy between the band's debilitating interrup-tions and humiliations at the hands of its record company, and the treatment of conscientious objectors by the federal govern-ment. My father's profile suggested that the real story of *Surf's Up* was not the product being shipped, but the record the band had lost its chance to make.

My father's editor responded with a brief note. "The piece," he wrote, "doesn't quite work for our purposes." He did not offer to look at a rewrite. My father telephoned, full of rage; after their explosive conversation, he was not asked to write for the *Times* again.

For three days after his rejection, he refused our company, taking sudden, solitary walks or lying on the bed in rumpled clothes. He was nearly silent, ignoring my mother's attempts to console him. A few times he said out loud, "I'm a failure."

• • •

LATE ONE FALL afternoon, when we were roughhousing, my sister's foot caught my father between the legs, and he yelped. The sound made me laugh. He glared at me, and then what I hadn't seen in some time began again. He yelled and smacked his free hand against the bare floor beside Amanda. Furniture and framed pictures rattled; his spittle flecked her face. All three of us screamed. He yelled at my sister never to hit him *there*, but she kept bawling, terrified of his crimson face and his wrenched-open voice.

And then I understood: This was her first time. I held myself as still as I could, waiting as always for the storm to pass, but admiring my little sister's lungs, her outrage. When she screamed, I could hear that she had reason to, that what he did was wrong.

Afterward, he held Amanda to his chest and told her it was all right. Even he seemed surprised, as though someone else had upset these children, toppled this chair, bruised his hand, which he sat and rubbed. Later, choked up, I told him that he'd scared me.

"Come on, lad," he said, sounding hurt, as though I was being hard on him. "It wasn't anything to be afraid of. What's all this about? Come on, now."

My sister and I and even our mother followed his lead. Someone else must have terrified us. It could not have been our Jimmy. He was the charming one, the man of a thousand pleasures and amusements.

But when he was out, I heard my mother on the phone to her friends from her consciousness-raising group. All she could do, she said into the black receiver, was to be *cheerful and positive and bland*—then she laughed an unfunny laugh. She said over and over that she was *walking on eggshells*. I thought a lot that fall about eggshells. Once they cracked, you could break them with the touch of a finger.

• • •

WE WERE HAVING dinner, and it must have been getting close to winter, because the city sky was already brown and the streetlight already shining outside while we ate. My mother had a consciousness-raising meeting that night, but no one talked about it. She dished out everyone's servings as usual, measuring out the big firsts, the smaller seconds, the portions always the same.

We were finishing when she saw the time on her watch and jumped up from the table. She kissed us each quickly good-bye, and told Amanda and me she'd see us in the morning. While she was putting on her suede coat in the other room, my father called, "Are you sure you don't want me to come?"

She walked slowly back into view, mouth open as if about to answer. She stopped in the little hallway, one arm in her coat. She closed her mouth, opened it again.

He put his hands up, as though her look was a gun.

"Joke," he said. "*Joke.*"

She pulled on the other half of her coat and started her good-byes over again, kissing me and then Amanda, who giggled as if it were a game. Amanda closed her eyes and raised her head for more kisses, but my mother was already hurrying to throw the barrel lock, pull open the door, get out.

IT HAD ALWAYS been that when my father's voice rose, my mother's went weak. Sometimes she wept, and the sound coming through the door at night faded until it was only my father saying no, please don't cry—sometimes in a pained voice, sometimes in frustration: How could they have a discussion if all she did was cry?

But now his anger fed hers. When his voice lashed out, hers hardened, matching him grievance for grievance, his frustration against her disapproval. Her words ricocheted through the apartment, banging into my memory. He was doing it again—didn't he see? He'd done numbers on her all her life, fucked with her mind. He was a bully. The words were all the worse when I didn't know what they meant. He was haughty, he was superficial. He was intolerable. The sounds of these words seemed pure vengeance. Later, when I recognized one in a book, it flew at me like the back of a hand.

In the mornings after these fights, we didn't talk about the night before. I tried to think about other things. The holidays were coming, which meant presents, and then New Year's Eve, when we would stay with my friend Peter at his house in New Jersey. In wood shop, to welcome the new year, I was building an airplane, with real wheels that turned.

BACK IN OUR apartment after the disastrous New Year's Eve, and still without my father, my mother made phone calls. I listened from my room while I watched my two green-and-black turtles. They lay in their faceted glass bowl on the windowsill, nearly submerged in still water, facing apart— dead, both of them, for all I could see. I listened to the crisp whisk of my mother's finger in the telephone dial, the unwinding sound like a fishing line playing out. She had cut my father loose. What would she fish for now?

The buzzer sounded and a small man came to the door, wearing an old leather tool belt and smelling of cigars. He was even shorter than my mother. I watched from the couch, kneeling with my elbows on the armrest, as he unscrewed the lower metal plate on the door and changed the bottom lock. He didn't need the whole thing, just one bullet-shaped piece. I wanted to ask him about what he was doing, how a lock worked and whether they could really be picked, and what all his different tools did, but it felt wrong to have another man doing the fix-it work. I only spoke to him once, to tell him that my mother preferred that visitors not smoke in our home, thank you.

The locksmith demonstrated the new lock and key before he left, but after he was gone my mother opened the door and tried it again.

"Very smooth," she told me, pleased.

I didn't answer. One more time, she snapped the key smartly. Then she pocketed the key, closed the door, and joined me on the couch.

"Are you feeling a little blue?" she asked.

The couch fabric was wide-wale corduroy, and I rubbed my fingers along it, first the cool, velvety stripes, then the rough spaces in between. I nodded.

She told me I had reason to feel blue, that we'd all been through a lot. She said again that my father should never have hurt us or scared us. She kept talking about him, and I had some trouble following her, but I understood that he was wrong, like the bad men in her stories. He could not be helped, but we could protect ourselves. We could lock him out of the house. When he had been out by himself long enough, she seemed to say, lonely long enough—when we had hurt him enough—then he would control himself. We would teach him to be careful around us. He was a violent man, and the thing to do with violent men was to hold them at a distance, lonely, uncomfortable, and full of blame.

Often, then, I had feelings I could barely make into words. My only guide was a welling up of *yes* or *no*. As I listened to my mother, I felt, *no*. Don't let this be our story.

FOR SIX WEEKS, my mother and the new cylinder kept my father out of the house. I remember almost none of it. Apparently she felt euphoric at first, free to write, take a poetry class, and socialize whenever and with whom she pleased, all without provoking jealousy or competition. I don't recall. Later she found that she missed my father, and she discovered to her surprise and anger that a single mother was even more tied down than a married one, since it fell to her to make every meal, clean every mess, solve every problem. I assume that during those weeks she worked on her poems, and on her freelance reviews of children's books and the records of new women songwriters. She must have recovered from her broken ribs.

My father must have visited, taken me out for a hamburger or an ice cream cone, joked with me and half-apologized and tried to make me laugh. It seems as if only for sheer intensity of feeling, I ought to remember his visits. But I remember none of that.

For most of my short life, I had watched my parents as closely as I could, listened for their changes of mood, reached for whatever understanding I could grasp. Now I refused. Mostly what I remember is pressure in the top of my head, a feeling like getting a headache but not having it yet. The pressure lessened, I found, when my mouth fell slowly open. It eased a bit more if I let my eyes unfocus. Things in front of me—toys, food, my small, impotent hands—lost substance, divided. In my memory, at least, I sat quietly the six weeks my father was gone, head down, mouth open, eyes slightly crossed, awaiting my father's return to break the spell.

ON VALENTINE'S DAY, my father picked me up after school in the Big Yard. He walked me home and up the dark stairs, but when we got to the door, instead of knocking for my mother to let us in, he reached into his pocket. He took out his big key chain, and I cringed. I was afraid he had forgotten. But his keys turned both locks, and as he held the door for me, he winked. He'd met my mother for lunch, he said, and she'd asked him to come back. Inside the apartment, he twirled me through the air, saying that things would be better now.

He didn't stay that night, but he ate dinner with us, taking his usual place at the long table, and he helped put Amanda to bed. After he left, while my mother cleaned up the kitchen, I brought the blue stool to the doorway, so I could watch. Water whistled out of the faucet and steamed in the steel sink as she piled up dirty pots and pulled on her rubber gloves.

"I never thought I'd let him back," she said.

I didn't answer.

"He's convinced me he can reform. I made my conditions clear! And he accepted them. He's ready to do whatever it takes."

Her voice sounded as though she was giving directions to a stranger. It was the voice from the phone calls I overheard, a voice of all the answers. She started to scrub the broiler pan. Her arms looked thin disappearing into her wide rubber gloves, but when she put her back into the scrubbing, she looked fierce.

"He's never going to hit, or scare us," she said. Hair was coming loose from the barrette holding her ponytail, and she pushed it aside with her forearm. "He's going to be supportive of my writing, and wherever that goes. And do you know that he found a real job?"

Glumly I said I knew—from now on he'd be working for a little record company, which meant out of the house all day long.

My mother rinsed the broiler pan, and stood it on the drain board. Her news should have sounded like *welcome home*, but instead it sounded like *we'll see*. My father was on probation. She was talking about him as if he was a child, a child given rules and strictly judged on whether he followed them. But she didn't even treat us children that way.

IN THE EARLY dark of winter evenings, I learned the new sound of my father coming home. Instead of sneakers, he now wore leather shoes that gave a sharp report on the wooden stairs. Tired from a long workday and the rush-hour subway ride, he took them more slowly than before. I usually heard his approaching steps, but if I didn't, the cat did, and his light thump down to the floor alerted me. My father's key scratched in the lock, and my mother and toddling sister came to the door as well.

He kissed us, suit full of smoke and winter, and Pepperwood dragged purringly against his leg. I watched carefully as he and my mother embraced. They were both even thinner than before he went away, and ringy-eyed. Once he was home, they snuck quick kisses almost every time they passed. They fluttered around each other, easily startled, seeming short of breath, at once frightened and grateful, like people who have seen a car accident. In the cramped kitchen, the sound of one rummaging for a snack often drew the other, and they hugged or laughed—how hungry they were! On the couch, when they sat reading, they touched shoulders or at least knees. Weekend mornings, it was late before they climbed down the ladder from their loft bed.

Then they might make brunch, a celebration that carried us into the afternoon. While my sister and I hovered by the warm kitchen, my mother made pancakes, or my grandmother's recipe for cornmeal waffles, and my father fried the bacon and ran hot water on the frozen orange juice canister until the yellow ice fell into the Tupperware jug. He shook the jug so hard that when my mother poured the juice, it foamed.

We ate at the long table in our usual seats, boys facing boys and girls facing girls, with my mother at the kitchen end, so she could get up when someone needed something. She didn't get as excited about eating as the rest of us, but you could tell she was glad we felt good. She ate some of her pancakes or waffle quarters plain, to appreciate the recipe, while my father and I poured on syrup, or slathered on dark jam. I couldn't believe how much he ate. I tried to keep up, and at the end pulled up my shirt to show him my stomach, which he palmed approvingly.

"Look at that basketball!" he said. "That's quite a basketball."

In these second-honeymoon days, it felt again that I lived in the family my parents had promised. Often while they cooked, we listened to the Beatles' white album, and my father sang along with "Ob-La-Di, Ob-La-Da": the husband and wife who both wear makeup, the wedding ring that rings. Before bed, I had what we called "story," a book story followed by a one-to-one conversation, parent with child, about the book and wherever else it led us. Afterward, I lay on the top bunk in the purple-brown glow from the street, and listened to the musical murmur of my parents' voices until I fell asleep.

But in time, my parents began fighting again. I woke up to his voice rising, shouts, a crash, my mother yelling for my father to stop. It was over quickly, but the next night it was *her* voice that rose, asking how could he expect her to *trust* him, how could he think she could even be *comfortable* beside him?

That was only a flurry, he said, compared to last time. *Only a flurry.*

But she was not placated. He had to learn to control himself. She didn't feel safe, and until she did, she wouldn't make love with him anymore. (I was not quite six. How could I have understood this on my own? When I was in college, and it mattered to me most sharply, I asked her if I remembered it right, if perhaps I had made this fight up. She gave me an odd, pained, sympathizing look, as though seeing me in a hospital bed. She nodded yes, it was true. She didn't seem surprised that I had known.)

I was waiting for the big change to come, the last, worst fight or the happy reunion, my father sent away forever or welcomed home for good, one simple story to live by. But my father could be both banished from his marriage bed and asleep in it, our hero and our parolee.

MY MOTHER GOT a job as a children's book editor, and sometimes she was sent on special trips by herself to conventions. The first time, a lady from Jamaica came to cook and clean for us, and my father bought a *Playboy* magazine and left it on the wooden side table. (I knew *Playboy* was dirty. Matt Sampton's first-grader brother had shown us a picture of naked ladies touching boobs to make lesbians.) The next time my mother was away, the magazines made a small stack. I found them on a Saturday while my sister and I were wandering around the apartment, restless.

"Hey," I said. "The dirty magazines are back!"

Amanda came to look.

"Shovaniss!" she shrieked, the way girls yelled it at the playground. "You're a shovaniss!"

My father sat at the desk, staring at her.

"Chauvinist *pig!*" I yelled, remembering another of the words. Amanda and I began to oink and snort.

"Margaret is *gone!*" my father yelled, standing up. "I can read *whatever I want.*"

The boom of his voice knocked us silent. He grabbed the little pile of magazines and carried them away. After that, I never saw them again, and I knew not to mention them. Sometimes, though, I wondered whether he'd thrown them out or hidden them, and why.

MY MOTHER WAS home from her business trip, and my parents were reading at opposite ends of the couch when I announced that I needed to talk to them.

"Is something wrong?" my mother asked.

I said I wanted her to tell me what making love was.

My father barked a laugh. "Greg?" he said. "You know we've talked about that." His look asked, What are you up to?

"*It's all right,*" my mother said, too loud. She put on a smile. "Why don't you sit down, so we can have a nice conversation?"

I sat between them. My father looked at me sideways, as though I was being difficult. He put his hand on my shoulder and kept reading his music magazine.

"We're always happy to talk," my mother said.

My father turned a glossy page. I began to wish I hadn't started this.

"Well," she said. "Now, let's see. When the mommy and the daddy are both feeling very comfortable and lovey-dovey," she began, looking over my head at my father. There was a pause, and then, as she continued talking, he got up and took his magazine into the bathroom.

My mother's words came out more or less as they had before, but instead of reassuring me, they filled me with questions. "The man puts his penis in the woman's vagina"—it sounded familiar, like putting a dish in the oven, but it didn't sound fun this time. And what exactly was this "lovey-dovey"? These questions hadn't bothered me before.

"Is there something more you wanted to talk about?" my mother asked, putting her hand over mine.

"No, that's all," I said.

"We're always happy—"

"*No!*" I said. "That's all." I slipped out of her grasp and slid to the floor, maneuvered around the coffee table trunk and ran-walked to the doorway.

"It's really okay," I said from across the room.

Soon I began having a recurring dream. I dreamed I was asleep in my bed, and that I woke in the middle of the night. I zipped lightly down the bunk bed ladder rungs, walked past the dinner table and through the vestibule, and silently opened the door to the living room. High above me on their loft bed, my parents slept peacefully together. The dream shifted the angle of the bed, so I could see up over the wooden edge to their pillows. Their dark heads were close, nearly touching, reliable as a constellation. The cat appeared at the top of their ladder, silhouetted by the window. He ran down a couple of rungs, then thumped to the floor. I heard his paws clicking toward me, felt his soft fur brush my calf. He trilled warmly, a greeting from one night watchman to another.

At the far corner of the living room, I turned the doorknob and walked down the steps to the bathroom. I did my business standing over the bowl, then I effortlessly retraced my steps through the dark apartment; I knew my home by heart, and I moved through it with the assurance of an Indian brave. Finally, I dreamed I settled again into my warm bed, and slipped easily back to sleep.

I was startled out of the dream by the touch of urine going cold against my thighs. The first time, it must have been confusing, but soon the clammy sheets clung with a dreary familiarity. I fumbled down the ladder, bumped through the dining room and into my parents' room, where I stood ashamed on the floor beneath the loft bed and called their names. My mother's newly woken voice was a croak. I said it had happened again.

The first few times, they were surprised, tender—it could happen once in a while, they said, even to a big boy who went to school. I shouldn't worry. My mother went to rinse the soiled sheets in the bathtub, while my father made up my bed with fresh ones, first covering the wet spot on the mattress with a towel. He talked to me as though I'd stubbed my toe, speaking in soothing tones, sympathizing with my embarrassment. I went back to bed feeling rescued.

But as the dream came more often, my parents grew concerned. In the middle of the night and again in the morning, they asked what was wrong. It was a question I found difficult to answer. They asked if I liked my new school, whether I felt sick. From time to time my mother put her hand on my forehead, to check for fever.

"Cool as a cucumber," she said, sounding almost disappointed.

She brought me to the doctor. He had a waiting room full of toys, including a magnificent toy bus made of wood, big enough to straddle and ride. In the little white examining room with the smell-less smell, he let me check to see how much I'd grown. The answers to his questions were all "no." He examined me very quickly with his cold stethoscope and his cool hands, barely at all, and he told me to put on my clothes, and to meet him and my mother down the hall.

When I opened his office door, I saw them standing between his file cabinets and his broad desk, speaking in low tones.

"Are there tests you could do?" my mother asked. "Or should we see a specialist?"

I couldn't hear his reply.

"But we don't have that many sheets!" she said. She made the joke in the girlish, cajoling voice she saved for men in charge.

"Margaret, Margaret," the doctor said, his voice rising.

"What do you want me to say? The kid is pissing on your marriage."

That night, when I stumbled into the dark living room to wake my parents, they answered quickly in gruff voices, already awake. My mother said something fast and sharp, said it not to me but to my father. There was a long silence, and then he made the trip down the ladder. Pushing up the sleeves of his striped pajama top, he stripped my bed roughly, saying nothing. I followed him to the bathroom, where he rinsed the sheets in a rush and threw them down in the tub, the wet mess smacking the porcelain. Back at my bed, I hoped he would let me help a little in putting on the fresh sheets, but he worked too fast.

"Come on," he said. "Let's go."

His watching eyes were all impatience. I climbed the ladder and squeezed into the bed; he'd made it up too tight. His breathing was too hard for only having made a bed.

"You have to cut this out," he told me. He stood on the ladder, leaning over me.

"I know that."

"We aren't going to get up every night and clean this mess just because you can't find the bathroom."

"I can too find it."

"Then *cut it out*."

"I can't *help* it," I said. He of all people, I felt, should understand.

"You're going to have to help it," he said.

"But there are things you can't *help*," I said. "There are things you can't control—"

"*No!*" he yelled. Then he yelled it again, louder, and again, until it didn't even sound like a word. His mouth opened, his lips bared teeth. The collar of his pajamas rode the taut cords of his neck. Inches from me, as though leaning in for a goodnight kiss, he yelled one long, awful note. When he ran out of breath, he smacked the bed beside me, keeping up the barrage. I shut my eyes and braced myself. He'd smashed furniture, punched walls, shattered windows, hit my mother. He had no self-control, she said. She had been right all along: Now he would hit me.

His blows fell inches away, banging the bed against the wall in an awful rhythm. As he screamed and smacked the bed, my body dug into the mattress, a helpless thing, a creature under his control. From below, my sister joined his screaming. They sounded as though by screaming they escaped to somewhere better than this bed, tossing now like a small boat on high seas. I cried out, but though my throat burned I felt no release. I was still on the bed, still thinking. This surprised me—surprised me so much my eyes opened. My father's red face screamed, his mussed black hair shook wildly, his teeth gleamed yellow in the half-light. But his eyes watched me carefully. He wasn't going to hit me. Some part of him was measuring out the terror that would do the job. His anger was no act of God, no storm beyond mortal control. It was a bomb tossed through a window, a protester's terror, methodical. And his method worked: Under his roof, I never pissed the bed again.

In the morning, his voice was still ragged. He sat at the table over brunch, drinking tea with honey. When I passed my mother the butter, she rested her hand on my arm. She offered me extra scrambled eggs. Amanda seemed not quite awake— suddenly grumpy, wailing over nothing, then gone again. All day, I felt myself holding back, moving carefully, giving my father room. I kept my distance, didn't take his hand or invite him to see what game I was playing. This choreography of subtle snubs proved surprisingly easy to pick up, but it wasn't enough.

As the days passed, I evolved a protest. I took silent vows: in all my life to be no man like him. If he would rage, I would be calm. If he would yell, I would be cool understanding. I would learn all the frightening, reckless damage he did, and do none. I would show that he was wrong, wrong in his ways and wrong in his heart, too hot, too selfish, too much a coward to live what he promised. I would not be what he would make me, not his creature, not his thing, not his, not his, not his.

Don't Cry

■ ▌ ■

I CRIED MORE OFTEN than most of the second graders I knew, though not as often as some. It didn't feel like something I chose, but Chris, one of my teachers, disagreed. She wanted to teach me to quit.

Chris took crybabies out to the hall. On the tiled floor, she stood me at arm's length, her long, skinny fingers holding my shoulder as if to make sure I didn't come too close.

"Don't cry," she said—once, again, several times, in a flat, unchanging voice. "Don't cry." I had a rule with myself not to answer if I could help it. We stood stiffly together, listening to the sloppy noises I was trying not to make. She looked down at me with her olive green eyes.

"Stop now," she said. "There's no reason to cry." I was still shuddering with feeling, but the wrongness of her words got through. To her, I never had reason to cry. A few times I'd seen her speak softly to a distraught student, but these lucky few who were spared the humiliating trip to the hall were almost always girls.

After several trips outside with me, Chris tried a new tactic. "Big boys like you shouldn't need to cry," she said. "And I know a fine way to stop. Would you like to see?"

"I *have* stopped," I said. I had caught my breath by then. I turned away from her, toward the yellow classroom door.

"I can show you a special trick," she said. "Something so you won't need to cry anymore. Wouldn't you like that? No one would ever have to see you looking like such a wet, splotchy baby."

It wasn't the taunt about looking like a baby that got me. It was the promise about not even needing to cry. I wanted that terribly.

"How?"

Just asking set me off again. I dragged my arm against my running nose. But this time Chris didn't look disapproving. She stared at me with the pitted olives of her eyes, and crouched down close, her knees making lumps in her long gauzy skirt.

"All right then," she said. "First, we make our hands into tight fists." She wrapped her damp hands around mine, pressing down on my knuckles until my nails bit my palms. "Then we squeeze our eyes tight. . . ."

As she told me this, still gripping my fists, she shut her own eyes, tightening her face until she looked as if she were fighting tears herself. Through her pinched face she said, "We clench our fists, and we lock our arms, and then we count slowly down from ten."

Chris counted aloud for me. Grief wants your chin not up but tucked into your collarbone, your chest not out but hollow, a cave your knees can close. But now with Chris I fought grief, posting my arms away from my body like sentries. At the end of her count, she stood up and opened her eyes. She still held my fists in her hands.

"There," she said. "You see?"

Her trick worked. With my arms stiff and my fists ready for a fight, my eyes blinded, my mind given to this prayer of numbers, I could jam my feelings down my throat.

That weekend I told my mother about my new accomplishment, boasting a little, demonstrating my technique—as if it was the latest thing they were teaching in school and I was the first to master it.

"Are you sure that's what Chris told you to do?" she asked. She was on the couch, pulling staples out of press releases, so we could reuse the paper. I nodded.

She looked past me, toward the desk she shared with my father, where a band of late afternoon sunlight lay across the polished brown wood and the neatly stacked file folders.

"Well," she said. "That's ridiculous. I mean really, in this day and age, to even *tell* a child a thing like that . . ."

Relief flooded through me. The crying trick worked for a while, but afterward, as I now admitted to myself, my throat burned as if I'd been screaming, and my stomach felt like I'd gulped swimming pool water.

"It is *perfectly* okay to cry," my mother said.

"Like on the record?" I prompted. I was hoping she'd say more.

My mother looked puzzled. Then she said, "Yes! Just like on the record."

She slid the door on the stereo cabinet and got out *Free to Be . . . You and Me*, a kids' record album with a matching book. She'd heard about it at work, and brought it home for Amanda and me.

We listened to "It's All Right to Cry," and we looked at the matching pages of the book. My mother pointed out a picture of the singer, Rosie Grier, a big, broad, black man, a pro football player. It was understood somehow that a man couldn't get more manly than a big, black football player. This big man sang that crying was the way to let sadness out.

My mother nodded, and explained again that crying was "natural." You sweated to get rid of heat, went to the bathroom to pass waste, and cried to get rid of emotions. And you had to keep doing these things—the temperature went up and down, meals moved through your stomach, and feelings "changed and changed and changed," as they said on the record. It was all healthy and normal and natural, and although a lot of people made fun of these things, those people, my mother explained, were just being crude.

At the end of his song about tears, Mr. Grier the football player promised, "It's all right to cry, little boy." My mother smiled, and her smile asked, All better? She offered to listen to the song with me again, and when I shook my head, she lifted it off the spindle and slid it away in its sleeve. The matter was settled.

And yet. I wanted to believe her, and it certainly impressed me that Rosie Grier was on the side of crying. But I worried that what made him so impressive also made him useless to me. He was a football player—no one who valued his life would call him a sissy. But I was just a regular boy, and I couldn't shake the feeling that my tears were a disappointment, a failure. A voice in my head argued with Rosie Grier, saying that what my mother said made no difference. *She was a girl.*

Boys were different. We had to operate ourselves like remote-control cars, trying for speed and daring moves, with no thought of a crash. Control took strength. If you held pain inside you, mastering it with your will and your fists, then slowly the sadness in you hardened into strength. Hadn't I felt strong when I forced back my tears?

I didn't believe this, exactly. But for years I could only cry unashamed alone. Only alone could I let my elbows find the nooks of my waist, and my wrists cross protectively over my belly. My head bowed, my teeth clenched, my eyes squeezed closed. It was like squeezing into a cave, a cave the dusky red of my own eyelids. I was both the cave and the boy inside the cave, and at moments I could see what I hadn't seen before, shadowy feelings, silver flashes of thought. It was the most trustworthy place I knew. Only alone could I give in, and let my shaking body gather itself together.

Mixed Doubles

■ ▌ ■

THERE WAS THIS girl on the bus to day camp. There were many girls, of course, but this one, Ann, an eight-year-old like me, stayed in my mind. She rode on the small minivan that took us Chelsea-and-upper-Greenwich-Village kids to the meeting point for Manhattanites. She was also on the big yellow school bus that gathered us all up and brought us to the Staten Island ferry, and then to the Y camp in that greener borough. The ride on the big bus was much longer, and I would have liked to sit next to her, but on that bus the bench seats were divided boy-girl.

I sat with Danny. When we weren't singing along to "Miss Lucy Had a Steamboat" and other songs of filth and innuendo, we talked about yesterday's baseball scores or our chances of completing a collection of Lincoln head pennies. (Not including the rare 1914-D, of course, and certainly not the 1909-S VDB, of which—as we both could have told you—only half a million had ever been minted, and which was not even for sale at the numismatics and philately department at Gimbel's, and which therefore, we agreed, didn't count.)

At school, Danny was my best friend. He unrolled his Yodels to eat them—creme filling first, then cake, then the chocolate coating, which he peeled and set aside as the dessert of the dessert, as he called it. He was passionate about the Mets, and he collected strange facts he saved to tell me: When his parents took him to an est seminar for kids, he was taught that if you had to whizz but couldn't go—if, say, you were on the camp bus—you should imagine a river or a waterfall flowing, and this would make the waiting easier. We subjected this technique to detailed study, making use of ourselves and our friends to collect data.

Until I noticed Ann, I'd been a loyal friend to Danny. When his parents made him get dressed up and go to *The Nutcracker*, just because his little sister was in it for three seconds, I went with him. But now on the camp bus, my thoughts wandered. I scanned the aisle for Ann's shiny dark hair, which was usually done up somehow, in barrettes or a dancer's bun, occasionally in ribbons. Danny seemed to feel my attention go, and if he couldn't get it back by asking questions about the National League standings or the games we played at camp, he watched the traffic out the bus window and left me alone with my longing.

Sometimes Ann knelt on the green bench seat to face the girls behind, back straight as a grown-up's, chin high, showing no fear of the grumpy-voiced bus driver with his mirror trained on us kids. It was so like her, I thought, to face the wrong way if she felt like it, and to roll her eyes heavenward when the driver scolded, as though she couldn't imagine how a man could be so plodding and predictable. Unlike most visibly unusual kids I knew, she didn't seem sad. Most girls dressed in jeans or shorts and T-shirts, but Ann came to day camp wearing dresses with ruffled skirts, tights, and black patent-leather sandals. In her fancy, old-fashioned clothes, she reminded me of something I couldn't place, and it was one of the pleasures of watching her that I would feel I almost knew what she reminded me of, that it was tantalizingly close.

One morning, I walked up to her in the camp parking lot. I had decided it was time to introduce myself. To my surprise, she seemed to recognize me.

"Oh," she said. "You again."

Before I could think of a comeback, she ran into the crowd of kids.

Long hours later, at the start of lunch, I raced down the hill from the soccer area to beat her to her cubby.

"Oh! You again!" I said, when she found me there. "What are *you* doing here?"

She looked at me with her mouth open, then she tossed back her head and laughed. That laugh made me feel like the cleverest boy in New York.

After that, when I watched her on the bus, she would wrinkle up her face, or stick out her tongue, and hide behind one of her girlfriends. When our groups passed on a path, walking with our counselors from one activity to another, we would have another chorus of "You again!"

"Him again."

"Oh, no! It's *that girl* again."

When Ann's group had swimming, my group had free play in the field beside the fenced-off pool, so we'd be ready when it was our turn to get changed. I could sometimes slip down to the pool fence and look for her.

It was still permitted for a second-grade boy to be friends with a girl. I'd made Play-Doh animals with Lesley Kaufman, nursed orphaned kittens from an eyedropper with sad-eyed Tena Cohen. I'd colored eggs with Theresa Ghent and her mother, but only once—when I came home with my Easter basket and my new understanding of the Resurrection story, my father got a rare inspiration to talk about our Jewish heritage. I considered all these girls my friends.

But I felt different around Ann. When I saw her, even if we didn't talk, my breath came faster. When she was gone, I'd think about when I could be near her again. I wanted to tell her how I was going to play for the Mets, how in my family we all called each other by our first names, how my parents were making a new life so we could all be happier than when they were kids. I wanted to tell her everything, but so far all we said was, "You again!"

Now as Ann screamed and laughed through free swim, the sound of her voice curled my fingers around the chain-link fence between us. I began to make up a song. It described a boy and a girl who always teased each other and played pranks, until one day everything changed. "It used to be a game," went the chorus, "but now it is a game of love."

AT HOME THAT night, the song still played in my head. I climbed up the bunk bed I shared with my sister, looked at the New York Pets arranged on my blanket, and climbed back down. My new garter snake was lying as usual on his rock in the glass bowl, flicking his forked tongue at nothing. I looked through my board games and toys. Nothing was interesting.

I pulled open the drawers of my little desk. Behind the shoe-box with my pencil collection, I found a small, black, three-ring binder and a package of lined paper still in its plastic wrap.

Amanda came to investigate. "What's that for?" she asked. "You don't have school."

I took the notebook and paper up to my bed with me, along with some masking tape and a purple marker to make a "keep off" sign. Something was happening, and I was going to write it down, the way my parents had in California.

Amanda was still watching me. I looked at her in her pig-tails, her fuzzy summer sweater and her floppy shorts, so very little. I turned my back to her and opened the notebook on my lap. On the lines of the small pages, in print, I began to write about Ann, though I wrote much less than what was in my head.

I wanted to bring her up to my bunk bed and get under the covers with her, where it was warm and dark and private, for a slumber party of just two. We could hold hands and rub noses—maybe she would want to touch tongues. We could tell each other secrets. I wanted Ann to know every possible thing about me, and I wanted to know every possible thing about her. I felt like the songs said:

> *I saw her standing there.*
> *Do you want to know a secret?*
> *I want to hold your hand.*

I sat in the droopy center of my top-bunk mattress, writing a few slow sentences in unerasable blue ink. Despite the purple "Gregory—Private—Keep Off" sticker I'd made, I worried that my secrets would be discovered. Yet at the same time, I almost wanted to be found out. As the last line of my first journal entry, I wrote, "Greg loves Ann Horowitz!!!" It was the jeer of the kids who would gather to taunt us if we were caught. At the moment I heard them in my head and wrote it on the page, I didn't care if they yelled, or sang embarrassing songs—"Greg and Ann sitting in a tree . . ." But before I went to sleep, I scratched out the line with a pencil.

MY COUNSELOR THAT summer was Todd, a man with skin so pale it was pink. He wore a white windbreaker to keep the sun off him. Through its translucent sleeves you could see the damp black curls of his arm hair.

Todd lacked not just the complexion but the temperament to be a day camp counselor. He believed that the highest virtue for little boys was strict obedience to his rules. When one of us broke a rule, he was subject to a fit of screaming, and then we were all punished together, to learn responsibility to the group.

"You know what we're going to do?" Todd always asked. "We're going to sit in the sun and stink." He arranged us in a circle on the grass, with enough space between each boy and the next to make sure no one spoke. Then we sweated out the punishment in the summer sun. I wanted to yell at Todd, but I kept silent. I wanted to run away, but I stayed where I'd been put. Once in a while as we sat, Todd announced the time we had left. Then he said, "Here we are again. You know what we do. Sit in the sun and stink."

None of the boys responded to these reminders, and none met his eyes. Sometimes when he spoke he sounded plaintive, like a child no one would play with.

Even worse to me than the loss of game time was how easily we boys could be made to wait and suffer and pretend we didn't mind. Somehow each of us was prepared for frayed-voiced men like Todd, red-faced and unreachable, wild while claiming to be disciplined. In our silence we agreed there was nothing to be done but wait. I hated the sweaty boredom and the shame, but most I hated that we made such good hostages.

The punishments were said to answer specific misdeeds, but as they grew more frequent I came to hear Todd's words about stinking as the chorus in a dirty song, like the ones we kids sang on the camp bus, only mean. The chorus came around from time to time on its own. It had nothing to do with us, really, except that he was making us learn it.

Finally one night, after my group had sat and stunk for a whole Wiffle ball period, I told my mother about our punishments. She expressed shock—at him, fortunately—and she filled with a marvelous energy. I listened as she called Greenwich Village mothers in the camp phone directory. A few other boys spoke up that night. The story hummed along the phone lines. It seemed the moms knew about this punishing kind of man, too. By the time my mother got through to the camp director, Todd had already been fired.

It was the first I knew of a complete, political act, and it lit me up like fireworks. It wasn't just that Todd was banished from our lives, but that the moms said his grief was not our duty to endure. Those uppity Greenwich Village mothers deflected some of the usual misery that would have fallen into their boys' lives. We could save our strength for more useful trouble.

Mixed Doubles

• • •

MY BEST CHANCE to get to know Ann was on the minivan that picked us up in the morning. The trouble was, Ann lived earlier on the route than me. She took a window seat, and a plain, tall girl named Eunice took the seat next to her. I had to sit by a boy who unwrapped his bologna sandwich as soon as he was on the bus, squeezing it so tight he left finger marks in the bread.

Morning after morning, all the way across town, I looked out the window, waiting for the day I could reveal my true feelings to Ann. As I gazed, I could hear Eunice ask her questions. She had a low, nasal voice that buzzed like a duck's quack. How was Ann's weekend? What did she do? I hated Eunice for monopolizing Ann. She seemed freakish to me, but as a girl she had rights with other girls that I could only dream about. Ann answered with stories of the charmed life I didn't share, and Eunice quacked out more questions until we changed buses, and I got the consolation of Danny's company.

Then, one day during the last week of camp, finally, gloriously, Eunice was absent. I sat down beside Ann while she was staring out the window, and soon the van was turning a corner, pressing us together.

"Where's that other girl?" I asked.

"I don't know," Ann said.

"Is she your friend?"

"I guess."

That was all the chance I needed. I put on a Muppet voice, squeezing my throat tight.

"Hiya, Ann," I said, my whole head buzzing.

"You again!" she said, but tolerantly. It seemed I was at least preferable to staring out the window.

"Hiya," I said again. "Did you have a good weekend? Did you have a good night?"

Ann sat up straighter, and curled her hands demurely in her lap. She pulled her knee away from mine and pointed her chin straight ahead. Her big brown eyes still watched me.

"Did you have a good minute?" I went on. "Did you have a good second?"

She laughed.

"You're a mean boy," she said.

I leaned toward her.

"*Quack*," I said.

Ann put her wrist over her mouth to block the giggles.

"*Quack*," she answered. We laughed and fell against each other. The big kids practiced their withering glances, and the little kids watched us like a truly peculiar cartoon. I felt I had a chance.

When the van stopped, Ann was the first out. She ran through the gathering summer heat to her group of girls. For the rest of the day, she didn't so much as look at me.

THE NEXT MORNING, Eunice was back, and the boy beside me was strangling his bologna sandwich as usual. But when we reached the bus transfer point, Ann raised her arms in an elbow-unbending, finger-splaying stretch that didn't seem like her at all. At the end of the stretch, she brought her hands together flat over one shoulder, making a duck's bill. She opened it and closed it at me, and rolled her head back over the seat rest. Upside-down, she mouthed, "*Quack*."

I found her at lunch, down the worn path that led past the administration building and the sports facilities for the older kids. She wore a polka-dot dress, black on white, and black sandals. Eunice sat next to her on some flat rocks, in a big brown T-shirt and ragged-edged jeans shorts. In a play, they could have been a mommy and a daddy.

"It's the you-again boy!" Eunice said.

"His name is *Gregory*," Ann said, shaking her head. "He's coming for a walk with us."

It was the first I'd heard about it.

Eunice looked anxiously back toward the counselors at the covered picnic tables. Ann started walking, and we followed her up the path, to the top of a rise.

"Look," she said.

Stretched out in the August sun were a row of green tennis courts, where older kids were playing in pairs, a boy and a girl together, brilliant in their all-white clothes.

Ann leaned over to me, and stage-whispered in my ear, "Mixed doubles."

I'd never heard the expression before.

"What?" Eunice asked. "What is it?"

"Mixed doubles," Ann whispered again, even louder. She giggled. Both girls looked at me at once.

Eunice asked me, "Do *you* know?"

I thought about mix and match. Mix was when parts were different, match was when they were alike. Ann and Eunice were a match, but Ann and I would be a mix. Ann could mean that mixed doubles was us, I thought. But as soon as I thought it, I knew it was wrong. It was too much what I wished.

"Sure I know," I answered Eunice. "Don't you?"

"She doesn't know," Ann said, mock-sad.

"Mixed doubles," I said, shaking my head.

"Well, you'll have to tell her by yourself!" Ann called. She ran back down the path to the lunch area, her dress fluttering in the wind she made, her sandals kicking up brown puffs of dirt. I caught up with her behind an old tree.

"I think we lost her!" I said.

Ann looked away.

"You don't really know what it means," she said.

I looked at the tree bark.

"It's from *tennis*," she said.

"Who cares about tennis?" I said. "What's so great about tennis, anyway?"

"My dad's always going out to play tennis," Ann said.

"Tennis is stupid," I said.

"Yeah," she said, bringing her face close to mine. "Stupid, stupid tennis."

"Ann!" a girl cried. She was walking up the path from the arts and crafts barn. "Ann! Come on! We're going to do *pliés*."

Ann left me under the tree.

Little orange ants were walking along the thick, ridged bark of the trunk. The ants were too small to use the ridges as steps, so they had to climb down the valley of each one and back up the other side.

I heard heavy footsteps. Eunice came and looked at the ants, then at me. She didn't sound like she'd been running, not even a little.

"You don't have to tell me," she said. "It can be your secret." It was as though she read my mind.

"It's nice to have little secrets with someone, isn't it?" she asked. She sounded as though she wasn't sure, as though it was a thing she'd only heard about. She was playing this all wrong. Why wasn't she trying to get me to trade secrets?

"I just made up what it means," I said.

She looked at me, doubtful, maybe suspecting a trick. Finally she asked, "How did you know you could make it up?"

"I don't know," I said.

Even her smile was sad.

THAT NIGHT I walked into the living room full of sudden purpose. I used the magic words—"There's something I need to talk to you about"—and right away my father's attention focused on me. He had put on his fancy red-and-blue beaded headband; he must have had one of his sociology night classes. My mother came over and joined him on the couch.

"Something important happened," I said. "I thought you two should be the first to know."

My parents glanced at each other for a moment.

"Is something wrong?" my mother asked.

"It's Ann!" I blurted. "From camp. She said good-bye to me today!"

I'd hardly said anything, but now the words dried up. My mother leaned forward, nodding, as though her nodding could draw out my words. My father grinned. He'd tease me for this, I realized, and she would say gooey mom things. What was I doing?

"I think we're going, I mean . . ." I said. "One day I'm going to have to get married!"

My parents just kept watching me, an amused grin and a sympathetic nod. They had no idea what I was saying. My face felt hot, and my hands began to shake. I was trying to put my parents on notice. What I really wanted—suddenly it seemed a provocative, dangerous thing—was to shame them with my example. To make them talk to each other again about making a new, happier life together, and all the things they seemed to be forgetting. In school this past spring, we had studied about the pioneers, but when I brought home stories, my parents had acted like it was just a history lesson, covered wagons and muskets. They didn't talk anymore about being pioneers themselves.

Could they hear my criticism? I checked my father's face for signs of anger, but there were none. My mother tipped her head to the side. Her eyes were bright and shiny. My tongue was dry in my mouth, and it took an effort to stay standing up facing them.

My father reached down for the knapsack at his feet, and loaded his school things in, yellow notepads, textbooks, pens.

"I have to get to class," he said, "but I definitely want to hear all about this tomorrow." As he left, he gave my mother a quick kiss, and me a big, burlesque wink that stretched one whole side of his face.

My mother was still looking at me with her bright, wet eyes.

"We would be very glad to hear as soon as you have more news."

I nodded, sighing.

"Would you like me to talk to your new friend's mother about a play date?"

THE WEEKEND AFTER camp ended, my mother walked me to Ann's apartment. We were met at the door by Ann's mother and a big, barking sheepdog. Mrs. Horowitz laughed.

"That dog," she said, "is the most jealous thing you've ever

73

seen." She made parent talk with my mother. I stood looking at the big, hairy animal, wondering where its eyes were.

"Ann, darling!" her mother called. "Your friend is here!"

The dog started barking again. Ann's mother grabbed it by its hidden collar and pulled it near her leg. I slipped past, into the sunlit living room.

Until now, I hadn't thought my family's apartment dark or small, but this one was all golden light and gleaming surfaces. Ann lived in a chandelier. I half expected the young couples from *The Nutcracker* to dance in from the next room.

My mother called my name a couple times, and finally I turned. She made a hurt face, but I just waved and turned away. She was no help to me here. When she'd gone, Ann's mother called, "Come say hello to your friend!"

Ann appeared barefoot in a doorless archway. She said, "Hello, Your-Friend."

This was happening a bit fast for me.

"Come see my new animals!" she called, running away. I followed behind.

"This is my room," she said, leading me around like a tour guide. "These are all my animals. These are my *china* animals, and these are my *glass* animals." She reeled off names, telling where they came from and who'd given them to her—often, her father. He seemed to travel a lot. There were several shelves of each kind of animal, china and glass, and Ann talked me through all of them, sometimes adjusting their shelf positions. A few times, she looked at me expectantly for a second, but I didn't know how to join.

"Can we play with them?" I asked. "That jockey could ride on that horse."

"Oh, no," she said, "they're *much* too fragile."

I never knew what to make of fussy toys like these, toys you could hardly touch.

"There's something I need to talk to you about," I said.

"There is?"

"Do you want to sit and talk?" I asked.

Ann was willing. She sat on the outer edge of the bed, her feet touching the floor. I wanted to take off my sneakers and sit cross-legged, but I felt shy.

"I need to tell you something."

"Okay."

"I guess you could say I'm in love with you."

"Oh." She stood up and looked around the room. "You haven't seen my antique dolls! Would you like to see them now?"

She was waiting for my answer. I stepped toward her and kissed her lightly on the lips.

"Mwah," she said.

I kissed her again, closing my eyes. The kiss tickled my lips. Ann laughed, and rubbed her lips with a finger.

"You're funny," she said.

I explained that I'd known how I felt ever since the day by the swimming pool, and that I needed to know if she could love me back. We didn't have to tell our parents if she didn't want to, at least not until we got married. In my best grown-up voice I told her it was very important.

Ann scratched her arm.

"Do you think you could be in love with me?" I asked.

"Yes," she said, after a moment.

"Really? You love me? You do?"

"No," she said.

"You don't?"

"No."

"Oh. Why not?"

"Um," she said, "I just remembered something. You wait here."

I listened as she ran in fluttering ballet steps across carpet, bare floor, carpet, and floor again.

"Mommy!" she said. "Can I have lunch now?"

"What about your friend?" her mother asked. "Don't you think he might be hungry, too?"

Ann walked back, in no hurry coming in my direction.

"Mommy says you have to come for lunch," she said.

Ann's mother made us chicken salad sandwiches, cutting the crust off Ann's. She sliced an apple for herself, and arranged it fanwise on a plate. She put all the lunch on a tray, then lifted it to the high table in the middle of the kitchen.

"Those apples look pretty," I said.

"Why, thank you," her mother said.

Ann stood up on the rungs of her tall chair to look.

"Oh, that," she said. "Mommy always does that."

"Annie!" her mother said. "Your friend can appreciate it if he likes."

"When does Gregory leave?" Ann asked.

"Aren't you two having a fun time?"

Ann was looking under the table. "Hello, puppy," she said. "What a wet tongue you have!"

"Maybe we could all play a game," her mother said.

Ann's mother brought out Monopoly, but Ann was more interested in feeding the dog bits of chicken.

"Ann, sweetie," her mother said several times, "come back and take your turn."

Ann climbed onto her stool, but by her next turn she'd slipped back down to the floor.

"It's you I love," Ann told the sheepdog. "I love *you*."

It came to me that I should take this as more of her teasing, that I should tell her the dog only loved her for her chicken, or that I'd never seen an apartment before with a girl for a rug. But my heart wasn't in it.

As I sat finishing my sandwich, I felt the old fear return, the fear that I was only a freak, worse even than Eunice. A freak from a family of freaks, who lived in a gloomy little apartment, with a father who didn't produce shelves of presents and a mother who didn't serve apples prettily on a plate. Why should Ann love me?

Ann led the dog into the sunny living room.

"I'm afraid Ann hasn't much experience with little boys coming to play," Mrs. Horowitz said. "I thought it might be a nice change for her. . . . I suppose she doesn't have so many friends over, what with her ballet lessons."

I perked up at this news—perhaps I didn't have rivals—forgetting for a moment that I'd already lost. Mrs. Horowitz must have seen the recognition in my face.

"Oh," she said. "You're interested in ballet?"

Mrs. Horowitz seemed kind. I thought about the question.

"Football players take ballet for balance," I said.

"Do they really!" she said. "Well, good for them. Dance is excellent for balance. But I suppose *you* know that!"

I wasn't sure what to say next.

"Do your parents bring you often, then?" she asked.

"I saw *The Nutcracker*," I said.

"Oh, I see," she said. "Well, that's not such a bad place to begin, is it? The toy soldiers are very nice."

She was right. That was a good part, the boy's toy soldiers coming to life to fight the man-sized rats.

"My favorite part was the dancing," I said. "Do you remember the part with the dancing?"

Mrs. Horowitz looked confused, and I was afraid I'd made a mistake. When I'd told my mother about the boys and girls dancing in couples, she'd told me how her best friend was sent to dancing school. She was sewn into her dress like a performing dog, my mother said, and she couldn't even go to the bathroom; Amanda and I were so lucky not to live in those times.

"The part in the beginning," I explained to Mrs. Horowitz. "When the boys and girls line up and dance together."

"When the children dance at the Christmas party," Mrs. Horowitz said.

"Yes! I like that so much. No one's fighting. The boys and girls know what to do, and not just because they have to. They like dancing together, boy and girl."

Talking to Mrs. Horowitz gave me an unusual feeling. She asked me questions, leading me, and I answered and asked her questions back. Our talk moved in a rhythm you could feel, like a dance—not the hair-shaking dance I did by myself to rock and roll, but a couple dance. She led, but it didn't feel as though she was doing something for me, as it had when she served lunch. It seemed we did this together.

"The way it is at the party—it's not like that at camp, or at school, or anywhere," I said. "Is it like that for you?"

"Oh," she said. "Well, that's a good question." Her laugh was odd. "It's not a question I'm going to answer, but it's a good question."

She didn't look angry.

"Those kids at the party," I said, "they must have had good parents."

"What do you mean?"

"The parents must have said, 'This is how you dance. You stand like this, and the girl stands like that.' 'Cause otherwise, how did they know?"

Mrs. Horowitz gave a play shrug.

I made my hands puppets, one teaching the other.

" 'Don't tease; talk, like this. And when you feel like you have to fight, you can try this, instead. And then you can know each other, and be happy.' "

Mrs. Horowitz laughed for a long time, showing red lipstick on her front tooth. Only as her laugh trailed away did she remember to cover her mouth with the back of her wrist.

"I don't know, Gregory," she said. "I don't know. Do you think parents can do all that?"

The intercom buzzed and the dog started barking and Ann told the doorman to send my mother up—right away, thank you! In the noise and good-byes I felt yanked roughly awake, as if from a dream.

A STRANGE THING happened that week. My father answered the phone and said it was for me—a girl. In my foolishness I thought it must be Ann. He held the black receiver up over my head, and he wouldn't give it to me until I jumped on the couch and yelled at him to stop fooling around.

It was Eunice. The quack of her voice cheered me up some.

She invited me to her apartment, which turned out to be a dense, dark place, thick with tall potted plants, and rugs layered on other rugs. When we took off our shoes, our feet sank in. There were more rugs on the walls, and heavy curtains that tinted the sunlight mustard colors. Eunice lived there alone with her mother, who talked to another woman most of the time I was there, and hardly said a word to me. There were few just-for-kids things, but Eunice was allowed to play with almost everything in the house—the piano, the many drums and percussion instruments, and the strange old wooden boxes and statues. Eunice played the piano for me, and I banged on a bongo drum. We never said Ann's name, but as we played we agreed we didn't have to mention her, didn't miss her, didn't need her, that afternoon.

When Eunice came to my house, the only instruments were my father's guitars, which neither of us could play. She picked my baseball mitt off the windowsill and asked if we could have a catch. I was surprised—I'd played catch with my mother or Amanda, but never with a girl my age. Still, I got her my father's mitt, and we threw a tennis ball on the sidewalk across from our building.

After a few throws, Eunice took off the big mitt and laid it on the sidewalk. She said she could catch better without it. I'd never heard of someone choosing to give up a mitt—we were almost always short mitts in games—but Eunice did catch better bare-handed.

More than usual, grown-ups passing by made comments. They came at us looking like they'd made a discovery, and that made me nervous. Someone said, "Nice day to play catch!" Someone complimented Eunice's arm, which turned her shy. A man with a mustache stood watching her, saying nothing. Finally he asked, "What the hell are you supposed to be?" He walked off before we could think of anything to say, his laugh like a wracking cough. But Eunice didn't want to quit. We played until the sun went behind the elevated highway by the river. The air was suddenly cooler, and all that was left was to go home again.

My mother was excited that Eunice had come over.

"Did you have a good time?" she asked.

"It was okay."

"You had a good time," she said. "I just think that's so wonderful!"

"Uh-huh."

"I think it's terrific that you would feel moved to play *catch* with Eunice. When I was a girl, I would never even have *thought* to play catch with a boy."

"I know," I said. "You told me."

She was standing over me.

"It's not such a big deal," I said, avoiding her gaze.

"Well, maybe not to you," she said, "at your age, but from my point—"

"Stop acting like it's such a big deal!" I yelled.

She took a step back, laughing nervously, as though I was joking.

"Nothing is any different, okay? We just had a catch. Everything is still the way it was before."

She'd stopped laughing.

"Is that so," she said.

Scrimmage

■ ▋ ■

K IDS CALLED SETH Lee dumb and mean, but that didn't seem to cover it. I'd seen him start a shoving match at assembly, with the principal standing right there, and he'd looked not mean but helpless, as though he couldn't stop himself. Last spring, in a kickball game his team was already winning, he'd slid into home, bare leg on asphalt. There wasn't even a play at the plate. The red-brown scab stretched from the top of his tube socks to the blue trim on his shorts. Lately I'd seen him talking to himself at recess, lost in an unshared world of made-up kung fu moves.

Seth wasn't in my class, but he was in Rudy's sports clinic, and on the first day he snuck up behind me in the yard. Lost in football dreams, I didn't notice him until I felt his breath hot on my neck. I spun, startled, and his fists shot up inches away. I flinched and jumped back, covering my face. In the middle of my spasm, I knew what he must have meant—not a sneak attack but a game of how close he could get before I noticed.

"You jumped!" he said, surprised. "You jumped off the ground! I scared you . . ."

I could have thrown my own fists in the air, startled him back, started us laughing. But he was right. I'd flinched, and now he knew—this was what I did. I cringed at screams, jumped at upraised hands, hid and cried and made secret vows. In my shame at his discovery I backed away.

"You jumped!" he said again, almost whining, as though I wasn't playing fair. Then in another voice, he yelled, "I made you jump—I saw you! You thought I was going to *hit* you! I scared you *good*."

I'd never been in a fight, but now my fingers tightened into fists.

"Jeez," I said, shaking my head, loading up the word with pity. "What's the *matter* with you?"

He tucked in his chin, and his straight dark bangs fell over his eyes. I'd stung him. But as I watched, he straightened up again and looked around, as though to make sure no one else was going to join me against him.

"What's the matter with *you!*" he cried.

He ran toward the boys gathering for sports clinic, and I let him go. I wasn't supposed to have killer impulses. I'd made vows. Never to engage in torture—to make no one cry "uncle," rinse no heads in toilet bowls. Never to snap a rat-tail in a changing room except in a fair fight my victim had joined by choice. Never to help give the fat kid his daily wedgie. Never to bloody a nose, blacken an eye, break a bone. To give no one cause to tell me to go pick on someone my own size.

In most schools, I suppose, and in most neighborhoods, no matter how close watch I kept on myself, my vows wouldn't have lasted a week. I would have needed my father's worst example more than I hated it. But my father didn't want that for me any more than my mother did, and his mother had offered tuition money to back up their ideals. Amanda and I were attending a new private school. Woody Allen, a neighbor, had written our untraditional alma mater:

Scrimmage

Very near the Hudson River
There's a place that sets my heart a-quiver
Near a street they call Horatio
Not far from the 8th-Avenue-and-14th-Street subway statio
Village Community School. . . .

Here, the teachers stepped into kids' disputes before they led to blows. We were taught to talk out our fights, that hitting was for babies. Here was a place where I could try to keep my vows. But now as Seth ran toward the waiting boys, I felt how hard it would be, the double life it would demand. I'd go on like a regular boy, sports and schoolwork and an annoying kid sister, but always with an eye on my father and myself, even when we were playing, even when we were happy. Maybe, I felt, my mother was up to this vigilance, up to keeping ever open one unblinking eagle eye. But I was eight. I didn't have the concentration, and I knew it.

MY FATHER SEEMED a little jealous that I'd be learning football from someone besides him, but still he was all for my taking Rudy's clinic. Not my mother. It was not going to be like playing baseball, she warned me. Football was macho—organized violence. I tried to explain that it was only *touch* football, that there was no tackling, and only the defense could block, but when I raised my arms to show her blocking I could see I only made it worse. She kept suggesting other classes I could take until I wanted to scream.

Maybe another boy wouldn't have cared what his mother said about football, but I didn't want to dismiss her. She knew things—she even played catch. Sometimes late on a weekend afternoon she would borrow my father's big glove. We climbed down the fire escape to the backyard, and in the slanting, smog-enhanced orange of the evening sun we threw an old green tennis ball back and forth.

She "threw like a girl," which is to say, she kept her elbow in front of her shoulder during the windup and heaved the ball like a catapult, rather than swiveling her shoulder and her wrist to make her arm a whip. But she threw harder and faster than I did, at first, and she liked to play with me. I was glad to have her as a partner.

She had nothing to teach me about the techniques and mysteries of baseball. Her chat was observation, not praise or pointers. My father called, "Nice grab!" or "Two hands!" or "Keep your eye on it!"—feeding my hunger for this amazing game. She'd say, "That was a high one." I had to ask her to throw me grounders, and to explain what they were.

"You know, grounders. On the ground. Like a ground ball. *Grounders.*"

My mother smiled, half apologetic, half amused.

I could hear as I talked baseball to her that, like her, I was new at this. As I explained to her bits of what I'd recently learned from my father, I heard something a boy might otherwise miss: *Baseball was strange.* Why would an intelligent person engaged in throwing a ball back and forth want the ball aimed at the ground? Why prefer a high fly that makes you run to one that falls right to you? The answers went back to the rules and habits of baseball, but why were those the rules? The more I tried to explain, the odder I felt. If baseball was strange, then boys were strange for playing it, and I was strange for being a boy.

When my father threw with me it was as if to say, *This is how we do what we do.* Not with my mother. Our "we" was not defined. The two of us talked between ourselves. There were no school programs, no televised professionals to show a mother and son the way. Even our equipment was borrowed. My mother didn't say, *This is what we do.* She said, *Don't leave. We'll figure something out.*

I'D INSISTED ON signing up for Rudy's sports clinic after watching him one day at recess. He'd risen up from his folding chair and eased himself toward home plate, an elephant of a man in a midnight blue windbreaker. To carry his belly, he walked with his shoulders rolled back, all breadth and dignity. A sun visor shaded his dark brown face.

"Time to bring it in!" he called. He cast his voice across the pavement, over kids' cries and chatter and the heaving noise of a diesel truck at the loading bay across the street. Rudy's voice got loud sometimes, commanding, but it didn't scare me. This was another reason I spent my last precious minutes of a morning's recess watching him.

"Bubba!" yelled one of the older boys from the outfield. He held up a softball. Rudy surveyed the space around him, nodded his approval. The boy had a good arm, but he put too much arc in the throw, and the ball came in high. Rudy didn't back up, didn't crouch for a jump. I thought the wild throw would sail over his head, but then he raised the wooden bat to it, snapping the bat back at the moment of impact. The ball fell docile at his feet.

"Hit one, Bubba!" a seventh grader called. I envied these boys the nickname. One kid with a mitt climbed the chain-link home run fence. He jumped to the sidewalk and crossed to the far side of Greenwich Street, by the unloading trucks.

Rudy picked up the softball and stepped up to the plate. He stuck out his bat, pointing with it over the fence at the boy with the glove. I'd seen his Babe Ruth style in the books I'd been reading. In time I would devour every sports book in the school library—sports technique, sports history, sports biography, the whole gray metal shelf full, even the books on rugby and cricket. When my last renewal was up on the story of the home run kings, I would stand it on our stoop in the sun, and photograph the pictures of Hank Aaron, Roger Maris, and the Babe with my new box camera, so I could put the great men in my photo album along with my friends and family.

Rudy tossed the softball in the air with one hand, and swung the bat with the other, connecting with a deep, solid smack.

"Did you see that?" someone asked in the stairwell as we raced back to our classrooms. "Bubba knocked it out of the park one-handed."

Out of the park. When Rudy took batting practice, the mis-shapen asphalt schoolyard turned stadium. Rudy was a dream grown-up, the biggest, most athletic boy we knew, bigger than our fathers and yet slow and soft in hand and face like us. He seemed a kind of missing link between kids and sports heroes.

Heroism was essential. In every sport we played, my friends and I copied our heroes' moves and mannerisms, knocked dirt from our make-believe cleats, spit pretend tobacco, and shielded our eyes from the imaginary glare of the night-game lights. On the backs of our baseball and football cards, we found greatness measured in statistics, ticked off in record years and percentages, specified in numbers that seemed all the more awesome when we only half understood what they meant.

My most devout sports friends were the Samptons, Matt and Josh. Their shared bedroom was packed with equipment and magazines, with sports-themed games and sports-logo deco-rations. On each visit, I brought my new baseball cards to sort. It was serious business. We had to determine which cards would join our permanent collections (to be passed on to our sons, as Mr. Sampton had saved his cards for Matt and Josh), and which ones could be traded or flipped. Cards from certain teams were definite keepers—the Mets and the Yankees, of course, but also the Dodgers and Giants, stolen New York teams, and the Red Sox and Royals. Cards of really talented players were worth keeping, as were cards rumored to be rare. But the remaining cards always made a big pile, and these players we sent to the Moon Dummies.

The Dummies were an all-loser team whose cards it was our secret project to produce. With enough patient erasing, the glossy finish on a baseball card wore away, and then the ink below. We could correct the errors that major league base-ball and the Topps Corporation had made when they'd hired and packaged these imposters. With our erasers and our Magic Markers, we traded them to the team they deserved. We black-ened their eyes, knocked out their teeth, drew them nerdy glasses and smashed them on their faces. We put them in new uniforms, pink and blue—"makes the men wink at you," as the taunt went. They were reassigned to new positions, Far Left Outfield, Rear Catcher. Finally, we corrected their names, rechristening them Dum-Dum or Shitbrain. . . .

It was surprisingly hard work. After a few minutes of erasing, my drawing hand ached. There was always the risk of tearing through the cardboard, ruining it. Among us it was understood that every reject had to join the Dummies. Even in such a gathering of heroes as the major leagues, men had to be viewed with a cold eye. What I remember best from those long afternoons is the pencil tight in my aching hand, the hot rubbery smell of pink eraser debris, and the sweetly distant rage I felt, disfiguring the faces of the men who'd let us down.

SETH AND I stayed out of each other's way during Rudy's clinics, but I kept my eye on him. I couldn't help it. At recess, at assemblies, before and after school, I had to know where he was, what he was doing. I got kids in his class to talk about him. Even the boys who disliked Seth repeated his stories with a kind of reverence. The shoving match in front of the principal. The shouting at teachers. The outrageous slide into home plate. One boy insisted that Seth was related to Bruce Lee, the kung fu master.

EVEN IF MY mother was weird about football, she didn't make me feel as tangled up as some of the other moms did. Jules Starkey's mother always had to make us vanilla milk, clanking long spoons in tall glasses and asking Jules how was his day. He said it was okay. The milk tasted like thin, warm ice cream, and she kept asking if it was vanilla enough, sweet enough. Jules looked at me sideways and said it was okay. When she took his glass to adjust the mix again, he turned on his stool to face me, puffing out his lips and cheeks and bugging out his eyes, as though he was being enormously squeezed.

Lukas's mother came home from her job and brought him hamburgers on a tray, and catsup or pickles when he yelled that she'd forgotten them—"Hurry up with those pickles, Mom! Mom, you're blocking the TV!"

Ethan's mother wanted to get us snacks, milk, water; or to spread peanut butter and fancy jam very slowly on sprouted wheat bread while she talked to us in her kitchen. "Ethan?" she would say from the doorway, her high whispery voice softening over the length of his name, drawing it out to three syllables, the two I said plus a little sigh. "Ethan? Are you boys ready for lunch yet?"

I tried to be calm around these moms, to be careful, to smile, but nothing really helped. We were too loud, too sudden, too strange. When we jumped up from their tables to go, they looked at us with mourning in their eyes. Their looks squeezed my chest until I felt the guilty wish that they'd hurry up already and let us go.

RUDY TAUGHT FORM. To throw a pass, you first cradled the football in your palm, resting your fingertips at the seam. You didn't *fling* the ball forward, you *rolled* it off your fingers, so it spiraled. When you ran with the ball, you cupped its pointy nose in the top of your palm, and hugged it to your side with your arm. It would be secure there, Rudy promised, as hard to drop as it was difficult for another player to knock away, even as you faked and cut. (We grinned at this, at the vision of ourselves dodging our way up the field, running for the end zone.) When you caught a pass, you had to pull the ball in with your hands, then trap it between your arms and your chest.

"Now, you may say to me," Rudy told us, putting on a high, boyish voice, " 'But, Bubba, I caught a touchdown pass in my hands, no trap, no form, just my hands!' You may say, 'But,

Bubba, on TV Larry Czonka holds the ball out at the end of his arm. It's almost in the grass!' "

He laughed, his bulk gently shaking. "You listen up now. Practice good form, and it will wait inside you for when you need it. It will be there when you have the luxury to hotdog *and* when you don't. Not just for one lucky touchdown, not just for one game. For every game."

While Rudy talked this way, so grave and mock-grumpy, boys looked at their sneakers and smiled, as though he was another grown-up making a wordy fuss over nothing. Yet he was easy with us, amused, tolerant even in impatience, and as the weeks passed, he won us over. His ease made me feel I belonged, a rare thing. Usually when I felt consciously *boy*, I felt at the same time out-of-bounds, too fast, too loud. Couldn't we cut it out? Stop it? Settle down? One evening at the end of sports clinic, I heard a mom say, "I've got two, which believe me is bad enough! But can you imagine? That poor man's got twenty screaming meanies to keep under control. . . ."

Around Rudy, boys formed a circle. I'd heard my mother put down a man as "a real one-of-the-boys type," yet with Rudy I wanted to be one of the boys. The form he taught was hard to get the hang of, but when you did, it felt amazing. For moments, my muscles moved me—there seemed no me at all. I could forget who I was, what I was missing, what I feared. For a too-brief instant I was an impulse made flesh—a dash upfield, arms up to trap the ball, running into the clear.

"TODAY WE TACKLE!" Seth Lee yelled, not quite at me but in my direction. We were waiting for Rudy in the Big Yard. Seth had tried to sneak up on me again, but I'd heard him coming.

"There's no tackling in Rudy's," I said.

"You're the quarterback, but Lee's bustin' through the line! Sneaks up and wham—tackled! Ow! That hurts! Now it's a pileup—loose ball! And Lee recovers the fumble!"

"*There's no tackling on asphalt!*" I screamed.

Seth shrank back and looked up at me, still as an animal. Then his arms and his head began to shake. It was as though he was having an earthquake.

"Ass . . ." he quavered, voice rising. "Ass . . . ass . . . phalt!"

He ran at me, then swerved away, tackling imaginary offensive players. I stared, expecting him to get embarrassed, tired at least, but he kept lunging and yelling and swinging his shoulders and I got sick of it. I wanted to shut him up, ram him with my shoulder like the pros did it, knock him to the ground. It would feel great to tackle, great to grab that enemy player and smash him, to knock the ball from his hands and run it for the touchdown.

Or forget the touchdown. I felt another game under the official one. Football was for crushing bones, hockey for swinging sticks, baseball for beanballs and sliding in with spikes bared. When I'd watched teams brawl on TV with my father, I'd sided with the referee, and yelled that the players had to cut it out, get the game going again. But now I wanted to throw a body and hear it smack against pavement. It would even feel good to tackle some girl, some frustrating girl who made you feel wrong and useless, who blamed you for everything even when she was the one who'd changed the rules. You could grab that girl and shove her down some stairs.

Seth stood still now, watching me, wide-eyed. I stood almost frozen, panting. My hands shook. I watched Seth, and he jumped straight into the air.

"Batman!" he yelled, as though he was the superhero, and I was the villain.

TODAY RUDY HAD promised us a full-size game, the real thing, what he called a scrimmage. In our hooded sweatshirts, we boys pressed toward him to hear the rules, bumping against each other in our excitement. Rudy stood talking in his long blue winter coat, which he always left open like a cape. He asked for questions.

"Bubba?" asked Seth. "Are we playing tackle?"

Behind me, one of the older boys muttered, "Does he ever listen?"

"Uh-duh," I added.

"Lee!" Rudy said.

"Yeah?"

"Stamp your foot."

Seth stamped the gray asphalt. A few other boys followed.

"How does that feel?"

"Hard?" Seth answered.

"Yeah, it's hard," Rudy said. "I thought *you* would know that."

Boys laughed.

"I don't care," Seth said. "I call we play tackle!"

Everyone was quiet.

"Jeez, Seth," I yelled across the circle. "I don't know why you want to get tackled so bad. You're going to be one giant scab!"

I thought this was pretty funny, but most of the boys turned back to Seth, who glared at me through the bars of his bangs.

"You don't play tackle where you're going to get injured," Rudy intoned.

A couple of boys stamped the pavement again. Others were miming long passes and brilliant receptions.

"What about on snow?" Seth asked.

"Could we just play the game?" I murmured.

"Bubba," Seth asked again, "what about on snow?"

In the distance I heard a siren. I could almost feel the circle focusing on Seth, working out his logic: Snow was soft, even softer than grass. Why couldn't we play tackle when it snowed?

Rudy was silent. Now, I thought, we would see what he was like angry. I watched him, his belly shaking in his open coat, and his breath coming in quick pale puffs.

"You're something else, Lee," he said finally, chuckling. "You are really something else. Snow."

I didn't think that was such big praise, but boys were looking admiringly at Seth.

Rudy walked back to the equipment bin, and returned with his long, loose shirt held out to make a bag for footballs.

"Bubba!" boys started crying, calling for balls. "Bubba, over here!" Seth wailed the name like a madman.

Rudy began to pass the balls to us, each pass a perfect spiral. The other boys jumped and waved their arms, dancing their boy moves, shouting the password, joining the club. I'd been growing used to this, but now the jumping and screaming scared me. I stood flat on the pavement, boys around me lifting themselves off the ground. I knew I ought to be studying them, copying them, learning to do what we did. I was pretty sure I could copy the moves, if I wanted to. But should I want to? Soon my body was among them, waving, jumping, but somehow I still floated behind, watching to see how convincing I looked.

LATE IN THE scrimmage, Rudy called for a delayed lateral to me. I made some yardage, cutting into a space cleared by a rush of receivers who'd lured the defense upfield, screaming for Rudy to see them. When the trick was recognized, four defenders came at me at once, including Seth. As I hesitated, picking a way ahead, someone tagged me out neatly from behind, and most of the boys slowed down. Seth charged with a war cry, and in the blur I saw others picking up speed again. Then Seth knocked a defender into me, and all three of us fell to the ground.

I had the ball secure in my hands, but Seth yelled "Fumble!" and the pileup grew, boy after juiced-up boy leaping aboard. I was flat on the ground with my face and hands on the football. The asphalt felt cold and sharp against my knees. The fall had knocked the wind out of me, and I couldn't yell at Seth to get off. Someone was giggling. Seth was still screaming about a fumble.

"Ball is dead," Rudy called from upfield.

Boys started climbing off the pile. I pushed a sneaker out of my face and rolled into a sitting position, babying my sore knees.

"Look what you did!" I yelled up at Seth. The cold and the breathlessness and the surprise of getting hit pressed some water out of my eyes.

The boys who'd tackled were walking away sheepishly. They knew they were wrong. But I wasn't finished.

"Look what you did!" I yelled again. "The play was over!"

I was still short of breath, and my words came out in gasps. My voice broke, and I choked up a little. This was how Seth always got into trouble, I knew, and now he'd hurt me. I had him.

"You are such a dumb stupid cretin idiot!" I yelled. "Do you have ears? Don't you know what no tackling means?"

I sniffed, scrunched up my face with emotion I almost felt, dragged my arm across my nose. My face was red, my gasps like the gasps of tears.

"I swear, you've got a problem, Seth Lee. You've got serious problems!"

I yelled for all I was worth, but at the same time, I studied him. Seth's face tightened, reddened. He clenched his teeth, and as tears came he hid the mess of his face in the puffy shoulder of his down vest, sliding it along his arm, shaking, burrowing, as though he could hide in his elbow.

"Look what you did!" I yelled again. Theatrically, I yanked up a leg of my jeans to show him my knee.

I had convinced myself that beneath the denim must lie raw hamburger dripping blood. But besides some redness and the imprinted pattern of the rough asphalt, my kneecap looked as it always did, a bare pale dome.

Rudy parted two watching boys and came up alongside me. I sniffled, rubbed my nose. He looked at my bare knee, looked me in the face.

"Don't cry," he said.

Rudy, too? He bent forward, his hulking body hanging above me.

"Don't cry," he said again.

He looked down at me without disapproval, calm as a

mountain. His two words rattled in my battle-ready mind, and in a few moments I recognized his tone. It sounded like, "Don't *fling* the football. *Roll* it off your fingers." These exaggerated tears were bad form. They were wasteful and flashy; they wouldn't help me play the game.

But I didn't care. Behind Rudy I could see Seth in the dimming light, standing apart from the rest of his team. Now, the other boys were keeping their distance, as though his impulsiveness was contagious and shameful. I had him where I wanted him now, hurt and lonely and full of blame. I'd spoiled his story. I'd spoiled it for both of us.

Angry Girls

■ ▌ ■

IT WAS THE end of lunch period, rainy and disappointing. Isabel Batler walked up to the teacher's metal desk,
pushing the sleeves of her turtleneck up past her elbows. The
classroom lights were out, and in the tarnish yellow gleam
from the windows she raised her thick, freckled arms above
her head. Batler was one of the first girls to grow taller than the
fifth grade boys, and she was wider through the shoulders
than any of us. When she smacked her hands down on the
desktop, the steel drawers rattled.

"Lukas Mucus!" she yelled.

Lukas Bergendorf sat on the gray carpet with a glossy
book showing the breeds of dogs. He pretended not to hear.

Batler stood by the desk, feet planted, arms crossed. She
glared at him.

"Lukas Mucus!" she called again.

From the floor, Lukas said, "That's not my name, okay?"

"Lukas Mucus, you are such a doofus!"

"That's not my name. It's not my name and it's not fair."

"Very clever," said Alexa Rockrimmon. "Did you hear that? What a clever boy."

"I didn't *do* anything!" Lukas cried, standing up. He walked up close to the girls. "Can't you just leave me alone?"

More kids were coming up from lunch. They looked around, then moved to the wall, away from the fight.

"What are you saying?" Batler asked. "That you haven't been dripping disgusting Lukas mucous all over the classroom?"

Lukas was getting over a cold, it was true.

"That your desk isn't full of disgusting mucousy Lukas tissues?"

This drew a few snickers.

"Your desk is disgusting. You're disgusting! You're the most Lukas Mucus anyone could ever be."

Alexa leaned forward to examine him.

"Oh, God," she said. "Why is he smiling?"

It wasn't a smile exactly, more a paralyzed grin, like a foretaste of rigor mortis. Lukas turned away from the girls, toward the rain-streaked window.

"We are telling you how disgusting you are," Batler said, "and all you can do is smile?"

From beneath her feathered hair, in a voice of pitying finality, Alexa said, "You really are a doofus." Her tone was almost medical. Hopeless case.

Our teacher came in the open doorway.

"What's going on?" she asked. Rows of fluorescent lights buzzed overhead and snapped on. "Why is everyone huddled against the wall?"

No one answered her question.

"Let's get started," she said. "Alexa, lunch is almost over. It's time to go back to your own classroom."

I took my seat near Lukas, who looked as though he'd lost something he loved. The angry girls could make you feel that way. Suddenly, after cold weeks of being ignored, came this public scrutiny. The girls who hadn't seemed to grant your existence turned out to have had their eyes on you all along.

They had watched Lukas, studied him, given him a pet name, made up a kind of poem. It was a cruel poem, a mortifying name, but I could feel how it might be hard to keep from grinning a little.

After the girls had last yelled at me, saying I only talked because I loved the sound of my own voice, I'd been scared to go near my friends, scared I'd contaminate them. Kids shied away, embarrassed by me—or by themselves, maybe, as I felt around Lukas, wishing despite our friendship that my seat wasn't next to his. All afternoon, when he sniffled, I squirmed. Silently I yelled at him to shut up.

Only once, near the end of the day, did he raise his hand. Kids lowered their heads, glanced sidelong at each other.

"Lukas?" the teacher asked.

At once, in every kid's head in the room—in mine, at least, and I was one of his few friends—the thought rang almost loud enough to hear: "Mucus!" The angry girls had marked him. Already I knew it would stick.

LUKAS AND TONY Fodor and I talked endlessly about Batler, but it was hard to get good information on her. In the school directory there were only two people listed at her house, Isabel and her mother. Her father wasn't in the directory at all, not even (like Tony's father) at a separate address.

We also knew, because it was a favorite story told around the school, that Batler's mother was the inventor of something called edible underwear. I'd seen it once, a pale pair of women's panties, orangey-pink, folded in half and bagged in clear cellophane like candy. Thinking about edible underwear troubled me. I could picture it as a gag gift, funny for a few seconds. But then what? I could tell I was missing the point. But Batler knew. She had glimpsed adult things, and this was one more reason I hesitated to tell her off. I was afraid of her comeback, afraid she knew something about us that we didn't.

• • •

BATLER WENT AFTER Tony next. He froze at first, and his face turned even whiter than usual, but he managed to stick to his plan. Tony believed we could get through to Batler, help her to see we were kids just like her. At his house one afternoon, he'd put on the Beatles for Lukas and me, drawing our attention to "We Can Work It Out."

Now he asked Batler, "Am I doing something that makes you mad? Because if I am, maybe you could explain the reason why."

No one had ever interrupted a denunciation before. Above us, the fluorescent lights hummed, and outside, the Big Yard rang with shouts. It seemed Tony had gotten through.

Batler took a deep breath.

"Because you're so annoying!" she yelled.

"You really do have an annoying, whiny voice," Alexa said.

"He's just trying to talk to you!" I said. "What's so bad about that? You won't even let him try to—"

"Blab, blab, blab, blab, blab!" Alexa said. "God! Don't you realize people have to listen to all this noise you make? I swear I've never heard such a pair of conceited little boys in my life."

After school I found Tony in the yard, holding on to the fence. His eyeballs were pink from the strain of not crying.

"Why do they have to do this?" Tony asked.

"I know. I know," I said, to quiet him.

"What did we do?"

"I know," I said again.

"You don't have to come over to my house if you don't want to," he said, voice starting to break. "I mean if you've got something better—"

"Come *on*," I said, glad for the change of subject. "Let's get out of here."

Tony looked at me, his pink eyes shiny with awful gratitude.

• • •

ONE NIGHT WHEN it was my turn to have "story" with my mother, I told her about the angry girls. She sat on the edge of my bunk bed with her legs down the ladder. There had been a girl who tormented her in grade school, too, she said. This was just a phase girls went through.

I tried to explain how they made it seem like *boy* was a disease. During free time, if you tried to join a game of crazy eights or Mille Bornes, or even just a group talking in a corner, they spit it at you: *"No boys!"*

"Well," my mother said, "you don't have to be friends with those girls. I'm sure there are lots of nice kids in the class."

"You can't just ignore them!" I shouted. "It's not like you can just talk to someone whenever you want to. They're changing *everything!*"

"Why are you yelling at *me?*" she asked.

It always frightened me to hear her sound hurt. I said I hadn't meant to yell.

She gave me a hug and a kiss good night. "Kids can be awful," she said in the dark, halfway down my ladder. "I know it. I really know it. But it does get better. School was just the same when I was a girl."

This was meant as consolation, I knew. I'd heard her stories. How boys and girls were kept apart, even when they went to the same school. How she'd gotten kicked out of dancing school for being a Jew. How she was so nervous talking to the first boy she liked that he gave up trying and asked her out by note. How she could barely speak on their first date, and he never asked her again.

But it was not supposed to matter anymore how things had been when she was a girl. The Fifties were the Old Country. We were supposed to have escaped.

I WAS WATCHING my friend Matt draw. Alexa came to look.

"More cartoons," she said.

Matt kept on drawing. All his characters wore baseball hats and enormous high-top sneakers.

"Why are you always drawing those dumb cartoons?" she asked.

"I'd like to see you do better," he said. He was decorating the baseball cap on a horse. He made the horse a Red Sox fan.

"Don't you get tired of wasting all your time?" she asked.

I would have argued with her, tried to make her understand. Matt didn't look up.

Alexa walked away. She didn't seem flustered or angry. She had the air of someone who had checked off a task on her list.

So it was true—you could ignore the angry girls, and they would go away.

"Why do you talk to her, anyway?" Matt asked. "It's not like she *does* anything." He looked at me from under the dark bill of his Yankees cap.

"But how can you just let her say those things?"

"Why should I care what she says?" Matt answered. He didn't have to finish the thought: *She doesn't cartoon and she doesn't like sports. Why bother? She's only a girl.*

But Lukas and Tony and I couldn't let them go. We might start out trying to ignore them, but then we gave in. We answered their questions, defended ourselves from their accusations. Soon not just Matt but most kids in the class were losing patience. They kept their distance from Tony and Lukas and me. We were an embarrassment.

THE YEAR BEFORE, everything had been different. My days hadn't been full of classroom humiliations. I hadn't found my place among the pariahs. All my attention was on Alison Eisinger.

We were studying how people lived in olden days and we got to making clothes. Alison was the only one who knew what a mordant was, a chemical you put on to fix a color in cloth so it wouldn't run out again when you washed it. I was impressed. That afternoon, the class did its own experiments with natural dyes, using beets and onion skins and spices, and we each kept a log of the colors we expected and the colors that turned out. I slipped over to the table where Alison was working.

"They come out the color of the thing that dyes them, only lighter," Alison said. "It's really quite obvious."

I felt an opening in my heart, as though a secret door had opened for the password, "It's really quite obvious."

By then I'd given up on Ann almost definitely. I invited Alison to my house, and the next week I went to hers. Then she came to mine again. It was a rainy day, cold for May, so we climbed up on my bunk bed to watch the water drops ski down the window, and to tell secrets.

I considered her for a moment, her yellow ponytails tied with white elastics, her knowing way of talking. This was some kind of girl who had climbed up the ladder to my bed.

"What a rainy day," I said.

"It's kind of a cold day, too," she said.

"Do you want to go under the covers?"

"I could go under the covers," she said.

After a while, I asked her if she minded kissing.

"That depends," she said.

The rain was soft on the windows.

"Depends on what?"

"On the boy and on the kiss," she said.

"Did you mind that?"

She made a thinking-it-over face.

"How about that? Did you mind that one?"

That night in my journal I wrote, "She has never been in love before. She doesn't mind kissing (or so I think!). She knows every possible thing about me, and I know every possible thing about her (I think). No one knows about our love except us and we are going to keep it that way."

•   •   •

BY THE FALL, Alison and her family had moved to New Jersey, and the new rules were in place. Fourth grade Catch-and-Kiss had been a better version of tag: The boys ran from the girls, and the girls tried to kiss them. I seethed with jealousy at blue-eyed Matthew Kaplan, the clear favorite among the girls.

"All right," he'd say, with fatherly gruffness, kissing girls hanging from him on all sides. "All right. You caught me! That's enough now. All right already."

But in the fifth grade Catch-and-Kiss, a caught boy threw off his captor and kept running. There were falls and scrapes, trips to the nurse, tears and screaming back in the classroom over who fought too rough. When a girl, even a girl Batler didn't like, came back to class late with a Mercurochrome stain and a Band-Aid, Batler was at her most enraged. Some games ended in pileups, with the girls too busy screaming "Got you!" to bother with any kissing. Boys who got caught were mocked by the girls, and by other boys who were still free.

"Burn! Burn!" boys yelled at those who failed to dodge their female pursuers. "You are so burned!"

The gym teachers, Kenny and Thomasina, seemed shocked. "What is this game of girls fighting boys?" Thomasina lectured us, when they tried to ban it. "That's no game."

MY FATHER HAD no explanation of the angry girls, but he had ideas of how to talk to them.

"Anything I say," I told him, "they call me conceited."

"You could tell them they must like conceited boys," he said, "since they're always trying to talk to you. Or say they must be the most conceited of all—don't they talk all the time?"

Those were good ones, I thought. When I felt down about school, my father would talk to me about the Mets, the prospects for Dave Kingman to beat Roger Maris's home run record. As the weather warmed up, I gave him daily reports of my batting statistics in Wiffle ball and kickball. My average that year hovered around .750, a personal record.

My father often made our school lunches, plastic-wrapped sandwich, piece of fruit, can of juice drink, trio of cookies. He began drawing cartoons and writing notes on the brown paper bags. "Faster than a salami sandwich," he wrote, "more powerful than three Oreo cookies . . . it's a bite, it's a snack, it's Superlunch!" Another said, ".750! .750? Two players put together don't bat .750! (This message brought to you by the U.S. Dept. of Lunches.)"

Down at the end of the long white Formica table, I showed my lunch bags to Tony and Lukas, and often other boys got interested. The bag made the trip up around the table, or kids came to look over my shoulder. Batler and Rockrimmon would be eating with the other angry girls, a safe distance away.

One lunch period, I forgot to bring my bag downstairs. When I went up to get it, the lights were out, but Batler was there, sitting on a desk with her elbows on her knees, staring out the window. I'd heard that Alexa was out sick this week. Perhaps that knowledge, and my father's coaching, made me bold. I took my lunch bag from my cubby, and walked over to Batler.

"You're friends with Alison E., aren't you?" I asked. Alison had been in New Jersey almost half a year, but saying her name still made my heart jump.

"So?" Batler said. She didn't look at me.

"I was just wondering if you'd seen her lately."

"She's in New Jersey. You can't just walk to her house anymore."

"She's in *Asbury*, New Jersey," I said.

Batler sighed. She turned to look at me with a slowness that suggested I was only barely worth the effort.

"She came to my house this summer," Batler said, "if you must know."

If you must know was a phrase of Alexa's.

"Well," I said, "she's coming to my house on Saturday."

"She is not."

"Her parents have to come to the city for a concert, so she's going to visit me."

Batler looked back out the window.

"You really shouldn't feel bad about it," I said. "She's only coming for a day and a night. She's not going to have time to see every friend and acquaintance."

Acquaintance had just been a spelling word. I'd taken a spying glance at Batler's test. She'd gotten it wrong in three places.

I walked out of the classroom, turning my lunch bag as I left so she could see the special cartoon drawn by my father.

THAT SUNDAY EVENING, I got a phone call in the middle of dinner.

"Greg?" said the voice. "It's Alison."

"Hi!" I said. "Wow. I didn't think I'd hear your voice so soon!"

"Gregory?" said the voice.

"Yes?" I said.

"I really, really love you!"

There were two or three fast clicks on the line, then dial tone. In my head I heard the voice of Pepe Le Pew, the cartoon skunk: "Oh, dahling, eez eet ze truth?"

In the morning I took Tony into the alley by the Big Yard and told him there was something I had to tell him, something so important that we'd have to wait to talk about it until after school.

"That's amazing," he said.

"It really is," I said.

"No, I mean it's amazing because I have to tell you something just as secret!"

In his silent apartment, the windows had been closed all day, and the smell was stale and stuffy. We split some strawberry yogurt his mom had left for him in the fridge, then we flopped on the couch.

"Tena was kind of avoiding me today," he said. "But that's smart of her, isn't it?"

Tony was right, public avoidance could have shown that

Tena was protecting the secret of her love for Tony. We lay on the couch and talked about tactics, about trust, about who in our class might be secretly sympathetic to our cause. When we got tired of that, we went to Tony's room and listened to "Do You Want to Know a Secret?" so many times I lost count. It felt like a good day.

Finally, as the weight of doubt lengthened the pauses between us, I asked Tony to tell me exactly, word for word, about his phone conversation with Tena.

She'd called him on Sunday night around dinnertime. She'd told him she really, really loved him. Before he could even answer, she'd hung up.

O N "H A V E A Nice Day" stationery decorated with a puppy, Alison wrote that she had not called me that Sunday night, nor any night since she'd seen me last. "Now," she wrote, "you'll never believe this, but, I have 8 boxes of stationery! I don't think I want you for a boyfriend anymore, just a friend. It's true."

Perhaps to soften the blow, she ended her letter with jokes. "Do lazy people wear shoes?" she asked. "Answer: Yes. Loafers!" Under each joke she wrote, "Get it? I do."

Tony and Lukas and I spent long afternoons trying to deduce who had tricked us. We named the mystery Case Catnip, after the effect the phone calls had on me and Tony. Our investigation began in 1975, and I was still noting possible clues in my journal in 1979. When we began, we agreed that the most important thing was to find the people who'd done it. They knew something about us. It was almost too enticing to stand, the thought of being known that way.

Weeks passed. We got nowhere. We stopped talking about the new rules and how to fight them. We knew when we were beaten. Now in class I rarely spoke. I clicked my bite-plate on and off my teeth, clicked it on, clicked it off, until even the teacher snapped at me to be quiet.

I kept a shoebox for pencils in my desk, and at the end of each morning and afternoon, while other kids found their friends and headed for the stairs, I searched the floor and tables for pencils that hadn't been put away. I added these to my box, and when it was full I brought it home, and brought back an empty one. Kids complained that I'd stolen their favorite pencil, the special pen that had been a present, the triangular plastic grip that kept the hand from hurting. They pleaded for their things back. I told them, *Finders keepers.* I never stole from them, as I always pointed out, and they had no proof that it was their property I'd picked up. If they wanted to keep their things, I told them—relishing the chance to enforce my own arbitrary and hurtful rule—they should write their names on them.

Another of my small satisfactions was taking the state's standardized tests. I was good at these tests, mysteriously good. As I penciled in the bubbles on the machine-scored answer sheets, and listened to the unhappy fidgeting of most of the kids around me, I pretended the lead ovals were machine-gun bullets spraying the class.

L A T E   O N   A spring night, I spotted a couple kissing out my window. Under the streetlight, they squeezed together as if they could fuse. Their arms were wrapped around each other's leather jacket. The kiss went on and on, an astonishing sighting, like the time my father pointed out a peregrine falcon, the fastest bird on the planet, he said, circling between the towers of two high-rise apartment buildings.

I watched, one hand on the cool windowsill. These lovers were showing the world. That was courage, I thought. I wanted to heave open the window, whistle, applaud.

The one facing toward me, mostly hidden, lowered an arm to squeeze a handful of buttock through black pants. It seemed a man's gesture to me, bold and teasing, but as I looked I saw the buttock he squeezed was small, the hips above narrow and unwomanly. The couple was two men. I jumped back from the window, knocked into my bed, feeling the rhythm of my pulse, my shallow breath.

I ESCAPED INTO fantasy books. In Narnia, Prydain, and Susan Cooper's Wales, lonely boys woke up on seemingly typical mornings and discovered awesome psychic gifts. Then one day, on a class trip to the public library, Lukas crossed over to the adult book section and found grown-up books on these subjects: developing your extrasensory perception; mastering the ancient techniques of telepathy, telekinesis, and clairvoyance. The books were long and obscure, full of words we didn't know, but to us this proved their authority, and anyway we could skim for the good stuff.

The power we craved most was telepathy, the ability to touch other minds. Lukas had been in love the year before with a girl named Lisa H. (All three of us referred to her without fail as Lisa H., as though to distinguish her from all the other Lisas across our great country who wished to be Lukas's girlfriend.) Lisa H. was in Colorado, and we knew it would be too great a feat for a beginner in New York to cast his thoughts to the Rocky Mountains, so we worked together, combining our psychic power to send a message such as, "Lukas still cares." After sending for several minutes, we cleared our minds and waited for a response. Then we compared our results—had we felt that we'd touched Lisa H.'s mind? Did she feel warmth toward Lukas?

Later we would sit cross-legged on the floor with a marble in front of each of us. Slowly we increased our concentration. We furrowed our brows and narrowed our eyes and squeezed tight our jaws until our teeth ached. We held our breath and sent all our psychic power into the marbles, to make them move.

After a minute or two of psychic concentration, as I was running low on breath, I saw stars. I gasped and looked around: The room felt brighter. It was impossible to say for certain that the marbles had not moved a little.

Disgusto

■ ▌ ■

O N A B I G square of drawing paper, I made a chart of the
sixth grade, showing the different kids' social standings:
who were the vain royalty and who the plotting aristocrats,
who the whispering advisers and who the unquestioning soldiers. I put myself down at the bottom, below the slaves who
would do anything, with the untouchables. Longing, sincerity,
heart's desire, open conversations like I'd had with Tony and
Lukas—these, I felt now, meant nothing. I set out to remake
myself.

I let it be known around the grade that I'd quit that sad
bunch of outcasts, Tony and Lukas and Tena Cohen. The two
boys kept their distance, though Tony stared at me sometimes
from across the yard. Tena began telling me I'd changed. I
walked her home down Greenwich Street, once, several times,
enjoying the flattery. A few days later she told me she really
liked me. She began talking to me where other kids could see
us. In my journal I wrote, "She is ruining my chances as an

actor in life!" I pretended not to know who she was, and soon she left me alone.

My camp friend Danny was shy and smart and very loyal; he'd never deserted me. Inspired by science fiction stories in which characters control the future, we drew up a detailed plan to become well liked, writing out the steps of our social climb and drawing a graph to track our progress. At the top of the final copy of the plan, we put our titles: he was a Mentat, a human computer from the *Dune* series, and I was a Psycho-historian, from *The Foundation Trilogy*.

There were two secrets, we decided, to a successful climb from outcast to commoner to nobility: to be seen with the right people, and never to remind anyone how we had let ourselves be treated the year before. (In a footnote to the plan, I wrote, "If attacked by Batler, fight to the *death!*") I dreamed I might one day set myself up as a king, like tall, funny, deep-voiced Jess Siegler.

But my coronation was a long way off. For now our plan ended with step six: Write a new plan. This popularity campaign, I suspected, could last a lifetime.

I tried to be as single-minded as possible, filling in the graph as I completed each step, and reminding myself to think of my schoolmates not as kids but as positions on a chart. I let show no more enthusiasm for girls than the popular boys did, and when the subject of a boy-girl party came up, I knew to talk as though all that mattered was what the girls would be willing to do in the kissing games.

But for all my plotting, I still went home with Danny, though his shyness might keep him forever near the bottom of the chart, a Lower Worker. And one Saturday afternoon, when my parents said I could bring a friend to a Mel Brooks comedy, I invited Matt Sampton, though he was a Warrior lacking aspirations.

Matt and I were sitting in the row in front of my parents, a position that partly eased the embarrassment of needing them to get us into movies, when a scene inspired my mother to commentary. The heads of a failing corporation sat around a conference table, talking about their marketing troubles. One of the men stood up to present the "secret weapon" of their new ad campaign, which, he said, would solve all their sales problems. He unveiled a redheaded woman, busty and beautiful, wearing a black merry widow, stockings, and very high heels. A toodling sound effect played, and the table rose a few inches into the air.

Matt and I laughed hard, rocking in our seats, bumping shoulders over the armrest. We were catching our breath as my mother leaned forward.

"Do you know why that's considered funny?" she whispered.

"Of *course!*" I said.

"It's okay to say you don't know."

"I got it! Why do you think I was laughing? Do you think I was faking?"

Beside me, Matt inched his back down the seat.

"Would you like me to explain?" my mother whispered.

"I got it!" I said again. "They all popped boners. Okay?"

Down the row and from behind, people shushed me. Matt was so deep in his seat that his knees touched the seat in front of him.

"Well," my mother whispered, "not exactly. You see, when a grown man sees something that excites him in a sexual way, his blood flows down to his penis. The blood fills—"

"That's what he *said*," my father interrupted. He sounded fed up with her, enormously fed up, like someone who didn't know why he bothered trying.

His voice snapped my mother back into her seat. She gave me a pleading look, as though I could rescue her just by saying yes, I was faking, I didn't get the joke. I had no idea what to do, so I turned forward again. Matt was still deep in hiding. It was bad enough that my mother would embarrass me this way. Worse that my parents were sniping in public. But what got me most was my mother's guess, that I was faking. My face felt hot with shame, and I was grateful for the dark protection of the theater. I hadn't been faking right then, but if I'd missed the joke, I'd have lied in a second. I did it all the time. I faked laughter. I faked annoyance with unpopular kids. I faked whole friendships. It was what you did. Only when my mother seemed to guess at my faking did I feel how much I hated it.

SETH LEE WAS planning a boy-girl party. He'd disliked me ever since Rudy's sports clinic, but by this time I had new allies—not the most powerful girls, but duchesses and such, and among the boys, Kevin Blair, the wild nicknamer. First I was Gregorio, because I'd been born in Italy, and then Oreo, Cookie-Face, Dessert-O-Rama. Kevin started in on Seth about inviting me to the party, and he wouldn't let up. I led Seth to think that no less a noble than Jess Siegler was planning to ride the crosstown bus with me. Seth found room for me after all.

He lived in a fancy apartment complex with an indoor swimming pool. We got the birthday presents and the pizza and the swimming over with, and then we got down to playing Postman. Six boys came, but of the invited girls, just two, both of them new to our school: Glenna wrote lyrics for a high school rock band, and wore brightly colored plastic earrings. Laura was a dreamy, private girl with fairy-tale blue eyes, who acted as though the world of our class, which so challenged me, could barely compete with the interesting things in her mind.

Beneath their perfume, the girls smelled of chlorine and blow-dryer heat. Their soft-lipped, enthusiastic kisses amazed me. When other boys got to go, I watched. We boys all locked our arms stiffly around their waists when we kissed, as if we were posing for a prom photographer. But these girls touched our hair, our necks, our faces. They leaned back and tipped our heads toward them like bowls, looking so serious that they seemed to be making a study: This is what it's like to kiss a shy boy. A tall boy. An overeager boy. A boy who really likes to kiss.

At the beginning of the year, I'd hardly dared talk to Glenna or Laura, let alone kiss them, but when I got home to my journal my triumph was overshadowed by envy. "We didn't have a variety!" I complained. But the trouble went deeper than lop-sided numbers. The boys had gone stiffly through the motions, but these girls had been *prepared*. I couldn't understand what we boys had missed. I had several well-meaning books to explain petting and intercourse, their mechanics and attendant responsibilities. One of these I'd bought in public at the school book fair, setting off a rush that cleared out the tall piles of books—blue covers for the boys' book, red for the girls'—and raising my standing in class significantly. But still I lacked crucial information. If I could have talked it over with Tony, we might have worked it out together, but Tony and I didn't speak anymore.

O N   A   R A R E family trip to see cousins out of the city, one of the men told a joke I didn't get. My father's laugh was like a dog's bark. I put a smile on my face, to keep up with the men, but then my father turned away from my cousin, and rolled his eyes for my mother's benefit. I froze, humiliated.

I waited until the next day, when I was alone with my father, to ask him about it. I sat down with him on the old wooden floor, while he got ready to fix a table lamp with a bad switch.

"Do you get that joke about how a JAP eats an ice-cream cone?" I asked.

The punch line wasn't words, it was a mime routine.

He said, "You mean—"

He made his left fist loose to show holding an ice-cream cone, and he stuck out his tongue to lick. But instead of licking the normal way, he put his other hand flat on the back of his head and pushed down, as though he wouldn't lick unless pushed.

"Yeah!" I said. "Why is she pushing her head?"

"She's not pushing her head! It's a *man* pushing her head."

He looked at me expectantly.

"What does he care if she eats her ice cream?" I asked. And then I finally got it.

"Oh," I said. "Okay."

Disgusto

I knew I wasn't supposed to, but I heard jokes as stories. I pictured a woman who hated ice cream and hated blow jobs, pictured her with the dark hair and dour expression of my cousin's wife. I imagined her with her husband's hand pressing her where she didn't want to go, and I thought how pissed off they both must be, how unhappy.

My father took out his toolbox and rummaged for the needle-nose pliers. Maybe, I felt, women didn't want what we wanted, and the secret in dirty jokes was that you forced them. Maybe my plan to become popular—my status chart and my schemes—wasn't just a trick for joining the kids who were growing up fastest. Maybe learning to push people down below you on your status chart *was* growing up. That could be the real joke: They didn't even want what you put in front of them, but there was your hand, pushing down.

"YOU KNOW THAT ice-cream joke?" I asked my mother.

"Ice cream?" she repeated. She was straightening up the part of the room we used as a living room. She fluffed a throw pillow on the brown corduroy couch.

"About how does a Jewish American Princess eat an ice-cream cone."

She seemed to be staring at the couch, though there wasn't anything on it except the pillows she had fluffed already. Her face was impassive, as it had been when our cousin told the joke.

"Don't you remember?" I asked.

"*Oh*, yes. That joke," she said, straightening a pile of magazines on the side table. "I sure do."

"Was it funny?" I asked. "I didn't see why it was supposed to be funny."

She stood back and surveyed the living-room area, hands on hips.

"You didn't, huh?"

"No," I said.

"Well, you know what?" she asked, turning toward me.

113

"What?"

"I didn't, either."

She smiled as though I'd made her proud—but for what? Refusing to understand how things were? Then she hugged me, though it wouldn't be my bedtime for a while.

I WAS HOPING Jess would have the next boy-girl party. He'd draw the most girls, I knew, and if he invited me personally it would help my standing. My father thought I should give the party myself, but I calculated that I was, at best, the most unpopular popular kid. Finally Seth had another party— "a 99% flop," I wrote in my journal. "The 1% worthwhile was that we played spin the bottle," but the feeling was all wrong. Besides the girls from the first party, Batler and another girl came, and though everyone kissed when the soda bottle pointed, you had to act like you'd hoped it would pass you by, as though by kissing you'd lost. Seth's mother interrupted us midgame, and Seth threw a tantrum, screaming and jumping until the furniture rattled. We were all sent home early.

TRISTAN AND I were trying to get to his backyard. From the hall, we could smell his older brother, Duane, smoking pot with his friend in the living room. Normally we would have sneaked past them to the back door, grateful to be ignored. For Duane, every moment seemed a chance to squeeze a reaction out of someone. When he wrestled Tristan, it didn't end when Tristan admitted he'd been beat. Tristan had to yell.

In the living room, Duane was saying, "That's an old one. Like the guy who gets out of jail and goes to the whore. Old and cold and full of mold."

"Sure, man," his friend said, "I think I know that one."

Tristan waved me on, but I hesitated. Duane had his sneakers up on one arm of the love seat and his head hanging down, his wavy, not-quite–Peter Frampton hair touching the floor.

"Whoa," he said. "Spies."

"We weren't spying, Duane," Tristan said, coming up behind me.

"Fuck a duck," Duane said. He sat up. "Now I've got to tell it. I wasn't going to bother, but these losers"—he gestured at Tristan and me with a hand that held a joint—"these losers don't know anything."

"We do so know some things," Tristan said.

"Yeah?" Duane asked. "Tell me one thing you know."

"I know Mom's going to be pissed when she finds out you're still smoking her pot."

"Why don't you tell her!" Duane said. He sat up on the couch and started flexing one arm, veteran of a million chin-ups on the bar in his room. "Why don't you tell her and we'll see how long you live."

"You think you're really tough," Tristan said sadly.

"You know what?" Duane asked. "I *am* pretty tough. You want to find out how tough I am? You want to come over here and find out just how tough I am?"

I knew I shouldn't, but I was staring at Duane, the rough way he tossed his head, the slow, hypnotic pumping of his forearm. I didn't know boys like this. He had something. He got girls, I was almost sure. He could help me, I thought, if he chose to.

"Come on, man," Duane's friend said. "Mellow out. I thought you were telling a joke."

"Look at this one," Duane said, pointing at me. "He's practically begging for it."

I examined the stained suede on my left Puma Clyde.

"So this guy gets out of jail and he goes to a whore . . ." the friend prompted.

"Right," Duane said. "That's it. A whore, first thing."

He interrupted himself to relight his joint with a purple plastic lighter. He took a long drag, staring at Tristan. We all waited while he held his breath, watched as he exhaled out his nostrils.

"The bastard goes to a whore," Duane said, "and he can't wait to eat her out. First thing. So he's at the whore's and he's eating her out, right? And he finds a pea."

"What?" the friend asked.

"He finds a pea. But he's been in jail for a long time and everything, so he keeps on eating her out."

"Gross," the friend said.

"And he's eating her out and eating her out and he finds a meatball."

"Get out!" the friend said. "Disgusto."

"So he says to the whore, 'If this keeps up, I think I'm gonna puke.' And the whore says, 'That's what the last guy said!' "

We all made laughing sounds.

"Oh!" the friend yelled. "That is foul. That is so foul! Duane, man. You're really grossing me out here."

"What's wrong with you?" Duane asked me. "Don't you get it?"

"Let's go outside," Tristan said.

"It doesn't make sense," I said.

"He doesn't get it!" Duane yelled. "Man, why do I even try? Why do I even fucking try?"

"It doesn't make sense," I said again. "I mean, the first guy. Why does the first guy go to a prost—what's he go to a whore for if he doesn't like it?"

"Listen to the big expert!" the friend said. He had himself a laugh.

"I mean," I said, "why did the guy want to eat her or whatever if he was going to puke?"

"The guy puked because the other guy puked first, Einstein." Duane shook his head at my youth and ignorance. He made a fist and started methodically popping his knuckles.

"But what about the first guy?" I asked. "He wouldn't have paid for it if he didn't like it, and if he liked it he wouldn't have puked. And he went to her first thing, right? He could have picked anything. He must have liked it."

For a moment the room was silent.

"It didn't really happen like you said," I told Duane.

"Who is this douche bag?" Duane asked the ceiling.

His friend cracked up again. Tristan jerked his head angrily toward the backyard and started toward the door. I'd blown it. Duane wasn't going to help me with anything. I could draw enough status charts to wallpaper my room, but I was never going to climb to the top.

"A meatball!" the friend cried. "Disgusto."

I WAS LYING in bed one night, half-dreaming. I'd been a prisoner, but I escaped from the dungeon up to a palace with a harem. The harem was full of girls I knew: Laura and Glenna the kissers, beautiful Alessandra who used to be my babysitter, even Alison who was still in New Jersey. I had escaped from the dungeon into the king's quarters, and now the harem guards thought I was a guest. Even though I cared about these girls, I had to be just as rough and demanding with them as the other men, so I didn't create suspicion and reveal my true identity.

The story rolled like a movie in my mind, and I ground my front against the bed, the firm mattress, the smooth, cool sheets. Sometimes, when I did this, the fantasy crossed into dream. I fell asleep. Other times, after a while, I felt a sweet burning, hot and cool at the same time, radiating out from between my legs.

This time the good burning came, and after a moment I reached over for my pajama bottoms, but they'd fallen off the bed. I switched on the reading lamp with the locomotive on the shade. Reflected in the light that burned my eyes I saw for the first time one clear drop, syrup-thick, shining at the tiny mouth of my penis. I was amazed—first at this proud little shine of come, and then at how ignorant I'd been. I'd thought masturbating was only when you grabbed yourself—*jerking off*, that vigorous pumping of hand on dick. You jerked and sweated and, when you were old enough, out shot this sticky white goober. The names for it were all jokes. But if it counted as masturbating to lift the top sheet in the summer and let it fall breathily against you, if it counted to press against the mattress and picture the someone you most liked in the world pressing back toward you from the other side, then I'd done it all sorts of times, without even knowing.

I straightened the lampshade and leaned my head back against the wall, understanding something two years later about my first summer at sleepaway camp. When our bunk had mandatory rest period, I'd daydream and grind against the mattress, and afterward the junior counselor smirked as if he wasn't sure whether to laugh in my face or admire me. Now it made sense. There I'd been, ten years old, masturbating in public to pass the time.

I felt the warmth of a blush on my face. In my embarrassment, I switched the lamp back off and slid under the covers. The strange thing about those afternoons at camp was how they hadn't felt the way the words made it sound: *whacking off, beating your meat,* or what this kid from Boston said, *poundin' the flounduh.* That kid cracked me up—sometimes it felt just like that, the whole sweaty experience one big dirty joke. But mostly, it didn't. Mostly, I found, when I tried things for myself, other people's names for them left so much out, they lied.

Like *dry humping.* In a couple of years, when I finally lay with a girl in my arms, and the two of us moved and pressed together through our clothes, my skin would feel as though after fourteen years asleep, it was finally awake. My dick—I thought of it then, no matter what it did for me, as a curse word, a *dick,* as in the insult, *suck my dick*—my so-called dick would feel ready to blow a trumpet solo. But the only words I'd have for this glory would be *dry humping.* It wasn't that I wanted to replace these dirty jokes with old-fashioned words like they had in the kids-and-sex books—*parking, necking, foreplay, excitement phase*—but where were the words for dirty earnest?

·   ·   ·

O N E   E V E N I N G   I N   June my father called me in to hear a song on the radio. It was hot and wet out, and the fans were humming.

"Know this one?" he asked.

I was amazed. Since he'd quit music reviewing and gone to sociology school, he'd stopped listening to anything fun. When I brought home "Convoy" or "Rubberband Man," or the hits of the Bay City Rollers, singles I bought after hearing American Top Forty, he was willing to listen only once. Yet now he was hurrying me to the stereo, to name the song before it ended.

"That's disco," I said.

"You don't like it?" he said.

"Disco sucks!" I said. It was what the older boys said at school.

"I don't know, lad. It would sure be great to dance to. . . ." He raised his eyebrows.

"Really? That?"

"Are you kidding? That could make anyone want to dance." He did a few dance moves, rocking his hips up and down. In the heat he wore cutoffs and no shirt. It had been years since I'd seen him dance.

"We're going to have a dance at the end of the year," I said.

"Yeah? At school?"

"Yeah, but I don't know if anyone's going to *go*. There aren't enough chaperons, and important girls are saying they're going to boycott. It's my last chance for a couples dance." My high standardized-test scores had gotten me into Hunter, a public magnet school: no tuition. I'd be starting there in the fall.

My father was still shaking his hips, moving his bent arms in small circles like a runner, but with his fists palm-down.

"This music sure is different from when I was in sixth grade," he said. "It's different from when I was in *college*. It's more . . ." he danced toward the overstuffed, yellow chair and danced back to me, thinking about it. "It's more *lubricated*."

I looked up at him, not understanding, but he was listening to the deejay.

"Could we talk about girls?" I asked.

He laughed so hard I jumped.

"What?" I said, frightened. "What's wrong?"

"Nothing's wrong." He laughed. "We can talk about girls anytime you like." His chest was still pumping in quiet amusement. We sat down cross-legged on the rug, where it was cooler.

"What if you're on a date," I said. "I mean, if you were on a date, how would you even know if she wants to be kissed?"

"A kissing question!" he said. "Okay. Let's see. There are three telltale signs. . . ."

"Really?" I asked.

"No."

"Oh," I said.

He winked.

"So how do you know?" I asked.

He shrugged. When I stared at him, he just grinned.

"You really don't know?"

"I sure didn't," he said. "A lot of it is just a surprise. The first time a girl put my penis in her mouth—whoa, was that a surprise! What's going on here? Nothing ever felt like *that* before."

"What about masturbating?"

"That tends to be less of a surprise," he said.

"No—I mean, do girls masturbate? 'Cause if they don't, they must think we're pretty weird."

"Some of them think we're pretty weird anyway."

"Be serious!"

"Well . . ." he said. "I don't think they . . . *find* masturbation as fast as boys do. But maybe that's changing."

"But they like it? When they . . . *find* it? Do they like all this stuff?"

"Do they like it?" my father repeated. "What's not to like?"

He leaned forward, grinning at me, an enormous, baby-glad grin that echoed across his face: His lips grinned, and the corners of his eyes; his dimples grinned sideways. His ribs, visible on his long, skinny frame, made a chorus grinning in harmony, and his crossed legs rose up grinning from the floor.

. . .

THE DANCE WAS held in the school cafeteria, which doubled as the auditorium. For a PA system, there was a dark blue record player with fold-out speakers. Borrowed Christmas lights flickered would-be disco ambiance, but daylight still shone in the windows. Streamers drooped from the ceiling. Even when most of the grade had gathered, the room dwarfed us.

Of the parent chaperons, my father was the only man. He looked happy enough doing the twist with one of the moms, but besides the two of them and a few girls closed off in a forbidding circle, no one was dancing. We'd eaten lunch in this room for years. Most of us had thrown up here.

"What's the trouble?" my father asked. "Everyone feeling a little shy?"

"Some of the boys want to open the equipment locker. They're saying it's still light out, so they might as well start a football game."

"Aren't they in the mood?"

"This is still just the cafeteria," I said. "It doesn't feel any different."

My father went over to the teacher by the record player and looked through the pile of 45's. "Disco Duck," a gag song about dancing waterfowl, ended and "Undercover Angel," a gag song about a guy and a centerfold photo, began. The wide wooden dance floor was empty.

My father had worn a satin baseball jacket, shimmery blue, to walk to the dance, a promo gift from his rock and roll days. Now he put it on again, and held up one hand to me with his fingers spread: He'd be back in five.

I didn't think much about where he was going. Maybe he just wanted a break. But when he came back, he was running. The flashing Christmas lights shimmered on his satin jacket. Here was something for us to look at—a tall, shimmering dad with a dandelion explosion of black hair, running through the elementary school cafeteria with a record-album-sized Crazy

Eddie bag held aloft like an Olympic torch. Kids pointed, edged forward to look at the mystery gift and the man with the enormous grin on his face who didn't seem like a chaperon at all. I ran to the stage, to see what he'd done.

He pulled the *Saturday Night Fever* sound track out of the bag and a few kids called out in recognition. The deejay teacher put on the disco album. My father started dancing the way he'd danced in our apartment, dancing as though it was the most natural thing in the world. A few girls started dancing with him. The sky outside had finally darkened, and the colored lights sparkled.

Boys crossed the dance floor, as though they were just there to check out the new addition to the record collection. I unfolded the cover, passed it around, and as kids gathered, my father danced over and gestured for the boys he knew to join him. Embarrassed but not unwilling, Danny and I started dancing near the girls, and then more boys, not to be outdone, followed. On the next song, my father danced over and slapped me five. Kids started slapping each other five. Soon I noticed some actual couples, boys and girls dancing together, in public.

It was not the way I'd seen it in the *Nutcracker* party, but it was pretty great. Between songs, kids told me what a cool dad I had, the hero of the sixth grade dance. A girl named Jenny had an envelope with a card inside for me, but I had to promise to read it in private. Batler was dancing with a group of her girlfriends. I wasn't even thinking about my status chart.

I WANTED MY father to talk to me about home runs, going all the way. I knew that if I asked him straight out, he would give me the facts, but what I wanted wasn't the familiar facts. I wanted the good kind of talking, the kind from when we talked about kissing. I couldn't think how to ask for it.

One night that summer on my bed, finally, sleepily, during the evening private talk I still thought of as "story," we stum-

Disgusto

bled onto it. He was doing most of the talking. When I realized what was happening, I didn't look up, didn't meet his eye. I didn't want to do or say anything that would interrupt him now, his voice so sleep-gravelly and sincere.

"The thing is," he said, "there are all these worries, and all these rules and rumors. All this terrible stuff about reputations, or there was. . . . And do you have to get married, and is it a sin. All that."

He waved his hand slowly in front of him, as though to clear the air.

"You do have to learn about not getting pregnant. That's a real thing." His voice turned fatherly for a moment. "It can seem like a really complicated deal. God, I don't want to have a *baby*, not now. And then you hear about these scary diseases, you have to be smart about that. You don't want to get syphilis or gonorrhea or something, your brains falling out your ears."

I laughed, very quietly.

"There's all this worry, and they manage to make it all seem really fraught and complicated. But okay, you learn about it, you use your head. It's not so complicated, really. You just have to learn to pay attention for a moment before things really get going. And then after all that, one night you're alone with this girl, and you want to be there, and she wants to be there. . . ."

He was talking by now almost completely to himself, as if he was working it out right then, discovering it as he said it to me.

Confessions of a
Gender Traitor

■ ▌ ■

M Y PARENTS HAD their blowups. The visible triggers, if any, were tiny things. One all-afternoon screaming match was about my father's hay-fever-season habit of leaving used tissues out. Another was about drinking soda from the bottle, instead of using a paper cup, selfishly leaving his backwash (my mother said) for the next person. There was a fight about the dangerous way he opened apple juice bottles, smacking them on the bottom to break their seals. (Once when I was little, a bottle had objected, shattering in his hands and leaving him with a tight scar across his palm.)

Other fights seemed entirely procedural, as though my parents couldn't even agree what to fight about.

"That is not the issue!" he would scream.

"This is your problem!" she would yell. "This is not my problem! It's *your problem*."

My mother left another job. Her career as a children's book editor was plagued by hostile men—"arrogant," she called them, "obnoxious," and "conceited." One boss might like her ideas, but soon he was gone, and the next was "impossible." My father's sociology degree had gotten him a new job in public relations, but he too hated the man he worked for. Hatred of the man in charge seemed like a fact of nature. Jobs were sellouts, careers shams. There was nothing to be done.

After my father got his public relations job, we moved a few blocks south to a larger apartment, a rent-stabilized duplex with separate bedrooms for my sister and me, a TV den, two bathrooms, a staircase the cats raced up and down—"a bourgeois palace," my father had complained, at first. But even with the extra space, my parents seemed increasingly agitated and jumpy, like animals in too small a cage.

My eighth grade year, my second at Hunter, the fights came more often. Mention of Jimmy Carter could bring one on. So could mention of inflation. More than once, Amanda and I asked to be excused from the dinner table, then fled, nearly running, as my father launched into his speech: If anyone had ever told him that one day he would make the enormous sum of thirty thousand American dollars a year and still only live like *this*. . . .

But he was still fun outside the house. Sometimes he took Amanda and me to brunch with his friend Eric, who worked in the music business. Eric wore dark sunglasses and leather bomber jackets, and his stiff black hair grew in a sharp, dark arrowhead at each temple. He talked to my father about new rock music and beautiful women. Stevie Nicks, he said, had the sexiest voice of any woman he'd ever heard. I hadn't known that a voice could be sexy, but now I began to listen.

Our game at brunch was to flirt with the waitress. When she came by with the check in her hand, looking tired at the end of her shift, asking if there was any last thing we needed—one more coffee refill, maybe?—everyone turned to me. I ordered another fresh-squeezed orange juice. She wrote it down, turned to the men. I kept talking. Eggs sunny-side up, two, no, make that three; sausage, hash browns, marble rye toast, a side of honey—an entire meal as though I'd just sat down. Amanda grinned, a coconspirator. We were happy if the waitress scanned the men's faces, asked if I was kidding, if I really thought I could eat that much. Then came the assurances. This? This was only an appetizer. You haven't heard of him? You must not have worked here very long. We won if she lost her composure, if her job face fell away and the woman underneath revealed herself.

Afterward, we listened to new rock albums together. We sang along to The Cars or Fleetwood Mac, all of us playing air guitars and knee drums. Eric started Amanda and me listening to New Wave bands like Split Enz, The Clash, and The Jam, also to smaller bands I heard nowhere else. He taught me about looking for nonalbum tracks on the B-sides of singles, about preferring the small record boutiques that carried European imports to the big bland chains.

When I telephoned girls, I played this new music on the living room stereo. I felt as though Eric and my father were friends hanging around to give me confidence. If the calls were long—if my mother was out, or too busy to enforce her ten-minute phone limit—I lay back on the couch with a girl's voice in one ear and my music in the other, and pretended we were talking in bed. From the bookshelf above, the spines of my mother's books stared down at me. I hadn't read them, but there they stood, waiting:

Woman in Sexist Society
Root of Bitterness
Male Chauvinism!
From Reverence to Rape
Woman's Fate

ONE WINTER NIGHT, as I sat at my desk by the window, I read and reread the same assigned line in *Latin for Americans*. Upstairs, my parents thundered at each other. I read the line again. There was a knock at my door.

"Can I study in here?" Amanda asked, quietly.

This was completely unprecedented. Usually I made it my

business to keep her away from my things, my friends, my skin if we sat side by side.

"Yeah," I said. She closed the door behind her and sat down at the edge of the throw rug, as though unsure how far into the room her welcome extended. I took my book and some loose-leaf paper and sat down next to her, leaning with her against the door, hoping to keep out the storm. I could feel her long brown hair tickle my elbow where my sleeve was rolled up; her shoulder warmed the side of my arm.

The noise from upstairs subsided. We wrote in our notebooks. Then our parents' voices started rising again, from hard-edged statements to theatrical exaggeration to full-throated anger. Soon could come projectiles and broken glass. I looked at Amanda to see if she was working, but she was staring at the rug. Almost as soon as I looked at her, she turned to me, and without a word we jumped up and ran upstairs. We pushed open my parents' bedroom door.

They froze. They were red-faced from screaming, their chests heaved, my mother's long hair hung in her face, but for a moment they stood perfectly still, looking at their children standing in their bedroom doorway.

"Stop it!" Amanda yelled.

"Can't you stop yelling?" I asked.

"We're only having a disagreement," my mother said, just as if she was saying, "It's about time to go to sleep."

"We have things to work out," my father added. He wasn't as good at hiding the edge in his voice.

"We have to be able to talk to each other," my mother said, reasonably.

"You're not *talking*," Amanda said.

"Can't you just stop it?" I pleaded.

"*A couple has to discuss their disagreements*," my father growled. When I heard that fraying tone I was six again, with my father standing above my bed. Now once again I flinched, shrank into myself. He didn't even need to scream at me. I was already making myself tiny.

Amanda and I slunk back downstairs. We sat again on my wooden floor and opened our books. Amanda started crying first. I leaned against her, and then, as she was beginning to quiet down, I joined in. I cried hard, wild, and smacked my back against the bedroom door. I knew it scared her, but I couldn't stop. I had relaxed around my father, relaxed as though I could trust him. Yet he still scared me silent when he wanted to; I still let him.

I suppose these fights weren't so bad, objectively. My father hadn't hit my mother, as far as I knew, and my mother hadn't locked him out of the house. I was older—a man, in the eyes of the religion we didn't observe—and I could understand more. But most nights, when the yelling began, I sat balancing on my cold metal windowsill, rocking hard against my fourth-floor window where it was cracked. I spoke to God, who didn't hear from me much otherwise, and asked for courage, the courage to roll through the cracked glass and out of this life.

There was self-pity in this prayer, but also something like a crisis of faith. There was nothing in these fights to keep alive our old stories, nothing to make us seem the pioneering family braving hardship to reach a better life. All we seemed to have left were versions of what had gone wrong. But it helped to have Amanda beside me. That night, I didn't take my usual seat rocking against the cracked window.

Finally our parents couldn't ignore the noisy grief coming up through the floorboards, or perhaps they finally wore themselves out. They climbed downstairs to comfort us and put us to bed.

THE NEXT DAY at Hunter, through the judicious use of cheating, silence, and lies, I got around the fact that none of my homework was done—until Latin. Mr. Kizner was a big, funny, demanding man who had been part of the D-Day invasion. While we translated Caesar's campaign in France, Mr. Kizner sometimes told us about his own battles—the sodden misery of amphibious landings, the confusion and the terror and the awful noise. On the marquees of big East Side synagogues, I'd see him listed as a guest lecturer, speaking on the connections between ancient and modern Jewish life. He was old enough to be my grandfather, and I liked to imagine (despite my parents' brief, bitter stories to the contrary) that he was what my grandfathers had been like, before they died.

Once in the hallway, I'd felt so overcome with admiration, I saluted him. He took hold of my arm, lowered it to my side, and said, "Don't ever do that in front of me again."

Today I started out class making a show of looking between my looseleaf and my open textbook, but my mind was at home, and I slumped down in my seat.

"Greg," he said, "would you translate the next line?"

"No."

"I don't think I heard you," Mr. Kizner said, walking down the rows of desks toward mine.

"I can't do it," I said. "I'm not prepared."

Through the wall, you could hear the quaver of the tiny French teacher with the curved spine.

"That's not like you, Greg," he said.

"My parents were fighting," I said in front of everyone. "I couldn't concentrate."

My classmates stared at their desks as I was transformed into The Kid Whose Family Is Fucked Up. I knew I should have crafted a better excuse, but my heart wasn't in it.

Mr. Kizner stood above me, rocking back and forth slightly. "Do they do that often?" he asked.

I thought about the question until kids began to fidget.

"I don't know," I said.

Mr. Kizner called on another student to translate the line. For a moment, before he walked away, he rested his thick hand on my shoulder.

W H E N I G O T home from school, no one mentioned the fight the night before. We ate dinner as usual at the stroke of seven, my mother measuring the portions onto all of our plates. A

129

thick silence settled over the apartment. It lasted all winter and into the spring, broken by cheerful impersonations of normality. I covered my notebook dividers and margins of my math homework with New Wave lyrics about the bitter ironies of love. There was a new Elvis now, Elvis Costello, who didn't sing "Love Me Tender." He sang, "Sometimes I think that love is just a tumor/You've got to cut it out."

Hunter was uptown on the East Side, and to get there I rode three subways. Afternoons, as I changed trains, a hole seemed to open inside me. To fill it, I would buy one Three Musketeers bar in the station, and sometimes another to carry me the six blocks home. There, I listened to my angry music, and stole from my mother's stash of bland, no-brand cookies, trying to lose myself in my homework. The plastic numbers on my clock radio flipped down, one at a time.

To distract myself from the empty feeling, some afternoons I went to Eighth Street, to flip through the posters of the Dallas Cowboys Cheerleaders. Hunter had no cheerleaders, no football team, no pep rallies, no jock in-group, and I was grateful I'd escaped all that. But when I saw the Cowboys' cheerleaders with their knowing smiles and their short-shorts clinging so high above their boots, I was sold. Before then, I'd given my private attentions to the unsmiling bra models in the Sunday magazine advertisements. They stared out at nothing as though hypnotized. But the cheerleaders looked like they knew what was up, that all their jumping and dancing and chanting was a ruse; they were on my TV screen and in the photography studios, traveling the country and getting known around the world *because they were sexy*. And they knew it. To look at them, you'd think they relished it. This astonished me.

On a flight back from a sales conference, my mother saw a movie about the cheerleaders. I wanted to hear all about it, but most of what I heard was my mother's disgust. The women were trained to smile and flirt, she said, even half-naked in freezing rain and snow, even when they felt sick and miserable. They were made to back into rosebushes, she reported, and to keep smiling while the thorns tore their skin.

"It's just so barbaric," she said. "No one cares how they feel, no one cares that there are *human beings* inside. All anybody cares is that they look *pretty.*"

When my mother talked, I could feel the misery of faking your feelings for a living. But when I was alone in my room that night, and the next, I'd picture the moment when my favorite cheerleader, a small, dark-haired woman, brushed against a rosebush, feeling smooth leaves and moist petals and now and then a thorn against her bare skin. In my version it was hot and sunny out, and she didn't worry about a scratch or two. She had better things on her mind.

In stores, I lingered guiltily over the cheerleaders' pictures, knowing I could never bring them home.

THE ONE THING that made me forget my afternoon emptiness was to ride downtown with Susie Steinbach and Rosa Rodriguez. Susie lived up in the Bronx, and Rosa all the way out in Forest Hills, but their ballet school was across from the clock tower of the Jefferson Market Library, near me. While we talked, I tried not to give away that I was watching them, how they balanced the weight of the dance bags over their shoulders by jutting out their left hips. I followed along with them, knapsack slung casually over one shoulder, amazed at my good luck. It also seemed to amaze other guys from school, who stared from across the platform.

Often we took the Lexington Avenue line, so we could walk west on Eighth Street, which was their idea of Greenwich Village—head shops, hippie jewelry makers, stores selling pins of album cover art. Young drug dealers called out to them, wishing the ladies good day, keeping up snappy patter: "Marijuana—check it out!—*real* nice grass. Marijuana—check it out! . . ." On Eighth Street, it was us and drugs and rock and roll.

Susie and I teased Rosa for being so polite, yet so judgmental. When she got shoved on the subway or the street, she apologized. "Someone ought to," she said. But once the offender was out of earshot, she ranted at how impolite he was, how badly trained. We were studying the Russian Revolution that year, and I called her the Little Czarina.

The two girls teased me for padding sentences with the words "silly" and "basically," which they said made me sound like a nerd. We complained about the injustice of teachers' past test questions, and we cagily compared grades. I tried to get Susie and Rosa to appreciate *Dune*, without success. Susie talked Rosa and me into reading *The Women's Room*, her favorite book.

Today the topic was the shy girl from Eastern Europe in our health-ed class.

"Can you even believe that?" Susie asked. "A thirteen-year-old girl who doesn't know what an orgasm is?"

"I bet my mom didn't know," Rosa said. "In Cuba? I bet she didn't know what a *boy* was."

Susie and I laughed. Rosa added, quietly, "I'm still not sure she knows."

We had a moment of silent mourning for Rosa's social life: She wasn't supposed to have boyfriends.

Then Susie asked, "What's this?"

She made a face, eyelids drooping, lips pursed weakly.

"What?" I asked.

"You sure you don't recognize it?"

Rosa sniggered.

Susie leaned in toward me, strands of her dirty-blonde hair slipping down like a veil. I smelled her conditioner, her sweet perfume.

"What, already?"

She gazed at me from under hooded eyes, breathing heavily, her face in a seeming ecstasy of fatigue.

"What is it?"

"Blower's cramp."

"Hey, that's pretty good!"

"What," Susie asked, "as opposed to all the bad jokes I tell?"

Jokes could vanish from my mind as fast as a night's dreams, so I repeated the parts of this one to myself, planning to tell it to Rafe at lunch, or to Tucson and his older brother Al. But it was no good. Susie didn't tell real dirty jokes. Her blow-job face seemed almost noble, as if she'd given her all, the best she had. It was a face that could never appear in a guy's dirty joke. It didn't wrench your stomach.

Most days we wound up at the bagel place just a couple of blocks down from their ballet school, where the girls bought the last of the day's many diet sodas.

"Do you know that guy John?" Rosa asked Susie one day.

"Which class?"

"I don't know. He hangs out in the courtyard at lunch."

"What does he look like?"

"I don't know, brown hair. He's sort of short—not really short, just sort of."

"How many boys in the grade *don't* fit that description?"

"Hey!" I said.

"Sorry," Susie said, "but you guys really have to work on the height thing."

"Don't worry," I said, looking up at her. "In a couple years you'll be a functional dwarf."

"Like me," Rosa said. Her list of what she viewed as the disappointments of her body included, as well as her too-cute-to-take-seriously dimples, her too-curly hair, her calves, her thighs, her ass, her waist, her breasts, the dark hair on her arms, and being too short.

"Do you ever notice," Rosa pressed on, "that the whole time John's talking to you, he's talking to your tits?"

"Doesn't that just drive you *crazy*?" Susie asked. "You want to take him by the chin and be like, no, really, I do have a face, it's right *here*."

"Oh, my God!" Rosa laughed. "Yes! You know the guy I mean?"

"Does it matter?" Susie asked. "Don't they all do that?"

"Oh, sure," I said, offended. "Every single one."

"You said it, not me," Susie said.

"But you don't think that," I said. "I mean, you don't really think that."

Susie raised her eyebrows.

"Do you?" I asked.

She was a genius at the ambiguous dramatic flourish, the gesture that gave nothing away.

"You can't be saying all guys are alike," I said.

Susie stared at me. I looked at her wide almond eyes, her slanting cheekbones, the curling fullness of her lower lip.

"Maybe," she said, "you ought to quit while you're behind."

"Wait," I started to say, not meaning to sound so pleading. "This is silly. It's not always the same, right? I mean, if someone's staring—basically—"

"Not 'basically'!" the girls chimed together.

"Okay! Okay. If someone's not-basically staring at your tits, I mean, not really staring but just looking at them—looking at them a lot, though, so you notice them—"

"—staring?" Susie offered.

Rosa giggled.

"Just wait!" I said. I had their attention, at least. "Someone looking at your tits. Is that ever, I mean could it ever be, you know, a compliment?"

The two girls were watching me, amused, but as they recognized the question I'd been stumbling over, they looked at each other, and then down at the table.

"It's not really a compliment . . ." Rosa said, in the exaggeratedly patient tone some women use with children. "I suppose it's sort of nice to know you're not *deformed* or anything—"

"First thing I worry about when *I* get up in the morning," Susie said.

"But is it *ever* something a girl likes?" I interrupted. "Is it ever something good?"

I was having some crazy fit of sincerity. I had to know right away—sooner.

I looked at Rosa for what felt like a long time, not at her tits—though honestly it was hard not to, with the thought in the air and Rosa sitting up straight so the table wouldn't make her look short, her white cotton blouse unbuttoned two buttons, revealing the brighter-white edge of her bra—but right in her dark brown eyes. Embarrassed, she turned to Susie.

"No," Susie answered. "How could it be a compliment? I know my tits are there. I've checked."

Rosa cracked up at Susie's outrageousness.

I knew it was time to let the question go—past time—but my head was crammed with it. What was a guy who went for girls supposed to do? Ignore what they said, because you knew best? Assume girls were liars? Wouldn't they admit to one single moment when a girl would be right to relish a boy's eyes on her?

I couldn't ask my questions. Even in the privacy of my own head, just thinking about looking at these girls, and what I could see—Rosa's hypnotizing ass, Susie's amazing small tits like a French model's—tangled me up. In my journal, when I described a girl's looks, I followed up with an apology. And now at our regular table, I could sympathize with how used and ignored Rosa felt with a boy who only talked to her boobs; envy this John for the good long look he got; steal a glance in the meantime at Susie's beneath her white leotard (noticing that she almost definitely caught me looking and didn't seem to be saying anything about it); and berate myself for not even having the decency to keep my eyes off her tits when we were talking about that exact male problem.

"Why do guys *do* that?" Rosa asked. "What are they *thinking*?"

Susie nodded, letting it stand, and the girls withdrew from me into private girl-thoughts.

"Nothing," I said. Susie and Rosa looked up, surprised.

"Guys *aren't* thinking. They look at a girl and they shut down their brains."

Rosa laughed.

"Really! You remember you were saying how nice everyone was after you were up so late writing that social studies paper? How Larry and Matt and Havana all told you you looked so pretty? That wasn't being nice."

"But I'd slept like two hours," Rosa said. "It was all makeup!"

"Guys don't know when it's makeup," I said. "Guys are *ignorant*! They don't know which girls dye their hair. They don't know when you like them and when you're just flirting. Half of them are probably mystified why girls use more toilet paper."

This got a laugh.

"I'm telling you," I said. "Guys are idiots."

FROM THEN ON, I had a sure way to catch the interest of almost any Hunter girl. Isn't that the problem with guys? I'd ask, getting a conversation going. Don't you hate that about guys? It got a laugh, then a look to see if I meant it. And I did. I'd mock anything guy, even things I loved—science fiction even when Danny was listening; sports even in the middle of gym. I didn't feel I was talking about me, only about *guys*. Whose side was I on? I didn't know. I made myself the girls' conversation slut. I'd talk about anything.

IT WAS A summer-hot June afternoon, too humid for walking around. Susie and Rosa and I went straight for the air-conditioning of the bagel place. Between them, as usual, the girls had one bagel with cream cheese and two large Tabs. Susie pulled the bagel apart, and both of them scraped the cream cheese off onto the paper wrapper, until the white film left was almost thin enough to see through.

"Is that all you want?" I'd asked, the first time I'd seen this. "You could take a pat of butter."

"Are you high?" Susie said. "Butter has like three times the calories."

Now Rosa pushed two leftover quarter bagels and the mounds of cream cheese toward me. "Would you eat that?" she asked. "Please? Because if you don't, I will."

I spread on some more cream cheese, but its sweaty sheen

began to bother me. Being around Susie and Rosa made me feel the little roll of stomach that hung over my belt when I sat down. I started scraping some cream cheese off again, and the plastic knife snapped.

"Amateur," Susie said.

Rosa offered me her Tab, but I said I didn't like the aftertaste.

"Oh, I'm sorry," she said. "I forgot. I shouldn't have ordered diet."

"Rosa?" I said.

"What?"

"It's your soda," Susie said. "You don't have to apologize."

"Oh, I'm—" Rosa said, starting to apologize for apologizing, but she caught herself. We all laughed, and it felt for a moment as if we'd been in Rosa's head together.

I liked them both so much.

"It's almost time," Susie said, looking at her watch.

Rosa slurped down to the end of her soda and then sighed. Then she put her hand on her stomach, making a face.

"I have to get up," she said. Susie slid her chair forward, making room. "God, I shouldn't have eaten so much."

Rosa stood before Susie and me, her designer jeans skin-tight. She could only get them on lying down, she'd told us, with her mother to help pull. The jeans squeezed in at her waist, clung as though wet to her hips and thighs. Below the metal button, fanning out left and right from the fly front, the denim wrinkled.

"Look at that," Rosa said. "Isn't that gross?"

"I have that," Susie said.

"You don't have it like I have it."

"Yes, I do."

"Have *what*?" I asked.

"Don't you see?" Rosa said. She slid a finger in between her denimed knees, and pulled it slowly up in the narrowing space. My breathing shallowed.

"They *touch*," she said, meaning her thighs. With a restrained *ugh*, she pulled her hands in toward her chest, balling her fists and quivering in self-disgust. Behind her small fists and her white blouse, her breasts gently shook.

Most guys, I knew, just let girls run themselves down. It wasn't their department. And among guys in our grade, the word was Susie had a problem. She was too sarcastic, too standoffish, and the reason was a swelled head. Because she knew she was sexy, the explanation went, she'd gotten spoiled, and Rosa could easily go next. You had to be crazy to give either one an excuse to get any more full of herself.

But I wasn't going to be held back by any guy rule. I wanted to tell them they were wrong about their bodies, that I carried whole movies of them in my mind. I wanted to tell them about how boys debated which of them was sexier, debates like the ones over which was the best group, the Stones or The Who. The point wasn't to settle the question, but to explore it, caress it. I wanted to tell them about the older boys I'd overheard watching Susie stretch, using her locker door as a barre.

"Look at that leg," one said to the other. "Couldn't you just eat that leg?"

But I'd watched myself watching them. When Rosa displayed herself, spotlighting her flaws, offering herself for public humiliation, I thrilled. Yes, it was awful that when she felt heavy, she punished herself with a long day in her tightest, most uncomfortable jeans, jeans that finally managed to make her sweet ass look fat. It was awful that everyone had to hear all day how revolting she was, awful and yet fascinating, breathtakingly sexy. Who was I to tell Rosa she could relax around me? Wasn't I her problem?

WE CAME OUT of the bagel place into the hot, wet breath of the day. The sun slanted over the low West Village buildings, raising the dirty-oven smell of concrete and blacktop. We walked slowly up the block to the ballet school.

"God, we're going to sweat today," Rosa said.

"It's not air-conditioned?" I asked.

"Yeah, right," Susie said.

"In the summer it's so gross," Rosa said. "We sweat right through our leotards."

"Wow," I said. I intended sympathy, but in my mind I saw the girls flushed and panting, the sweat gathering between their breasts, sliding down their poor maligned stomachs.

"What a surprise," Susie said. "Look who's back."

She cocked her head across Sixth Avenue, at the construction workers sitting on the steps of the Jefferson Market Library.

"Can I just ask a question?" Susie went on. "How much fun is that? I mean really. You've got your sandwich and your can of soda, and you're sitting in the shade watching girls sweat. How much fun could that be?"

I didn't answer.

"Well," Rosa said, "in we go."

The girls kissed me good-bye, the kisses quick and sophisticated—more about seeming cosmopolitan than about me. Still, they leaned in toward me, brushed close, and for a minute I felt I was living in one of those movies in my mind.

The girls vanished through the narrow ballet-school doorway, and I was alone on the street. I crossed to the shaded side of Sixth Avenue, and walked over to the library steps as nonchalantly as I could.

Five guys with dirty work clothes and clean, muscular hands sat theater style, all looking up at the dance studio windows across the street.

"Come on, teacher," one guy said, "send your students to the head of the class."

"Where we can see 'em!" said another.

Up behind the tall second-floor windows, teenage girls in leotards gathered, stretching. They raised their hands high over the prim buns of their hair like bra models in the Sunday ads, presenting their breasts. It was luxurious to look, and not be careful, and not second-guess myself. I could stare at my complicated, elusive ballerinas as long as I damn pleased. The ceiling fans above them spun lazily.

"Got some very attractive girls at that dancing school," the guy nearest me said.

"I know," I said. "I noticed."

"Hey—" he called to his buddies, "I said there's good-looking girls over there, and this kid says, 'I noticed'! " He laughed with his mouth open, and I looked for cruelty, but I didn't find it. He was young, not so far out of high school, I guessed. If Susie and Rosa had met him, they'd have fallen over each other to talk to him. My shoulders tightened in competition. The construction worker caught me staring.

"You noticed, huh?" He laughed again.

I wanted to tell him I wasn't what he thought, some kid here to gawk. I knew these girls. I knew these girls better than he ever could. But what exactly did I think I could tell this guy? *We have really great conversations?* That wasn't going to cut much ice on the job site. *We flirt a lot after school?*

A couple of the other construction workers leaned forward to get a look at me, and apparently what they saw made the joke even funnier. To them, I imagined, it would seem simple. I'd had a whole school year to work on these curvy ballerinas, front row seats at the seasonal striptease, watching them shed their winter coats and leg warmers, unglove their hands. I'd been there as they pulled off their sweaters in the spring, and bared pale arms and paler shoulders to the heat of summer. Could nature have given me a bigger hint? Yet in the past ten months, I'd barely gotten to first base.

I sat on the steps, breathing the hot, heavy air, wondering what reason I could give for not making moves on Susie or Rosa. (What to do? Who to leave out? How to keep the connection?) Maybe, I thought, that was my real problem: I thought too much. Maybe manhood only asked one thing: a firm, unwavering ignorance. To grow up and get laid, I had to stop thinking about what girls felt and thought and wanted—stop thinking, in fact, as much as possible. Stick to the one thing men were meant to have on their minds.

MY PARENTS HAD grown ever more restrained after the fight Amanda and I had interrupted, and when they asked us, perfectly calmly, to sit down in the living room with them for a serious talk, I knew what was coming. My mother explained that my father had taken a small apartment. My father added that it was very close, nearby. My mother began explaining the difference between a trial separation, which is what they were getting, and a divorce.

"No!" Amanda said, jumping up from the couch, instantly, brilliantly hysterical. "No, you're not getting either one. I won't let you! *I won't let you.*"

My marvelous sister screamed, she cried, she flailed her arms and her head. Her hair swung through the air like a banner that yet waved. I sat unmoving, deep in the couch, watching the pain on my parents' faces, and filling with love and gratitude for my beautiful, banshee sister.

My mother stood up from her chair and gently put her arms around Amanda, who broke free, still howling. In my head, a voice like the narrator of a documentary described how reasonable my sister's response was, how appropriate. Finally she tired out, and my parents got back to their script. They explained that nothing had really changed. They still loved Amanda and me, they'd just be living in two different, yet nearby, places. The narrator in my head observed that in their own ways they were as hysterical as my sister.

My mother put her arms around Amanda again, succeeding this time. I got up and walked quietly to my father, who sat in the overstuffed chair. He wore big thick glasses with brown plastic frames, and behind them his long face was pale. I raised my hand in the air, and he seemed to flinch. We both froze for a moment, and then I lowered my hand onto his shoulder. Maybe they had only scripted the group presentation—I could tell he didn't know what to say to me one-on-one.

"It's all right," I told him. "I understand. It's all right." I squeezed his shoulder. Then I walked slowly to my room and lay on my bed, my sneaker heels catching on the thin blanket. I tried to think of nothing, but "Helter Skelter" was screaming through my head.

•   •   •

THE LAST TIME my parents had seemed content together
had been a Sunday of spring cleaning. We all had jobs assigned
from my mother's list, and in addition, my sister and I got a
quarter for each load of trash we carried downstairs. My father
put on paint-speckled jeans shorts and an old yellow T-shirt
with the name of a band across the chest, a band he'd believed
in during his rock critic days, a band that never made it. I
helped my parents roll up the Oriental rug Grandmother Jane
had given us, to take to be cleaned and stored for the summer.
On the bare floor where the rug had been, my father spread out
newspapers, then got down his toolbox and the fans from the
closet.

As he loosened the screws of the fans' protective cages, he
sang to himself. As usual, the tune was right, but he didn't
have the words straight. He was singing about French kisses. I
knew the song from my radio, knew he was jazzing it up a bit,
putting an extra *oomph* into "French."

All my father did was wipe the grime off the blades and the
cage, and oil the little engines with 3-in-One oil, but when he
was done, and the five fans stood gleaming in a line, my
mother stopped to admire them, and to smile at him. My father
could rewire lamps when they got old, he could spackle and
repaint holes in the wall, he could clean and oil the fans. Mean-
while my mother was in the kitchen, doing things he didn't
know how to do. This wasn't how they'd meant to live together, but for that afternoon at least they seemed glad to have
each other in the house.

After all the chores were crossed off my mother's list, I asked
my father if we could have a catch on the side street. He was
nearly forty, but gangly and loose from the heat; in his bright
yellow T-shirt, his cutoff jeans, and his fielder's mitt, he looked
like a teenager. We threw on the sidewalk in the late afternoon
light until a woman I'd never seen before walked by. She had
big eyes made up to look dark and wide, black hair that fell in

shaggy curls, and lipstick red as barbecue sauce. She stopped to talk to my father, rocking one heel of her high, shiny boots.

I could have thrown my father a high fly, tricking him away from her with a chance to show off. I could have screamed, "Come *on*, Jimmy!" But instead I wandered among the parked cars, and in time I found an old tennis ball. Putting the hardball aside, I rediscovered my old game of throwing a tennis ball at the base of a wall; if it hit the wall first, it came back as a skimming grounder, but if it hit the sidewalk first, it bounced back as a pop fly.

Every few throws, I glanced up the street. My father had a grin on his face, and a look of relief, the look Amanda got on a summer day when we'd climbed the three flights of stairs, and we were finally standing by the biggest fan in the apartment. I couldn't remember the last time he'd looked that way.

My
Don Juan Complex

■ ▌ ■

UP BEHIND ME came Havana Perdiguero. I was at my locker, spinning the dial on my combination lock. I heard the slow tapping of his shoes on the hallway tile. Most of the ninth grade had already left for the day.

"I got something to say to you," Havana called.

I turned to face him. Like me, he was of about average height, with dark hair, and skin the drama-group makeup crew would have called olive. His gray dress shirt shone like silver, and his snug designer jeans were streaked pale down the center of each leg, where an iron regularly pressed them smooth. He kept coming, crowding me now, tipping his head back until he seemed to loom.

"You know what your problem is?" Havana asked, chin in my face.

Over his shoulder, where the nearly empty hall turned the corner, I noticed his guys, five or six of them by the lockers. I could feel my heart beating.

"I didn't know I had a problem."

He smiled cheerlessly. "Yeah, I bet you didn't."

Another guy, I imagined, would think of a way out of this, but all I came up with was something Havana once said about music: "Oh, The Beatles. Those five faggots."

"You got a problem all right," he said. "I've seen guys like you before, always on the make. Your problem is, you got a Don Juan complex."

I'd never heard of a Don Juan complex, but I could guess. Even now that I was going out with Rosa, I was promiscuous in glance and conversation and friendship. It wasn't normal.

In the narrow space between us, Havana raised his forefinger higher.

"I . . . *love* . . . Rosa," he said, as though *love* was a word a guy like me couldn't understand. "Rosa, she's like a sister to me. You touch her—"

He stopped himself short, leaned back, looked down at the red-and-black tile floor. I *was* Rosa's boyfriend, after all. Even though she wasn't allowed on formal dates, it was pretty likely I'd touch her somewhere. He waited a beat, then puffed out his chest and tried again.

"You mistreat her," he said, "I kill you. You make her cry, I kill you. You hurt one hair on her head, one single hair—I kill you."

I'd never been cornered like this, but I knew what he was saying. *Keep away from our women.* I tried to back away, felt a combination lock hard between my shoulders. I imagined Havana and his guys as a Latino gang in deepest Queens, gold chains around their necks, scars on their faces from the fights that protected the honor of their women. I thought it might almost be worth getting beat up to have the rules that clear.

But then he hesitated, looking at me for a cue, and I couldn't help thinking about that hair. One *single* hair?

"It's all right, Havana," I said, surprising us both. "Rosa's great. We all love Rosa. She's going to be fine."

He narrowed his dark eyes at me, took a step back. Even I

knew this wasn't the right tough-guy move. I turned my back to him, and pulled out my windbreaker and knapsack. His loafers tapped back toward his friends.

As I reached the end of the hall, he yelled, "Don't make me tell you again!" But his line was late, and his guys were still by their lockers. I let the stairwell fire door smack shut on his words.

I ran down the stairs two and then three at a time. Fear buzzed through me like too much coffee, but my speed was celebration. Havana and his boys weren't going to come after me; if they did, they wouldn't know what to do.

ON THE PHONE after my brush with Havana, I tried to give Rosa a blow-by-blow of my escape.

"There's no way that's what he said," Rosa interrupted. "That's not even how he talks. He doesn't drop his—his helping verbs, or whatever they are."

"I'm telling you exactly what he said!"

"What is *with* you guys?"

"Me? You're including me?"

"God!" she yelled. "Havana isn't even *from* Queens. And Vago is Armenian—that's not exactly Latin heritage, in case you didn't know."

She tried to tell me again about Havana's friends, how Larry was only mean when he felt insecure, how Antolin was the gentlest boy she'd ever met. I didn't care. They were still a group of guys, and any guys who hung out in a group were guys who'd have no use for me.

I'D MET AARON at my friend Tucson's weekend Dungeons and Dragons game, but his real love was social intrigue. He got the story on every argument and every school couple he could, and when there wasn't enough new ninth grade gossip to talk about, he made his own, conducting informal surveys of who would consider going out with whom, and then reporting the conversations to his friends. He was brusque and invasive and disarmingly frank, and almost everyone answered his questions. I admired him hugely.

After I broke up with Rosa—I said her mother's rules were puritanical, she said it shouldn't matter to me—he called me with the news that Ronnie Wiener, the class oracle, had proclaimed my romantic career dead.

"Who's he going to go out with now?" Ronnie had asked Aaron. "Who'd want to be his next victim?"

To Aaron, perhaps, this was just the day's wild story, but I'd been waiting for this moment, dreading it. When my class had started Hunter in the seventh grade, we were a motley, socially confused bunch of A students from all over the five boroughs; the school had only gone co-ed a few years back, and no one seemed to know how guys and girls were supposed to act together. But now, I was afraid, the grade was coming to its senses. My strange ways were being discovered. I spent too much time with girls, and too publicly. It wasn't just my suspicious number of girlfriends. I came to school early to see who was hanging out in the hallways. I passed notes with Sarah and Kyra, held hands in the hall with Josine, joked with Joanna before and during Latin. There was something wrong with me, befriending all these girls. Boys would close ranks. Girls would be warned away. I'd be cast out again.

I got pretty emotional on the phone that night with Aaron. I dragged the heavy black rotary into my room and sat at my old desk, digging with my thumbnail in the soft, flesh-colored wood beneath the veneer. I pitched my voice low, so my mother wouldn't hear, but Aaron didn't make fun of me. I felt like a freak, I told him. I didn't fit in with guys, but I couldn't reach the girls, either—I'd gone out with Rosa, and Susie before her, but I'd lost them without ever really feeling like I'd "had" them. Maybe, I said, Ronnie and Havana were right.

I told Aaron that when I slept over at my father's new apartment, he would get up in the morning, turn on the shower, and sob. My father thought the shower noise hid the sounds.

Aaron was silent for a few moments. Then he said, "I hate

that kind of stuff." He told me to come sleep over that weekend at his mom's place in Stuyvesant Town. Between them they had all the Beatles albums, and we would listen to them in order. He said that if you timed the marathon so you reached "Here Comes the Sun" at daybreak, it felt really good.

AARON AND TUCSON said to come play ultimate Frisbee after school, that it was a cool game and co-ed. The game moved like soccer up and down the courtyard, a rectangle of gray asphalt behind the redbrick school building. After a couple of throws, the disc flew wild, skittering along the ground and scraping to a stop. The other side took possession, and one of the guys on my team yelled, "Guard your man! Guard your man!"

"Or woman!" cried Heather, sprinting across the field.

"Or person!" cried Joanna.

Again, players dodged and weaved, and the Frisbee swooped in unplanned directions. After giving up a touchdown, we reassembled at our end of the playing field. From his end, Aaron yelled, "What's the score?"

"Who cares?" came the oddly cheerful reply from Eleanor.

"We can't play if we don't know the score!" Aaron yelled.

"Aren't we playing now?" asked Heather.

I laughed out loud, then looked around nervously, but no one seemed offended. Aaron called out a score, and instead of confirmation, the other team sent the Frisbee sailing back toward us.

As the November afternoon waned, the sun got lost behind apartment buildings. The colder air hardened the plastic disc and stiffened our fingers.

"Do you have to pass so damned hard?" Joanna yelled at Aaron.

"I didn't think it was that hard," he said.

"Well, it was."

"I guess I don't know my own strength."

"Well, *learn* it."

In a game full of commentary and jokes, Aaron's sharp voice was the most frequently heard. He was tall, over six feet, even standing hunched over as he did. His dirty-blond hair stood in the rounded mass of curls kids elsewhere called a Jewfro. He argued for keeping score, for continuing to play until the game was won, for team captains evenly matched in ability and knowledge of the players. Although I often agreed with him, these disputes made me nervous. I thought I knew what was going on: Guys arguing for what they always argued for—playing to win, interpreting the rules to benefit your own team, pushing until the end. Girls resisting. Most of the inexperienced and unathletic players were girls, and most of the players who wouldn't throw to them were boys. I imagined the girls wanted a kind of antigame, a game that took revenge for all the old schoolyard exclusions.

But it wasn't true that the boys were all of one mind. Tucson, Aaron's closest friend off the field, would have nothing to do with his game attitude. He told Aaron to calm down, to stop yelling, to shut up already and let us just *play*. If I'd had to choose, I would have sided with the girls and Tucson, but I didn't want to choose. I wanted Aaron to argue for keeping score, because I loved to play defense, to become at once a sheepdog and a geometry whiz, feeling where the disc would appear, and at what angle.

The girls played harder than I'd realized. They all looked great to me, running in their jeans and sweaters, but they played for real, and screamed and cursed when they missed a throw. I'd never noticed how much longer a girl's legs were than those of a boy the same height, or how quick those long, light legs could make them. Some afternoons, the teams were well matched and the mood was right, and everyone kept score with Aaron, cheering and groaning until the game was finally won.

That winter we played three, sometimes four afternoons a week, whenever we could gather the bare minimum six players and there wasn't too much ice on the ground. The wind spun dried leaves and discarded sandwich papers in little tornadoes, and we began the game awkwardly bundled in coats and scarves—all except Thads, in his light wool sweater and jauntily tied scarf, who seemed not to believe in the weather. Gusts jerked the Frisbee up like a puppet; our shouts and the slaps of sneakers on the winter-hard pavement echoed off the courtyard walls. We coughed in the cold dry air, and on the worst days our eyes watered, but slowly we warmed up, shucking our coats on the redbrick stairs. In winter hats and layers of sweaters, we sprinted through late afternoon light, the heat from our bodies winning us if not easy summer then at least promising spring.

We disagreed about the score, and whether to keep score, and whether to keep arguing, and whether we were in fact arguing at all. Aaron yelled, and Joanna yelled back, and by winter break they were a couple.

RAFE CAUGHT MY eye in the hall, motioned me over to a narrow window that didn't open. He wore a baseball jersey with the sleeves pulled back to his elbows. He tipped his head toward mine conspiratorially, long boyish bangs falling in front of his eyes.

"You know Andrea?" he asked.

"Sure," I said. "She plays ultimate sometimes. Why?"

"Wow, man," he said. I found it hard to tell if Rafe was joking.

"Wow what?" I asked. Andrea was an ace Latin student, the shyest girl I knew. She wore sweaters as shapeless as ponchos.

"She's pretty big, right?" Rafe asked.

"Andrea?"

"She's big," he said. "I'm telling you." He made his hands bra cups.

"Jesus, Rafe."

"She's like the biggest in the school! Have you seen those things?"

"Rafe, man . . ." I said.

"How much do you think they weigh?" he asked. "Just one of them. You think a pound? It's got to be at least a pound each."

"You're saying you like *Andrea*?"

"You're the one that knows her!" he said. "What do you think? You think three pounds, altogether? I think it could be three pounds."

"I don't really see you two as a couple," I said.

He hugged his arms to his chest and rocked his shoulders from side to side.

"She's so big," he said, rocking. "Sooo big. Have you seen those things? I'm telling you, man, have you seen them?"

IT WAS TOM'S first ultimate game, and I could tell that he was nervous about it, that he didn't understand that it wasn't the kind of game you had to be nervous about. Tall and quick, he intercepted a pass and spun around, looking for a receiver. I was far behind, but Andrea was near the end zone. Tom ignored her. She trotted in, self-conscious as always but unguarded, totally open. Tom was looking everywhere but at her, yelling for his team to get moving. He threw to Cilento for the score.

As the team gathered for the throw-off, Tom said, "I think I'm getting the hang of this."

"Nice grab," I said. And then, "You know, Andrea's on our team."

"Oh, yeah?" he said, his voice carrying self-consciously. "Andrea? Were you open?"

"Right, yeah, I suppose I was," she told her arm. When she got shy, she tended to talk to her elbow.

"You need to speak up!" Tom announced. He had a handsome, foxlike head, and he held it high. "You need to yell and let me know you're there."

"Yeah, well, no," Andrea said. "I suppose. I know. But I'm not really much of a yeller. . . ."

"Anyone mind if I throw off this time?" he asked, holding up the graying disc.

"Andrea isn't much of a yeller," Eleanor repeated. Tom lowered the disc and looked at her.

I was afraid he was going to say, "I'm sorry." I'd been spending a lot of time with him lately, and I knew how his apologies came out like impatience. "I'm sorry," he'd say, "but somebody had to shut that guy up." Then he showed his fox-sleek profile.

The rest of the team, all six of us, were quiet now, looking at Tom. A wind-tossed white foam cup scuttled across the asphalt. From the other end of the field, Aaron yelled, "Let's go, people. Throw it!"

Standing there, wondering if the group would take to Tom, I understood for the first time that there was an "us." With him, Aaron and Tucson and I could be a foursome, like Eleanor, Heather, Josine, and Joanna, who'd been close since they were little girls; like Kathy-Amy-Laura-Mia, whose names the rest of us said as one word. Now that I could imagine a group of guys I could stand, I felt how badly I wanted to join.

"She doesn't like to yell?" Tom repeated. I was afraid he might laugh at all this fuss over shy, unathletic Andrea.

"No, no, well, yes," Andrea said, "I suppose that's true."

He shrugged. "Could you wave?"

"Wave?" she asked.

"Wave . . ." said Eleanor. She tipped her head forward, so her straight blonde hair shaded her eyes like the brim of a hat. She lifted one open hand in front of her chest and turned it in a slow-motion wave.

Josine leaned in and gave the same wave back.

"Hey, Tom," she said quietly, almost whispering. "I'm open."

We laughed, Andrea and Tom included, and as Aaron started yelling again, we threw off.

From time to time in our games, when Eleanor or Josine was open, she would give a little wave, rotating from the wrist. And every once in a while, Tom noticed Andrea, and threw to her.

My Don Juan Complex

.　　.　　.

MOST DAYS AFTER the ultimate game, the players who had time wandered together through the neighborhood. To the north beyond Ninety-sixth Street was Spanish Harlem, where we never went. To the east was the vo-tech high school, where a few students, provoked perhaps by stories of public school kids with private school futures, met Hunterites outside the subway station to take our coats and wallets. To the west was Central Park, but it was winter, so most days we straggled south down the concrete hill of Madison Avenue, faces flushed, hair wind-smashed, sweat stinging cold at our hairlines. Often we passed students from the Lycée Française, their matching navy uniforms displaying their school insignia. They gawked at us and spoke in French, wrongly assuming none of us could understand their cracks about our mussed, sweaty, makeupless girls.

At the Sweet Suite, we usually got the round tables upstairs to ourselves. We had hot apple cider to sip, ice cream and big oatmeal cookies to share. At first, girls mostly sat with girls and guys with guys, but the cramped upstairs blended our conversations, and as we crowded around the close-set tables, lines blurred.

Our talk amazed me—I hadn't realized how I'd been holding back. We talked about Rubik's Cubes, about Pac-Man and Centipede, but not so much. Josine wanted to know why it was only guys who told jokes—she did imitations of joke-telling, talking in a low voice and throwing her hands around, cracking us up. Tucson complained that reading *Catcher in the Rye* for English didn't mean someone was any less phony than before. Reagan had just been elected, and we wondered who had voted for him—some formerly Democratic dads, it turned out, when we compared notes. Amy and Mia wanted to know what was up with the girls who constantly fixed their makeup and acted baffled. Every Hunter student passed the same entrance exam, Amy said, and everyone knew it. Why did these girls pretend they were dumb?

In the evening, the afternoon's conversations would get

retold in phone calls, along with questions about homework and tests. In the morning, back at school, we heard who'd appeared in whose dreams. The boys seemed to spend as much time talking this way as the girls. My mother got tired of fighting me for the phone, and finally, like a girl in a sitcom, I triumphantly got my own.

ON THURSDAYS AND alternate weekends, when my sister and I visited my father for dinner, he loved to hear about my afternoons at the Sweet Suite, all the who-was-who and who-said-what, how the girls looked and what the boys thought about them. My stories got him reminiscing about his own high school afternoons at the soda fountain, about cherry Cokes and black-and-white sodas, Fats Domino on the jukebox and girls one booth over. It seemed to raise his spirits to hear that something like this was still going on.

One evening, as the two of us were making a salad, he interrupted the day's list of who had come to the Sweet Suite.

"The girls change and meet you there?" he asked.

"What?"

"After the Frisbee game," he said.

"Ultimate," I said. "No one meets anyone anywhere. The girls come with us. I mean, we go together."

"Aren't you all a little sweaty?"

"Of course! We're totally sweaty. You run practically the whole time."

"And you don't feel like you ought to take a shower?"

"We're just going for *ice* cream."

My father held some lettuce leaves under the water tap, then laid them on paper towels to dry.

"So you're with these girls in school," he said, "and then you play sports with them, and then you go out with them to this ice-cream parlor."

"Isn't that what I said?"

"And you're together the whole day? And you all talk to each other?"

"No, we march in silence."

Amanda looked up from her loose-leaf binder and flashed me a smile. She was putting on a good show of doing her homework at the little dinner table, which made me think she hadn't been doing much of it lately.

"I think that's amazing," my father said. "Just amazing."

"What's so amazing?" I snapped. "What?"

"They sound like friends."

"So? What are they supposed to be, enemies? What do you expect?"

He flinched. Sometimes he seemed like an immigrant parent, as if he didn't even know what life was like here. It made me angry, more angry than I could understand, and I wished it hadn't—I'd been glad to see him happy for a moment. He'd been separated from my mother almost six months, and now his mother, Granny Fran, was dying of cancer. He lived in this stuccoed, student-style apartment that embarrassed him, the bedroom barely wider than his futon, the kitchen appliances squatting in one corner of the living room, which was also the room we ate in, and where I slept on the couch, and Amanda on a fold-out cot, when we visited. Everything was rickety except the new stereo, which he told me, simply, he could not afford. When I woke in the middle of the night, whatever the hour, his light always seemed to be on, and I heard the mouse-scratch of pen on paper, or the ghost music that escapes headphones.

In the morning, when he was done weeping in the shower, I pretended I was still asleep on the couch. He stumbled past the white plastic shelves that precariously held the stereo, and back through the curtain into his doorless bedroom. I thought it would only depress him more to know his children heard what he wanted to keep secret.

The feeling was as bad with my mother back at our old apartment, though there was more space and privacy to hide in. When it was her turn to wash the dishes, she carried one of the old KLH speakers to the kitchen entry, not caring that she was spoiling the stereo effect. She liked a feminist musical called *I'm Getting My Act Together . . . and Taking It On the Road!* But most often she listened to Barry Manilow, singing along about people who get soaked in the rain.

Still, my mother knew how to keep busy. We saw more of Grandmother Jane, and of my aunt and uncle, and of my friend Peter's family. She threw an afternoon party so big that she felt she couldn't afford enough hors d'oeuvres. "F. H. B." she mouthed to my sister and me, her signal for "Family Hold Back," so we wouldn't eat the food she'd bought for the guests.

In the evenings and on weekends, she was on the living room phone with friends, telling them loudly that the kids were doing well, that we had adjusted to the separation, and things were getting back to normal, that everything was *just fine.*

But except for some dinners with his old rock-and-roll friend Eric, my father was on his own. One weekend he did go away with a man he knew from work, someone I'd never heard of who invited him up to his hunting cabin and sent him home with fresh venison and a bottle of moonshine. My father told me how this colleague, not even a friend, had taken pity on him for a weekend, a suffering fellow male waiting on a divorce. Describing it, my father sounded so grateful that the good meat went dull in my mouth.

"I SUPPOSE YOU'RE part of that clique," other kids began to say, though the ultimate games were open to anyone who showed up, and so were the trips to the Sweet Suite. True, we were mostly Manhattan kids, but not all, and none of us had ever been cool. But now we were *that clique, that new clique, that exclusive clique.*

"If they're going to call us that ridiculous name," Kathy complained, "they could at least say it right." The word was French, she said, *cleek,* not *click.* They didn't even know what they were calling us. And so we picked it up, referred to ourselves first as a joke and then for real as the Click—maybe, it seemed to me, because we clicked.

. . .

A A R O N A N D I were at Tucson's apartment playing Dungeons and Dragons.

"I told you what happened," Al said. Al was Tucson's older brother, and the Dungeon Master. The round wooden table was scattered with loose-leaf pages, soda cans, pencils, potato chip bags, and multicolored, polyhedral dice.

"I don't know what your problem is," Al went on. "I talked to him on the phone this morning and I told you exactly what happened."

"Sure, Al. Sure," Tucson said. He and his brother were both long and thin, but Al had a push-up-regime meatiness, while Tucson was slender as a girl.

"The guy's a friend of mine," Al explained to Aaron and me, then turned back to his brother. "His girlfriend left the party early. What part of that don't you believe?"

"Let's just play," Tucson said. "We search the lair of the gelatinous cube for treasure."

Al turned to Aaron and me.

"My friend's girlfriend left this party early. So he goes home with another girl, right?"

"Oh, yeah, right," Tucson said.

"Shut up," said Al. He scooped up some dice and rattled them in his hand. "So the next day his girlfriend calls him up and says, 'I heard what happened.' And he's thinking, oh shit, here it comes."

Al threw the dice and they clattered on the wooden table.

"But then," he said, "*she* apologizes."

"The *girlfriend* apologizes?" I asked.

"You're so full of it."

"Shut up, Tucson. Yeah, obviously the girlfriend apologizes, because *she wasn't there to take care of his needs*. Right? What's so hard to understand about that?"

Al looked back and forth from Aaron to me to Tucson. Tucson shook his head.

"Wow," said Aaron. He had a good poker face.

"So what happened?" I asked.

"Well, after she apologized, he told her to call him back later. And when she called, he said he'd give her another chance."

"It wasn't like that," Tucson said.

"You are such a baby!" Al yelled. "Do you realize that? You are such a fucking baby."

"And you're an asshole," Tucson told a soda can, somberly.

THE CLICK GIRLS named us: Now we were "the boys," or occasionally Tucson-Aaron-Greg-and-Tom, one word. When we weren't with the girls, we hung out in twos or threes on weekends, slept over at each other's house, browsed at The Compleat Strategist and Disc-O-Rama. We called each other on the phone to talk about girls, wrote out lyrics from our favorite rock albums and argued about which was superior. It was great. One day at lunch, Aaron brought us a mystery.

"How does Rafe get away with it?" he asked.

"With what?" Tucson said, already sounding wary.

"There are two periods of lab, right? For two periods every week I do the experiments and write up the report, and my so-called lab partner, Rafe, walks around pinching asses. He's like, Hey, Sarah, what did you get for number seventeen? *Squeeze.*"

"So?" Tucson asked.

"So how does he get away with it?"

"Girls like guys with those little-choirboy looks," Tom said. "A guy who looks like that, with his hair falling in his big eyes, he can get away with anything."

"No, I want to know how he does it," Aaron said.

"What, so you can get away with it, too?" Tucson asked.

I thought of accusations like these, also, but before I could decide what to do with these thoughts, Tucson spoke them. His radar for guy-phoniness and guy-deception was more finely tuned than mine, and in this one thing he seemed more decisive.

"Well, I want to know!" Tom said, grinning.

"Oh, so that's what you want to be?" Tucson asked. "Now you want to be Rafe?"

"It's not that he wants to be him . . ." Aaron said.

"Then what is it?" Tucson asked, angry. "Tell me what it is."

"I'm sorry I said anything," Tom said. "Jesus."

I thought I knew what Tucson meant. There was a choice to be made. But I was also glad it was Tucson saying it, because it left me free on the phone that night to tell Tom I knew what he meant. There were whole class periods when I could hardly sit still, hardly think from wanting to reach a hand to a girl nearby. With a hard-on hot and cramped against my thigh, it seemed years until I could get home and get some relief.

"Think about the girls in that class," Tom said on the phone. "Did you ever try to argue with some of those girls? Think about Sarah—or Kyra? Kyra would stop him in a second if she wanted him to stop. . . ."

Later that week, Tom and I turned a corner in the fourth-floor hallway and saw an older boy we didn't know, hurrying to catch up to Susie in her burgundy leotard and patched, clinging jeans. The older boy leaned close and said something in her ear, and at the same time he laid his hand on her ass. Just like that. They turned together toward the stairwell, still hand-on-ass, and disappeared from view.

"Did you *see* that?" Tom asked.

We found excuses to tell the story to most of the Click girls—what we'd seen, how calm and unoffended Susie had acted. Susie wasn't in the Click, but she was a good student and she ate lunch with us sometimes, and I thought she might carry some weight with them.

The girls who knew Susie pretty well all said it couldn't have been her, that she wouldn't allow herself to be treated that way. The ones who didn't know her seemed to blame her—she must really have become one of those play-dumb girls, they said, who wore feather earrings and cut the collars off their T-shirts and hugged when they met in the halls even if they'd seen each other an hour before. But the Click girls who blamed Susie weren't as upset with her as they were with Tom and me.

"Why are you guys so interested in this?" Amy asked, as though we'd revealed some heretofore unsuspected shallowness. She crossed her arms over her breasts. "Why can't you just let it go?"

One way or another, the girls all hated the story. Tucson was angry we were even talking about it, and Aaron was admitting to no position, just gathering opinions. Joanna said the girls were very disappointed in Tom and me.

That Thursday, Amanda was at a friend's. I sat with my father on our canvas director's chairs at the dinner table and told him about the uproar. He was dumbfounded, too, but not for the same reason.

"What I can't understand," he said, "was why you told the girls this in the first place."

Men weren't supposed to talk about these things.

"But even so," he went on, "what are these girls making such a fuss about? You haven't done anything wrong yet." He laughed, shaking his head. "As a policy," he continued, serious now, "I think you could just do what *you* want. Whatever feels right. If it turns out to be wrong, just apologize."

I thought that sounded great, and Tom couldn't get over that I'd talked to my dad about it. He called the advice The New Policy. In my journal that night I wrote, "The Policy is always reaching for the ass when saying hello to applicable people. Sounds dumb and sexist, right? Try being inside my head."

In school, though, Tom took the practical line. It was important not to piss off the girls in your crowd, and our girls would jump down your throat if you copped a friendly feel. He restricted himself to jokes, asking me in front of girls if I'd had any luck with the Policy, any news about that Policy—and if one of the girls took the bait he'd shake his handsome head and say it was nothing, nothing important.

I had more reasons for not following up. Where would it end? Say one day you felt good and what you felt like doing was giving a little squeeze. But you were told it was wrong, so you apologized. Then the next day you had a bad day, and what you felt like doing was screaming at a girl, slapping her, so you screamed and you hit and you were told it was wrong, so you apologized. And the next time, you knocked her down some stairs. . . . What was in my father's policy to stop you?

IT WAS LATE on a Friday night, and I was already in bed. Peter was visiting from Princeton for the weekend. His parents had patched things up with my mom after the long-ago disaster on New Year's Eve, and now the two of us visited each other for weekends about once a month.

Peter closed my bedroom door and stripped to his white briefs. He bent down, facing away from me, to unzip the sleeping bag. It was the moment when, alone, I would have masturbated, but instead I watched him, tall and slender and nearly naked. I looked at his little butt in his cotton briefs, and I could see how someone might think it was all right. He pushed his thumbs under the elastic at each narrow hip and slid them down his long legs. Wouldn't things be easier, I wondered, if I could just want *him*? What did I really know about being inside a girl? Maybe I'd like it with a guy as much, or more.

But I could feel that even if I got into that sleeping bag with Peter, I'd wake up beside him hoping to see a girl. I didn't actually know if I was straight when it came to sex, but when it came to romance, I was sure.

I folded my glasses next to the record player.

"I'm turning out the light," I told Peter.

"Go for it," he said.

By the end of high school, we had found rituals for our weekend afternoons in the city. We talked frankly in cafés about our girlfriends or the ethics of registering for the draft. We got haircuts together at Astor Barbers, and shopped for vintage jackets and slacks at stores like Andy's Chee-Pees and Alice Underground, a carpeted basement where jazz standards played. We picked out narrow-lapelled jackets, skinny embroidered ties, loose hipster slacks sharply creased. We caressed fabrics between our thumbs and forefingers, modeled for each other in curtained-off dressing rooms. Our clothes talk might draw a salesperson, often an intrigued man with gel in his hair and black eyeliner on his lower lids. There was lots of back and forth, sudden moments of hilarity. No salesman ever said he thought we were gay, and we never said we weren't. As we left the store I often felt we'd gotten away with something, something good, for which I had no words.

THE GIRLS HAD a gathering without the boys, an afternoon of tea and sandwiches. This was a private conversation, in theory, but Joanna liked to pass stories to Aaron, and Aaron liked to pass them to the boys. The lines of communication were open. Aaron told me the part where they went around the room and said what experiences they'd had with boys, and what they'd like to have.

Some of the girls had only ever really kissed, they said. Some had felt a boy's hands underneath a shirt or a skirt. That was how they talked about it, the type of clothing under which they'd been touched. They talked about when they thought they would sleep with a guy—maybe sixteen, maybe eighteen, at the rate I'm going, never. Amy announced she would do it this year, but she was a drama group actress and a tough talker. She might or might not have meant it.

Around the halls at school, outside the Click, I heard words for girls: bitch, prude, nympho, virgin, whore. An unsexy girl was a dog, and a sexy girl a cocktease or a slut, depending. Mostly the words got used on girls the speaker didn't know or didn't like. A girl's girlfriends were almost always *nice*, which meant you wouldn't talk about them with the other words.

But the Click girls weren't using the lingo. They'd talked about what they thought would happen, what they would like to do. Tucson and Aaron and Tom and I never talked that way. Tom lied about his Fire Island girls, and I told Aaron that I'd never slept with Susie or Rosa, but we weren't actually giving each other new information.

"What about Eleanor?" I asked. Lately in ultimate I'd been guarding her. Her blonde hair blew in my eyes, and I told her it was an unfair advantage. She said my height was an unfair advantage, too, and she left her hair loose. I relished the sight of her as she ran, her legs amazing in her low-slung jeans, the wind pulling her Icelandic sweater against her chest.

"She wasn't there," Aaron said. "I think she had some rehearsal."

He was silent for a minute, and as the line faintly buzzed I realized this talk would get communicated in the other direction.

After he told me about the party, he went through the names of all the girls who'd been there, asking me which ones I'd go out with if I could, and why.

"With a girl like Amy," I told him, thinking of her gutsy talk, "it's better to wait." I was showing off, talking as though Amy was a vintage wine we'd have to let breathe before we drank her. "Amy's the kind of girl to go out with for six months in the eleventh grade."

"Wow," Aaron said. "Six months? That really would be fucking."

It took me a few moments to realize he wasn't still mid-sentence, that he wasn't going to say *fucking unlikely*, that I was *fucking dreaming*.

RONNIE WIENER HAD a new theory about me, Aaron reported. She'd calculated the lengths of my Hunter relationships: a while with Paula, but seventh grade didn't count. With Anna, not even a month. With Eloise, six weeks and four days. With Susie, barely six weeks, counting the time she was home with an injured foot. And most recently, with Rosa, six weeks and one day. The conclusion was obvious. I had a six-week limit. I got a girl going and then I dumped her. It was proof of Havana's theory: I had a Don Juan complex.

I asked Aaron who he thought was hearing about this.

"I think it's getting around," he said.

"Even—I mean—in the Click?"

"Oh, definitely," he said.

AT THE SWEET SUITE, ELEANOR usually sat with Heather, her best friend. It was Heather who kept everyone informed of Eleanor's whereabouts when she was away on an acting job, and Heather who'd organized a group of us to see Eleanor in a kids' movie at the theater on Eighty-sixth Street.

Along with Joanna and Aaron, Heather made most of the Click's plans, but when she decided that she'd have the next party, it was Eleanor who called to invite me. On the phone, I heard in her voice a smooth, melodic elsewhere—Texas and Missouri, she insisted, reasonably. She came late to the party, still in makeup from a show, and we pressed together on an overstuffed chair, joking for hours in an odd, associative way until Heather decided that the boys would not sleep over after all.

Soon, after an ultimate game, as Eleanor and I reached the Sweet Suite, I said, "There it is."

"Sure enough," Eleanor said.

We turned our heads to look in the window as we passed.

"There it goes," I said.

"Sorry, Heather!" Eleanor called, though Heather was at least a block behind us.

We walked in silence until we crossed the street, and then I began our odd way of talking.

"So if a yogurt maker fell in the forest," I said, "and no one heard it, would anyone have lunch?"

Eleanor wrinkled her brow, playing at puzzling over a deep, philosophical issue. "It would depend on the yogurt maker," she said.

"Or the flavor of the yogurt."

"Or . . . the flavor of the forest."

"Mmm," I said. "It's hard to get good forest these days."

"That's the truth," she said. "They don't make them like they used to."

"Maybe they don't use them like they're made to?"

Eleanor looked at me disapprovingly. *"We* don't use a maid."

"Too bourgeois?" I asked.

"Too *clean.*"

At Eighty-sixth Street, I could have caught the express downtown. I didn't even glance at the subway stairs.

"You know I'm reading Machiavelli for that social studies paper?"

She nodded.

"Pretty depressing," I said. "How to plant information, to create a politically useful lie."

"Junior high school," she said.

"Yes!" I said. "And not just junior. I mean, if I tell someone something, I know who it will get back to. It made me realize: If I spent all my time at it, I could make people think all sorts of things."

"Are you kidding?" she asked. "If you spent *half* your time you could make them think anything you want."

We got to the end of another block.

"I had kind of a strange talk with Eloise, did I tell you?" she asked.

I was instantly nervous.

"She pulled me aside after Official. Asked did I think I could 'beat her record.' "

I knew what record: six weeks and four days.

"What did you say?" I asked, trying to sound casual.

"Not really anything," Eleanor said.

For a while I watched the sidewalk slide under my dirty sneakers, and wondered how much of a problem this was going to be. At Hunter there was no casual dating. You chose between friendship and Going Out, a minimarriage that began with a formal proposal. Maybe Eleanor was acting so calm, I thought, because she wasn't interested in me anyway.

"This is my street," she said.

"Look at it!" I yelled, feigning horror. In my nervousness I really howled.

"What's wrong?" she asked.

"Your street—it's filled with trespassers!"

She groaned at the joke, but she pulled her bare hands from her pockets and took one of mine. Her fingers were long and flat, and her palms at once moist and cool.

"What do you want to do?" she asked.

"Is anyone home?"

"Only Angela." Angela was her cat. "She's probably lonely."

"Someone ought to cheer her up," I said.

"I think she'd like that," she said, and pulled me by the hand toward her little apartment house.

Angela was accustomed to her all-female household; dark-furred and dignified, she had no use for me. She didn't even follow us into Eleanor's room, where the bed had big square pillows and a quilted white comforter.

The hot room hissed with steam from the radiator. I pulled off my sweater, and as I came out of its tent I saw Eleanor cross her arms in an X along her slender torso, then lift her own sweater up around her head. Beneath, she wore a white cotton shirt that she'd clearly outgrown. The seams where the sleeves attached rode up her shoulders, and the soft fabric clung to the whole braless swell of her breasts, even the side curves revealed by her raised arms. She pulled off the sleeves of her sweater, one and then the other, drawing the fabric of her shirt even tighter. It was a beautiful, artless performance, and it left me burningly aware that we were alone in the apartment— alone in her bedroom, where every night she took off her clothes.

"You look really amazing in that shirt," I blurted.

She pulled the sweater free, and her shirt slid up, baring her belly button. She said nothing.

"I mean it fits you really well," I stumbled on. "Not that it *fits* you well, but that the fit—"

She met my eyes and I stopped myself, alarmed at the foolishness pouring from my mouth. Still she didn't respond. It was as though I hadn't spoken. She threw her sweater over a chair and turned toward a chest of drawers. In the inscrutable silence, having just done one dumb thing, I reached out to set things right. I did what I'd done with other girls when I felt this way. I tickled her. Or tried—I pressed and vibrated my fingers below her ribs with what I thought was practiced expertise.

"Not ticklish," she said.

"Yeah, sure," I said.

She turned toward me and raised her arms again, sighing a little and looking toward the softly curtained window. I did my best—light touches in the armpit, soft pokes to the stomach—but she stood silent and still.

"When I was little," she said, "everyone tickled me. All the time. I taught myself not to feel it."

For a moment, I was aware she was breathing with control, concentrating on resisting me, but then it passed, and it was as though I wasn't touching her at all.

"Wow," I said, feeling creepy. "You're really not."

"I told you," she said.

She pulled open a jumbled drawer and picked a lighter sweater, and then she was dressed again.

"Are you hungry?" she asked. "I'm hungry."

I followed her to the dark, square kitchen. While she sliced the orange cheddar, I wondered how much of a fool I'd made of myself, and whether it would be a mistake to ask her to Go Out today. I suspected I was really blowing it. Eleanor was slapping together grilled cheese sandwiches, starting to fry them on the stove. Had there not been two sandwiches in the pan, she could have been alone.

Then I thought of Grandmother Jane. I spent weekends with her from time to time, just the two of us. Usually I arrived on Friday, in time for cocktail hour. Over the weekend we baked bread together, and talked about plays and movies and books and our own lives. Being here with Eleanor was no stranger than that, really—Eleanor at least wasn't four times my age. So I asked her why she salted the sandwiches, and why she pressed them with a spatula down into the bubbling margarine. By the time they were ready to eat I was pretty much myself again.

Smoke from the frying pan lingered in her bedroom. When we kissed, her mouth was still salty. She had an audition that night, so we both headed downtown. On the subway platform, I told her gravely, "There's something I need to ask you."

"What's wrong?"

"Nothing's wrong!" I said. "I just wanted to ask you to Go Out with me."

Eleanor pressed her thin lips white and looked at the subway tracks.

"That's a silly question," she said.

"Hey," I said. "Silly's my word."

She took a breath and let it out again.

"So will you?" I asked.

"Do you really think the words change anything?" she asked.

"You're saying no?" I blurted.

"No!" she said, raising her hands in exasperation. "I'm not saying no . . . but why do I have to say at all?"

"You don't want to be my girlfriend?"

"What have we been doing?" she asked. "What would you call this?"

"So you're saying yes!"

"*Unnnnn!*" she growled. "Stubborn boy!"

She leaned in to kiss me, but I pulled away.

"Are you upset that it wasn't a romantic setting?"

"Will you stop it?" she cried.

This wasn't the moment I'd been expecting.

"Is this about Eloise?" I asked. "Or Ronnie Wiener? Because—"

"Why are we wasting our time with this?" she asked. And then, more softly, "I've got rehearsals all weekend. I won't even get to see you."

"Okay," I said. "I'm sorry. I won't talk about it."

.   •   •

M A N Y   A F T E R N O O N S   W E   wound up at her apartment, on her high bed. She was new to this, it seemed, but ready. Often she mirrored my touches back to me. She liked to kiss full on, soft mouth wide open, lips deliciously salty with postgame sweat. She liked to drag her fingertips over my face, exploring, staring, and I felt studied, unnerved. But when I hugged her and pressed us together, she ground her hips slowly against mine, and the grinding together was very good.

I was surprised at the delicate thinness of her blonde hair. Parted down the middle, it left a line of scalp, pale and unprotected. Even the winter sun could burn it pink. Under my amazed fingers, her skin felt so moist it seemed oiled. She mostly wore blue jeans, but her life in them was nothing like the high drama of Susie and Rosa. Instead of struggling to fit herself into stiff, washed denim, Eleanor wore her few pairs day after day, playing ultimate in them, until they yielded to her shape. Under strong light, her denimed thighs gleamed, and when I ran my hands down her legs, the fabric left an earthy scent like a leaf pile.

I loved the surprising cool of her breasts, the pink peach-flesh tightening at the tips. She did not seem shy about the parts of her or me which we slowly, over the weeks, undressed. Some days, beneath the undershirt she wore instead of a bra, like a little girl, her back and even her chest were knobbed with acne. But she didn't tense, as other girlfriends had, when my fingers discovered a pimple. Except onstage, she wore no makeup, and she only worried out loud about her clothing for a family event or an audition. She said nothing about her complexion, her weight, her shape, the size of her breasts, the supposed failings of her hair. She didn't talk about her body at all. Fooling around, we were in another element, undersea in lightless water. Once she closed her eyes, they stayed closed.

Rosa had seemed boundaried like a playing field, these parts off limits, those in bounds. I'd learned the precise, invisible line on her clothes where outer thigh was deemed to cross to inner, where a touch brought her referee hand to stop play. With Susie the game had been to cross the lines, like taking dares: Frenching, second base outside the clothes, second-inside, third-outside, third-inside until someone, usually me, turned chicken. But exploring with Eleanor I sensed no boundary lines, no dares. What she pulled back from one day she might push into the next.

As we spent more time together, routines I'd mastered slipped away. I forgot to show up for my mother's precisely seven o'clock dinners, neglected to call home to report my whereabouts, lost the keys to my parents' apartments. One night, when I got home to my father's, I was singing to myself, dreamy, untroubled.

"You jerk," my father said.

"Don't call me that," I came back.

"You were supposed to meet us for dinner an hour and—"

"Don't call me names. I don't care if I was late. Don't talk to me like that."

I stopped, amazed at myself.

My father sat in a director's chair, blinking.

At dinner, he gave me a long talk about how I didn't understand how difficult his life was, and how I had to learn to be more responsible. But he never called me names again.

"TOM, MAN," TUCSON said. We were by the lockers. "I can't believe it, man. You're going out with Amy."

"Oh, you know," he said, turning his handsome head away, the picture of nonchalance.

"She's so beautiful," Tucson said.

"No kidding," I said.

"She's not *so* beautiful."

"What are you saying?" Tucson asked. "You don't think she's beautiful?"

"She's a good-looking enough girl and everything. I'm just saying I've had more beautiful girls."

"What?" Tucson asked.

"What do you want me to say? It's a fact."

"Just shut up. You're talking about Amy. She's, you know . . ."

"She's what, exactly?"

"She's—" Tucson looked over at me. "She's one of us."

"I'm not saying she's *ugly*. I'm not saying there's something *wrong* with her."

"Shut *up*. . . ."

"It's not that I blame her for how she looks, if that's what you mean."

"I can't listen to this," Tucson said.

"You understand, right?" Tom asked me.

I could picture what he meant. Amy had a weirdly tight way of standing, if you looked for it, with her shoulders forward, hiding her full breasts. And she had a lot of freckles, and her breath was sort of sour sometimes. This fault-finding was a skill you picked up somehow, a knack for looking at anyone, even statuesque, smart, funny, delicious, redheaded Amy, and seeing serious flaws. It kept things under control.

"Come on, Tom," I said. "It's *Amy*."

"I'm sorry, this is bullshit!" he yelled, striding away. "What is wrong with the guys at this school?"

ONE AFTERNOON, WHEN Eleanor and I were on her bed, we heard a key in the lock, and the front door opening. We pulled apart, already buttoning up our shirts.

"Mom," she said, when she opened her bedroom door, "this is Greg."

Her mother was taller than mine, and broader across the shoulders. She was wearing rough woven fabrics, a tunic and loose pants. Unlike my mother, she was letting her hair go gray. She looked at me, and then to the side—just like Eleanor when she was going to make a joke.

"Is it," she said. "I see. Well, then. *Hello, Greg.*"

She turned back to Eleanor, calling her Pumpkin and giving her a complicated story about a script and a director. Eleanor had told me that her mother was her agent, and I'd felt it was my role to act as though this was as normal to me as it was to her. Now her mother said that the director would love her to read for the part, but it had to be Friday, so if it was something Eleanor wanted to do, she'd have to change her time to see her father. . . . I couldn't follow it all.

For weeks, Eleanor's mother acted this way around me, mostly ignoring me but greeting me and saying good-bye when prompted, as though I were an imaginary friend and she knew better than to discourage Eleanor's belief in me.

HEATHER OBJECTED TO the Click's rampant pairing off. She griped that I blocked her friendship with Eleanor. Aaron got in her way with Joanna. These friendships went back most of her life, she said, and all this Going Out was the most damaging thing that had ever happened to them. Not that the couples were so happy. Tom and Amy broke up fast, then Kathy and Tucson tried and gave up; the atmosphere at Click parties was filling with resentment. When Eleanor and I withdrew to a back room, we could hear the complaining jokes we left behind.

My mother had told me how when she was growing up, friendships among girls were considered a way to kill time. If a boy called or came by, a girl was expected to ditch her girl-friends. But this was the Click, and Eleanor and I took the complaints seriously. I told her that my friend Peter was frustrated with me, too—when he came into the city he felt like a third wheel.

Eleanor and I made a plan. An old-fashioned set-up, a double date out of my father's stories of diners and drive-ins, was out of the question. But we thought that if we could get Peter and Heather together just to hang out and talk, they might fall for each other, and our problem would be solved.

The next Saturday I brought Peter over to Eleanor's apartment, which was even hotter than usual.

"Do I smell *turkey*?" I asked. "I thought we were just going to have tea or whatever."

"Well," Heather said, with a gasp, "we thought you boys might be hungry."

She looked at Eleanor, and they both went back into the kitchen.

Peter asked, "Is 'you boys' supposed to be us?"

I raised my hands to show I didn't get it.

"How much longer does it need?" Peter called. He knew a lot about cooking.

"Just a bit!" Heather answered, mom-chipper.

Eleanor came back and took a seat at the table. "What we've got," she said, "is a popper-upper that's not popping up."

"You mean that thermometer thing?" I said.

Heather appeared in the kitchen doorway. She was wearing an apron. "It can be *very* dangerous to eat food that's not properly cooked," she told us.

"Life-threatening," Peter said. "I believe turkey's up there with the Japanese puffer fish."

Heather stared at him, then retreated back into the kitchen.

"He was kidding!" Eleanor called.

"I know!" came the response, again a kind of gasp. Heather seemed to be sucking the first word of each sentence back down her throat.

I'd told Peter that Heather was a fierce debater in class, one of the most athletic girls in the ultimate game, and something to see at a party in her suede elf boots. But Peter wasn't going to meet the girl I'd told him about. She'd been replaced with this jittery, aproned housewife, panicked that her dark meat would poison us.

By the time Peter convinced the girls that the turkey's pop-up thermometer might be broken, its skin had cracked. Some larger force seemed to be at work, and even as Peter finally relaxed we could find no joke, no kindness to prevent this from becoming The Day Heather Ruined the Turkey and Spoiled Everything.

. . .

I DIDN'T KNOW what had gone wrong, but the Click was having a run of it. Amy and Kathy swore off Going Out, and kept to their oaths not just for a month or two, as my father predicted, but permanently. Kathy took me aside one night at a dance, and explained in half-drunk earnestness that it wasn't that she didn't like Tucson. She'd always liked Tucson. But it was too weird to Go Out with him, to be someone's Girlfriend, to have to live with that pressure all the time. How could she be His Girlfriend and still be herself? Even tipsy, she said this with force and polish, and I suspected this was a common feeling among the Click girls, a settled position.

Didn't I understand? I nodded while she spoke, feeling that I'd heard things like this before. "Marriage just wasn't *designed* for women," my mother said into the living room phone. "At a certain age, you realize that."

Joke-telling, sociable Josine turned out to have a secret boyfriend, because having a boyfriend in public was just too much, somehow. And at almost every Click party, cheerful, beautiful Laura broke down crying, helpless to explain herself, as though there was something unsayable and heartbreaking about being a young woman at a party.

WITH ELEANOR, ANYWHERE seemed romantic. On un-crowded subways, we held on to a metal pole and twirled opposite each other until the pitching of the train threw us together. At night on the phone, we talked and talked. Was it strange or wasn't it that Tucson and his brother Al were from the same family? Was Heather, so comfortable with Eleanor yet so tense around guys, gay? (Eleanor thought not.) We talked about her shows, and the books we read in English, and what it would take to become a playwright.

But we didn't talk when we fooled around, and especially not after. When I said her touches felt good, she seemed not to

174

hear. When I repeated myself, she sighed. If she responded in words, she might say, "I'm glad you came over, too"—as though I'd misspoken and she could correct me. When I slipped and told her she was beautiful, she said, "You're beautiful, too," an absent singsong. Once, when I insisted, she answered, "You should really go now."

I was slow to understand the problem. After all, she hadn't minded when I'd told her I loved her soft pink angora gloves, which she'd bought on a whim from a street vendor. I petted her gloved hands like kittens, and she didn't mind—in time she bought another pair, royal purple, and gave me one glove of each color. They were mismatched, and my father made faces when he saw them, but when Eleanor and I held hands, the colors lined up.

Yet she didn't want to hear that I liked her blonde hair or her crooked smile, or that she looked sexy. When I complimented a thinly striped blouse I savored for its close cinch at her narrow waist, the blouse disappeared. Like the outgrown white undershirt that had clung to her so marvelously, the blouse vanished from her wardrobe—I, at least, never saw it again. Then one day I told her that I loved the fit of her soft old jeans.

"Shhh . . ." she said, pressing a flat forefinger to my lips.

"No, I mean it," I said. "Those Wranglers really—"

"Difficult boy!" she cried. "Stop. *Please* stop."

I didn't understand what she thought I'd done wrong, and she wouldn't talk about it. Regular couples had Asking-Out conversations, how-do-I-look, secret-shame, how-far-to-go, dreams-of-the-future. But Eleanor refused that world, rebelled against every familiar line in the script. It felt as though she was teaching me to play an antirole, to learn which lines were never to be said. In most things she seemed easygoing, nonjudgmental, open to suggestion— "A perfect girlfriend," my father said. "A relationship with no stress"—but in this she would not be moved.

I told Aaron some of the things Eleanor wouldn't talk about.

He said that he'd asked Joanna to tell him her favorite part of his body. He'd offered that his favorite was her side, the curving slope from her ribs down to her waist and up again to her hip. Joanna had found this game preposterous, offensive. She refused to discuss it.

LATE ONE AFTERNOON in Eleanor's radiator-baked bedroom, after what seemed hours of shirtless passion, I slid my hand between her thighs. With her eyes squeezed shut, she turned her head down and away from me, as far as she could go toward the comforter. She squeezed her legs tight around me, and I traced the upraised seam of her jeans, up and down, on the fabric and on the stitching, to one side and then the other, until she clenched her thighs so tight I could barely move my fingers. As I fought a cramp in my hand, high, musical notes led each quick breath out of her mouth. Her body against me radiated heat, and the pale, crooked part in her hair flushed red.

At first, I felt surprised, proud, relieved. I'd read in my mother's copy of *The Hite Report* about how much women resented guys who left them hanging, and I knew Steve Martin's stand-up routine about the insensitive lover.

After a long moment, saying nothing, still with her eyes closed, she went back to kissing me, as though she had been in another room for a time, but now had rejoined me on the bed. She said nothing, acknowledged nothing, and finally I rolled away from her, to make her open her eyes. Her lids came up slowly, as though from sleep, and with a blank look she leaned over to continue kissing.

I felt alone, wrong, on the bed by myself while she went back to her closed-eyed, silent place, but I didn't stop. I rubbed against her, my rough, denim-coated pillow, and after some time, unexpectedly, I came in my pants. I almost didn't recognize the feeling, a sudden squeezing tight, an almost pleasureless spurt. Was that it? I had never imagined it could feel like so little.

．　　．　　．

I THINK IT was Mia who first heard about the Judy Chicago
exhibition. She said the artist set a dinner table with place set-
tings inspired by women's genitals. I wasn't exactly sure what
that meant. Mia wanted the Click girls to see it, just the girls. *No
boys.* Tom said what did we care—if they had a thing for weird
lesbo dinnerware, let them gawk. Aaron went crazy.

"The boys never leave the girls out of *anything,*" he said to
me, to Joanna, to the unhappy bunch of us gathered after
school to argue by the lockers. "Nothing. Not one thing."

"Oh, *please,*" said Mia, walking away.

"Name one!" Aaron called after her. "I mean it. Name one
thing we leave you out of."

"Come on!" Joanna said. "Of course you do. You play those
fantasy-whatchamacallit games, right?"

"You could come!" Aaron said. "Any time, you could join in."

"Don't hold your breath," said Amy.

"But the point is that you could come. We're not *excluding*
you."

"Would you just calm down?" Tucson said. "It's not such a
big deal."

Joanna went down the hall to where more of the girls were
standing, to try to broker a compromise. In the end, the girls
went without us.

"Do you at least understand?" Aaron asked me.

"I don't know," I said. "If it's really what they want to do,
they should do it, right?"

"But you're missing the point!" Aaron said. "It's like a
breach of faith."

"I don't even know what that means," said Tucson. "The
girls already left. Do we have to keep talking about it?"

EARLY ONE EVENING, when her mother came home,
Eleanor asked if I could come to dinner. They had a favorite
Chinese restaurant for hot-and-sour soup.

"Do you really think he'd like that?" her mother asked.

"Greg loves Chinese food," Eleanor offered.

"Does he," her mother said.

She'd still taken no interest in me as her daughter's boyfriend—didn't ask about my family, didn't flirt with me as moms sometimes did. She gave no indication, when I said good-bye, that she expected to see me again. But she didn't put obstacles in my way, either, and when my birthday came she took us to a Lanford Wilson play, as though I was Eleanor's new school chum. What I felt from her didn't seem to be dislike.

The restaurant was standard-issue Chinese—red paper placemats, plastic chopsticks, stubby water glasses with uneven rims. We were here for the soup. It arrived in white bowls, murky-brown and steaming, the spiciest, pepperiest thing that had ever passed my lips. After one square-bottomed spoonful the whole front of my mouth burned, and the heat didn't lessen when I bathed my mouth in ice water.

Eleanor and her mother continued to bring their spoons slowly to their mouths, with small noises that suggested the pleasurable discomfort of stepping into a hot tub. I tried eating some of the bean curd, then a slick, brown vegetable, but all of it burned with spicy heat. Eleanor didn't ask me how I liked it, and her mother didn't watch me struggle, but their politeness was their disapproval. When I asked the waiter for more water, Eleanor's mother allowed herself a smile.

"Don't feel you have to finish it," she said.

Inspired to do something else with my mouth, I launched into conversation—something lost to me now about a movie we'd all seen. I was just talking to talk, but apparently I said something so naively romantic that Eleanor's mother couldn't let it go.

"You have to understand," she said, in her clear midwestern voice, "there's really a very simple reason people get married. It's not love, or anything like that."

Eleanor stared out at nothing. I imagined this was old news

to her. In the silence, I wondered what these other things *like love* were supposed to be. I raised my spoon, thought better of it, put it down. The plastic clicked against my bowl.

"People get married," her mother continued, "because of timing. They have needs, things they have to do at certain times in their lives, things that are quite difficult to do on one's own."

She looked over at me, to see if I was attending to her words.

"It's burdensome to buy a home by yourself," she explained, "or to raise a small child. It's only reasonable to get some help."

Eleanor was still staring away from the table, but whether because she objected or because she agreed and didn't need to listen, I couldn't tell.

"If you get that straight now," her mother went on, "it will save you a lot of confusion. A *lot* of confusion."

MORE AND MORE now, when Eleanor and I fooled around, I got distracted. When I was alone and imagining it, I could make myself feel great, but when I was with her, I watched for the moment her eyes squeezed tight and she disappeared from me, and I went cold. Sometimes I admired her for her privacy, her self-protection—the world had its tickling fingers on her every day, mine especially, poking, prodding, demanding a response, feeling for the spot where a touch could make her a puppet. She would not give in, not respond, not cry out.

I learned to focus on small irritations, the sharp, sour taste her beloved black jelly beans left in her mouth, the acrid smell of old sweat, her oily, pimply skin. My mind filled with taunts.

You know, you aren't so pretty when you're covered with all those bumps.

It's not like a shower would kill you.

Don't you think it's time you learned to brush your teeth?

I'd heard girls complain about boyfriends who tried to control them down to the smallest things—what clothes they wore, how they styled their hair, their lipstick, their nail polish, the way they walked. I envied those guys a little. At least when a girl had to primp and worry and follow orders, you could be sure she knew you were there.

At night, I mocked her in my journal. Once I wrote, "In bed it's as if her interest, knowledge, and abilities are all inferior copies of mine. Making out with her is masturbating on someone else's hand. Sometimes she *completely turns me off*!"

At summer camp, I'd heard older boys grousing with weird, insistent pride about their girlfriends' sexual flaws. Guys who wouldn't usually admit to jerking off snidely bragged that they could give a better hand job themselves. At the time, I'd taken this for the usual macho bullshit. Now those voices were mine.

Though I said nothing about all this to Eleanor, our nightly phone conversations developed awkward pauses. We couldn't find anything about our friends or our classes to talk about. She told me she felt mysteriously down, "kind of depressed." When I asked her what she was down about, she said, "I don't *know*. . . ." If I pressed her, she said, "I suppose I'm just being silly. . . ."

ONE DAY IN *Rolling Stone* I read about a band called Human Sexual Response. They sounded perfect, exactly what I needed.

"A little New Wave New Culture?" my father said, riffing on my enthusiasm.

I bought the record the next day and took it home to my mother's house. I played it on the old KLH in the living room.

"That's an unusual name for a musical group," she said, reading the album cover.

After she hung up her coat and changed out of her suit, I put on the first song for her, "What Does Sex Mean to Me?" It had some good harmonies, and some pretty political lyrics, connecting intercourse and the cultural revolution, rhyming "China" with "vagina"—a rhyme which didn't embarrass me until I heard it with my mother.

"What did you think?" I asked her. I snapped off the turntable and sat back down on the floor.

"Well," she said. She stopped and thought, all sincerity. I didn't ask her opinion much anymore.

"I think they're asking a good question," she said. "And that line about worried women going off the Pill, that's certainly true. But they just keep asking what sex means. I don't really get that they have any insights to share."

I slumped down. She was right.

"It does have a good beat," she said.

Without going into specifics, I told her things weren't so good with Eleanor, that I felt far from her, and that she said she was depressed.

"You know, teenage melancholy is pretty common," my mother said. "Even when you aren't a teenager anymore." She said this smiling, but I didn't smile back. "Everyone has times they feel blue," she said.

I wanted to know why Eleanor and I felt blue.

"I don't think there always is a reason," she said. "It's just feeling blue. If you wait long enough, eventually it will go away."

MY FATHER'S ADVICE: Talk to Eleanor.

"I already talk to her," I said, annoyed.

"I mean talk to her when you mess around. Talk to each other. At the time."

"Oh," I said. I'd never thought of it, but now that I did, it sounded like a great idea. It sounded like me, exactly like a thing I would do. Maybe I saw this so quickly because I knew I wasn't going to try.

I broke up with Eleanor on a subway platform. At moments, as I gave my reasons and said the required words, she seemed to hold back a smile, no more impressed with Breaking Up than Asking Out. I watched her walk away, thinking she was even more beautiful than I'd realized. At least, I told myself, I wouldn't be hearing about my six-week limit anymore. We'd lasted almost six months.

Alimony

■ ▌ ■

A S MY MOTHER told it—and she could tell it loud and clear—her son had become a self-indulgent shopper: inflexible, unmindful of price, far more faddish at fifteen than when he was a boy. I had growth spurts, though she couldn't quite blame me for that. Worst, to her eye, was my weight. Uncontrolled. Who could tell what would still fit me from one month to the next? She would scold me in dressing rooms, not using the word *fat* but filling me up with it anyway, until the word weighed me down like the real thing.

I didn't have to put up with this, I knew. I had an out most kids lacked. I could trade our humbling mother-son shopping trips for a businesslike clothing allowance from my father, cash on the first of the month, no questions asked. If I chose, I could go further, quit all the mother-teen arguments at once. Like my father before me, I could leave her.

In my mind's eye, these choices stretched below me like a steep slope, almost a cliff. I imagined that one step down would compel another and another, until I was running just to keep my balance. There seemed no careful path, only headlong descent with no return. For now, I still shopped with my mother.

I followed her down the aisle of the department store, where criticism could lurk in any mirror or display case.

"Alimony . . ." I sang, not quite to myself. The song was a country blues from my father's rock-critic days.

"Alimony . . ." I sang again, louder. We hadn't taken out the record in years, but here it was, playing in me again.

"Please have mercy, Judge, Your Honor," I sang. "Alimony's killing me."

By the revolving doors, my mother stopped to button her winter coat and settle her white earmuffs over the dark waves of her hair. Then, as though the words had just occurred to her, as though she was only making a light remark to pass the time, she said, "That's quite a song to be singing, don't you think? Under the circumstances."

The circumstances: After a decisive separation, my father and she had divorced. I didn't know how much my father paid in alimony, or in child support. Sometimes he hinted angrily that she was keeping the child-support money for herself, but at the same time she always seemed strapped for cash.

I looked back at her, wondering if it was time for our next fight. Then she smiled. It was the imploring smile that offered a deal. If I would act as though this singing was harmlessly eccentric behavior, this mood only a passing teenage cloud, she seemed to say, so would she. *We could have a nice time together.* This is what my mother wanted, and I could hardly blame her. I knew the alternative. Lately we'd argued in her apartment until she stormed up the stairs and slammed her bedroom door. If I started to cry, she took a shower. Our simplest communications went painfully awry. But my mother and I weren't supposed to be people who screamed and slammed and then kept out of each other's way. We were supposed to be able to talk.

With Grandmother Jane, recently, she'd discovered they could have a *nice time shopping together* every couple of months, and in their often-strained relationship this was a joy. Last week, as though to demonstrate, she'd asked my grandmother to dinner after one of their trips.

"Did you have luck?" I knew to ask.

They looked at each other for a moment, straightening up in their seats, getting in sync.

"I'd say we had luck," my mother answered for both, coyly tipping her head.

"Maggie had terrific luck. That darling light wool suit will be splendid for the spring. It was the find of the afternoon."

"Oh, but it was *you* who did the finding!"

They rode the bus together to the Lower East Side, hunted bargains along racks of dresses and business clothes. Each knew the other's wardrobe, what she liked and disliked about her figure, her hopes for how she might look and who she might be. On these trips, it seemed, these two women on their own could satisfy each other. Grandmother Jane had a cold, ironic side—"The secret to happiness," she liked to tell me, "is low expectations"—but now the satisfaction of their lucky afternoon filled the apartment.

After my grandmother had gone home, my mother had suggested this shopping trip to me, for a Saturday rather than the usual hurried hour after work. It hadn't seemed crazy to think that we could find some of that luck, too—I *liked* clothes. And Amanda didn't seem to have any trouble shopping with her. Amanda stayed home with her when she got lonely, and held her when she got upset about my father living with another woman. If Amanda could do so much for her, couldn't I at least manage the occasional shopping trip? Maybe this was the thing that could bring us together again, like books when I was little, or like catch before I threw too hard for her.

I FOLLOWED MY mother through another set of revolving doors, down another long aisle and onto a rackety wooden escalator. We were still empty-handed. On the step ahead of me, she took off her coat and held it in her arms. What in the world was she wearing? Winter boots with high slanting wooden heels, and tight-fitting blue jeans with no back pockets. A man in a charcoal gray suit passed by on the down escalator beside us, turning his head to take her in. A few seconds later, a woman made a quick assessment, her eyes sliding back and forth, beads on an abacus. Unnerved, I turned my head to watch the wall going by, but would I have wished her otherwise? She was a divorced mother of two, pushing forty, beginning to dye the gray out of her hair, but she still had it.

On the next floor, my mother found me a room full of jeans, but they all had flashy labels on the butt pocket, disco style. In the Click we did not wear designer jeans.

"This entire room is on sale," my mother said. "Don't you even want to try a pair on? No?"

In the silence, she sighed audibly.

The next room, to my amazement and horror, held bell-bottoms and wide-wale corduroys. We'd worn bell-bottoms in the eighth grade, with black concert T-shirts and maybe a nostalgic button from a shop on Eighth Street: *End the War in Vietnam. Legalize Marijuana.* Back then, we'd sometimes said everything would be better if only we lived in the Sixties. Now I would rather have been caught dead than in bell-bottoms.

We were not having luck.

"Well," my mother said, "you can't wear *those* all winter." She meant my fraying jeans. "Let's take one more look and see if there's anything you'd deign to try on."

Finally we found some boring but acceptable corduroys, plain gray.

"What waist do you wear," my mother asked, "a thirty-two?"

"Maybe a thirty-three," I said, my heart sinking.

"Really?" she asked. "I don't think so. Let me see you."

She looked me up and down, evaluating, as though she'd never seen me before.

I put on the cords in a thirty-three and came out into the hall of the changing area.

"They look fine," she said. "How do they feel?"

"Kind of tight."

"Lift up your shirt," she said loudly. Behind her, I saw the Hispanic woman who unlocked the changing room turn her head to listen in.

"Those are the thirty-twos?" my mother asked.

"No. The bigger ones."

"I guess you've really put on some weight," she said, loud enough for the whole department to hear. "Put a finger in the waistband. Do you have any room?"

"I think I should try the thirty-fours."

"No, no, no. The thirty-threes will be fine."

"What do you mean?" I asked. "Why?" My own voice was rising. Behind my mother, the saleswoman was squinting at my waist.

"I don't want you moving up a size. If you get the thirty-four you're just going to settle into it, and then the rest of your clothes won't fit and I'll have to buy you a whole new wardrobe."

When I owned these pants, when I pulled them on in the morning, I knew already, I would return to this moment, the cold, scolding voice, this embarrassment, the evaluating eyes of strangers.

"I don't have the money to buy you all those clothes," she went on, and then hearing herself, lowered her voice. "You're just going to have to be more careful about what you eat."

"It's not your money anyway!" I wanted to shout. "It's not your money and it's not your life!"

But something stopped me. Why did I take this from her? I think it was because I believed her. I believed that I was fat. I believed that everyone looked with my mother's cold, evaluating eye, straight at my belt. Was that a little bulge hanging over? He can obviously pinch more than an inch. Which hole does he have that belt on, anyway?

It didn't matter to me then that my father's new live-in girlfriend—who said things like, "Wow, Liz Taylor's really porked up"—thought I was too thin. My mother was some kind of phenomenon. She seemed almost as thin as in the wedding pictures in the file cabinet. Her waist was smaller than her friends' waists, smaller than any of my girlfriends' waists, smaller than my father's girlfriend's, even. How could you argue with that waist? Shouldn't she know?

ON LINE FOR the cash register, waiting to pay for one pair of gray corduorys, waist thirty-three, my mother said, "I think I remember a nice candy store downstairs."

I looked at her but no words came. Since I'd stopped singing, I'd been having trouble finding my voice.

"You look like you could use a little pick-me-up," she said.

That wasn't how I would have described how I felt, but chocolate still sounded better than no chocolate.

I gazed through the glass at the deep browns and creamy whites, at the champagne truffles and the cordials and the chocolate-covered fruits. I felt as though things around me were coming into focus. Nothing was complicated about wanting what I saw in front of me, at least not yet.

"I'll have those Continental truffles, the square ones," I said.

"An eighth of a pound," she told the man behind the counter.

He said the minimum was a quarter pound.

"Oh, really," she said. "You can't just give us three pieces?"

With my mother, a treat was always three, three cookies, three sucking candies, three squares of chocolate, whatever small pleasure she was doling out. Unless it was a special occasion, you might have to take two at first, and then ask for the third once you'd finished.

A quarter of a pound made four pieces, it turned out. I sat down at one of the little round tables and pulled the chocolates out of the white bag. On my tongue, the sweetness stung pleasingly, and the dusky flavor went to my head.

"Wow!" I said, loudly. My mother sat back, startled, and at her sudden movement I startled too. We rocked on our stools, regaining our balance.

"Wow," I said again. I licked melted chocolate off my finger-tips. "Aren't you going to have a piece?"

"Oh, I really shouldn't."

In a few minutes, when the candy weighed heavily in my stomach and I imagined my jeans already squeezing me tighter, I'd regret this indulgence. But for now, even though I heard the judgment in my mother's voice, I was content. I lifted a whole piece to my mouth and closed my eyes. It was delicious, perfect—except that the alimony song was in my head again. I opened my eyes and my mother was watching me.

"You aren't even going to taste?" I asked.

"I was going to try one of my new cookies when we got home."

That interested me. There were cookies waiting at home that could compete with this?

"*What* cookies?" I asked.

"Oh, all right," she said. "Let's see if it's really that good."

It was a quiet moment, but what happened next stuck in my mind for years. She reached across the table and lifted the striped brown square with the thumb and forefinger of her right hand. She brought the candy back toward her, but not all the way to her mouth. With her left hand open to catch any possible crumbs, she leaned against the table and craned her neck up to reach her treat.

As I saw her strain like a little girl reaching for something high up on a shelf, I knew which cookies she'd meant. The kind she bought herself at the supermarket. They came in flimsy plastic trays she stored high in a kitchen cabinet, so she had to stretch to reach them. The cookies were all decorated somehow—with pink icing or technicolor sprinkles or brightly dyed cubes of dried, ambiguous fruit—and they were hers alone. Occasionally she insisted on this fiercely, though the truth was that my sister and I didn't like them. When she first tried a new kind—it was usually a new kind—she reviewed them for us, but even if she called them "delish," we could see by her unchanged face that they weren't. She was full of dieter's lies.

She bit off a small corner of the chocolate, then pulled her head back to a more comfortable position and fixed her gaze on the candy while she chewed. She nodded. It was a slow nod, and it reminded me of Miss Krilov, the junior math team coach, who nodded in just this way, measured and measuring, after a student put a solution on the blackboard. Miss Krilov, we all knew, still lived with her parents.

My mother put the chocolate back down in front of me. She wiped first her thumb and then her forefinger on an embossed napkin.

"Very rich," she said, still nodding. "They do a good job here, don't you think?"

In her voice I listened for some sign that she'd had the experience I'd had, for an echo of warm richness melting against her tongue, a hint of sensual delight that might have played along her arms. But it seemed she hadn't tasted at all. It was as if she'd only tested it, only fixed it with her eagle eye. She might as well have been scrutinizing a sexist ad in the subway, or squinting at my waistline.

For all this time, I'd wanted to believe that this careful scrutiny would protect us both, as much as anything could. I had tried to have eyes as sharp as hers for everything suspect and dangerous and unfair, to learn her eagle-eye blindness, to lock those things out of the house of my heart. I'd tried to be the best student of her I could, but as I thought of her bitter stories of a girl in the Fifties, and of what she was showing me now, I found I couldn't tell them apart. They seemed to hold the same miseries—scrutiny, isolation, keeping up appearances. The same female hell.

Across the table, she tipped her head politely to check her watch without my noticing. All day, as we'd gone out into the January cold and back inside the heated department stores, she'd been taking her earmuffs on and off. Her hair was parting, the spray-fixed waves of brown falling into two uneven halves, baring a ragged line of scalp white as an egg. I wished then that I could crack her head in two, wished that her cool, careful self would break, fall away, and let someone else out.

Someone who could protect herself, yes, of course, but who could also taste chocolate, taste a man—taste anything, anyone, whatever it was in her to taste.

Of course, there were things a son didn't want to hear from a mother, and had she actually broken out and tried to tell me about it, I'd probably have cringed and retreated to my room, to call a friend and complain that my mom was acting weird. But even as I went to my room, I'd have had reason to believe what I was now coming to doubt: that in living her way she had something to live for. That we both did.

THE NEXT SUMMER I finally asked my father and his girlfriend if I could move in with them for good. In my nervousness—not about their answer, but about the consequences of my decision—I asked offhandedly, as we were walking toward the kitchen. They pursed their lips, holding back smiles, like candidates on election night who pretend they don't know they're winning. Their faces said that the vote was in, that they'd beaten my mother in the race for True Parents.

"It's me," I tried to explain. "It's just me. I can't— It's impossible—"

My voice broke, and my knees gave way. I fell to the wooden floor. I screamed as I couldn't ever remember screaming, and swung at the floor with my fists. My legs pumped as though I was running; they squeaked and burned against the wood, turning me like a record until my father knelt, put his arms around me and held me still. I gasped for air, breathing the smells of floor polish and dust and my father's summer huskiness.

"It's all right," he said, resting his head on mine. "She's not going to hurt you. She can't hurt you anymore."

I stiffened in his arms. This wasn't what I'd meant, either.

Kiss Me

■ ▌ ■

IT WAS THE fall of my junior year, and for most of lunch period I'd been walking the school halls with Tasha, her hand moist in mine as she talked out her latest operatic family fight. Her mother, she explained, had bought her a sweater, a pouffy pink angora. Tasha had laughed out loud at the child-ishness of the thing, her mother had taken offense, and the fight had stretched through the evening, until her father was screaming at her to stop fighting. It had gone so badly that today she wore the sweater as a "peace offering," she said. It made her look like a little greeting-card girl.

The fact was, I didn't understand these fights. But I knew how to push her red hair out of her face, and joke with her, and put my arms around her while she tissued off the raccoon rings her tears made of her mascara. Sometimes I could talk her through, and we reached a high-ceilinged place where sadness lifted, and she would look up into my eyes, unblink-ing. After we kissed good-bye, it took concentration to walk a straight line.

But we wouldn't reach that place today. Tasha was a mess, and the November rain outside too bitter to walk in. In school we'd found no privacy. We liked to meet in the theater, away from our separate groups of friends, but today all four entrances were locked. So we walked the kid-crowded halls that ricocheted with shouts, music, the banging of locker doors. When Tasha stopped to cry, I stroked her back through the pink sweater. I didn't see Amy and Mia, my neglected Click friends, until I was pushing past them.

"Oh, hi, guys," I said. An afterthought.

Tall Amy crossed her arms and began to laugh—a big, stagey, mocking sound. Smaller Mia joined in, leaning toward her. They were drama-group leads, and their laughter rattled with the sarcasm of much older women, women with clanking jewelry and cigarette voices, rough and bitter. As I realized they were laughing at the sight of me and my sophomore, I lifted my hands in the air to show confusion, smiled as though they might let me in on the joke. The girls tipped their heads back and laughed harder. Mia leaned against Amy, who steadied herself against a locker as if the force of their hilarity might knock them down. Other kids were staring. A few began laughing along.

Tasha turned, asked why I'd stopped. She was still in Queens with her mother, fighting in the little stone-facade house with its view of the Manhattan skyline; she hadn't noticed my derisive friends. But she seemed changed as I looked at her, transformed by the laughter even more than by the sweater. Heat on my face, I hurried her around the corner, more ashamed than I could understand.

HOW DID YOU *meet her?* the Click girls asked me, as though just knowing Tasha was a suspect act. I didn't explain how I'd followed her down hallways and up stairs, not yet knowing her name, telling myself as I tightened with desire and self-consciousness that I was not just staring at her ass (her jeans pockets small and high, as though to give a better view beneath). She wore ankle-high black boots and midnight blue jeans sleekly pegged at the calves, a style I'd never seen before. Her alabaster face seemed to give light, and her thick hair, I thought, was red as embers. I shadowed her in crowds, telling myself I meant this single-minded, uninvited, shallow-breath stalking in a *good* way, if that could be. What could I have said to my Click friends that they wouldn't have found outrageous? *I think she's gorgeous? Check out that ass?*

To get near her, I hung around groups of musical-theater kids talking between classes, cut in on their conversations. Unlike the drama group, they had no faculty director. They were on their own. At their parties they played Ska and New Wave music—The Specials, Depeche Mode, the English Beat, what the magazines were calling the second British invasion. Tasha spent more time hunting import singles than I did. The Click listened to our parents' music—Simon and Garfunkel, The Beatles, the Stones—but this new crowd actually seemed to live in 1982. Some of them went down to the Village to window-shop sex toys at The Pleasure Chest and The Pink Pussycat Boutique. They had in-jokes from *Pink Flamingoes*. Two girls on makeup crew, Kerry and Wendy, called me over one day to tell me I was weird. It was a compliment.

ONCE AGAIN ON a Saturday night, Tasha couldn't get permission to come into the city. Joanna called, and I met her at Café La Fortuna, to share a wobbly table in a dark corner, eat crumbly Italian cookies, and talk about What It All Meant.

"Am I going crazy?" I asked. "Is everyone mad at me?"

"I wouldn't say everyone is *mad* at you," Joanna said.

Scratchy opera music played, some soprano. I suspected Joanna knew the aria.

"No one calls me anymore, practically, except you. I get these looks in the courtyard. Amy and Mia and Heather are barely speaking to me. There's a name for this, right? Being shunned?"

Joanna lifted her tea bag by its string and twirled it in

her cracked china teacup. Her straight brown hair hung matter-of-factly behind her back.

"I guess," she said. "I guess Tasha's just not what anybody expected."

"What's that supposed to mean?"

"You know. She tells people she's an *actress*, but of course she's not *really* an actress."

"What do you mean? She just got the dancing lead in *Anything Goes*, she's in her church theater production of—"

"Okay, okay," Joanna said, hands up at her shoulders. "I'm sure she does. I'm sure. But she doesn't get paid for it, right? You know how Thads is always saying we're only pseudo-intellectuals, that we can't be intellectuals because that's not how we make a living?"

"You're saying that after a *year*, everyone's still down on me because I'm not with Eleanor, the real actress."

"Nooo . . ." Joanna sang. She looked uncomfortable, but then she often did, shoulders high and tight below her ears. "I don't think it's just Eleanor. I guess, I don't know. . . . It's just, Tasha's not a very good *student*. Not that that makes her a bad person, but it's a fact, she's not. And she's *younger* than you, and probably all impressed that you're a *junior*, and that you live in *Manhattan*, on the *Upper West Side*. . . . It just seems like you picked someone so *easy* for you."

I wanted to tell her that to get to Hunter, Tasha took a car, a commuter train, and three subways—an hour and a half each way, on a good day. That she'd just gotten an A on her math unit test. That I talked to her about my life as frankly as I talked to anyone in the Click. That unlike most people, she could always hear the difference between my voice on the phone and my father's. I had evidence of her talents, her good character, her intelligence, but I saw it was no use—I'd just sound like a guy insisting he bought *Playboy* for the articles.

"I mean, she wears all this *makeup*," Joanna went on, twiddling her fingers to show prissy girlishness. "She chats at lunch with all her little fashion friends. She goes to those shows at the

Peppermint Lounge and Limelight. That's, like, trendy haircuts and little toy synthesizers, right? Is that music?"

I turned from Joanna's gaze, picked up a sandy cookie and looked at it for a moment. I meant to eat it, but in my head I saw the girls laughing at me again. I put it back on the little white plate.

"You're saying I'm with a cookie."

"I don't *know*. . . ." she said. She glanced down at her short, unpainted nails. "It just seems like, Oh. Look at that. After everything, Greg wants a trophy girlfriend."

She looked at me suddenly, and her long metal earrings glimmered.

"It's just," Joanna said, "what are you *doing* with her . . . ?"

". . . when I could be with one of us?"

WHEN TASHA AND I couldn't meet backstage or in the theater, we left each other notes. We wrote about her chorus performances and my guitar playing, about our fights with our mothers, about whether anyone really ran their own lives, or whether their lives ran them. I used sheets of loose-leaf paper, but Tasha's father was "in paper," and her notes came on stationery bordered in shades of cream or pastel. Her fountain pen ink was turquoise or fuchsia, and she sealed her most private notes with red wax.

"I love theaters," she wrote. "They feel so far from . . . from your predictable self."

Before the last performance of my play, she handed me a note:

> *Savor it. Tuck it away in your mind—all that you feel, think—and save it for a time when you need to have that experience. Save your feelings of experiences, because they are always useful to a person who needs a lot of emotion to make a play not be a play.*
>
> *Do you know what I mean?*

I didn't, exactly, but I reread that note even more often than the others. It seemed she'd gotten things switched around, calling the play an experience, which left real life as the thing you worked to make "not a play." She wore rouge, like Grandmother Jane, but unlike my grandmother she didn't blend it into her cheeks to make them look natural. The lines slanted down her cheekbones like war paint. Fair-skinned as she was, redhaired even to the soft arches of her eyebrows, she still edged her almond eyes in vivid black, letting the line trail back from the corners. For shows, she refused the makeup crew and put on her own natural-looking stage face, but in regular life she always looked, as my grandmother might have said, theatrical.

A few boys in school, like Jonathan, her director for *Anything Goes*, were wearing eyeliner and mascara, like the men in New Wave bands. The best movies that year, we agreed, were *Tootsie*, with Dustin Hoffman passing as a woman, and *Victor/ Victoria*, with Julie Andrews passing as a man. Peter's girlfriend in Princeton had made him and me up for a couple of parties. A little eye makeup made me feel quietly radical, which I loved, but it was for boys who fooled around with other boys. Most of the time, in my button-down shirts and my crew-neck sweaters, I didn't look theatrical at all, but I felt strangely at home around people getting away from their expected selves.

Still, sometimes the self Tasha picked embarrassed me. With girls from her grade, she spoke a Queens answer to Valley Girl, riddled with "like" and punctuated with exclamations: "Oh-migah-od! No way! No *way!*" She tossed her long red hair, simpered, called herself and her girlfriends lazy ditzes. The insults and the bimbo voice made me glance around in shame; so did her loud enthusiasms for kittens and chocolate and roses and Disneyland, though I enjoyed those things myself. She liked to tell me, "Enjoy the moment!"—calling it out as good-bye. I didn't mind it in a note, but I wished she wouldn't say it out loud.

Once I asked why she let people think of her as ditzy.

"Why should I let them know me the way you know me?" she answered. "They're not you."

. . .

ONE AFTERNOON, TASHA'S *Anything Goes* rehearsal was canceled at the last minute. We walked across Central Park to the new apartment on the Upper West Side that I shared with my father and his girlfriend, Ronna. On the way I pointed out The Dakota, where John Lennon had recently been shot. At home, I gave Tasha the tour, introducing her to our two young cats, showing her the closet-sized Manhattan kitchen with its narrow brown refrigerator, the living room with Ronna's white leather couch and her brown-and-white rabbit-hair throw.

Tasha went into the master bedroom, snapped on the bathroom light, opened the closet and bathroom doors, and peered in. I waited in the living room.

"You have to show me your mother's place, too!" she called.

My mother had kept everything as it was before my father left—for Amanda's and my sake, as she told friends on the phone. To give us the consistency and the continuity we needed. What she wasn't telling her friends was that I'd failed to appreciate her efforts. Hers was my real home, as she often reminded me, but now I lived with my father, and visited unreliably, and when we were together we mostly fought. I had no respect for her feelings or for her, she told me. I was obnoxious, haughty, insensitive, arrogant. We argued on the phone from my father's until she hung up on me.

While I stared out the window, Tasha wandered over to the dry-erase board where we left messages about whether we'd be home for dinner and where we could be reached. She pulled the cap off the red marker and wrote: "I love this apartment! Can I move in?"

She stepped out of her low boots and settled into the soft white couch, snapping the pages of one of Ronna's thick, glossy fashion magazines. She stopped suddenly to lean in for a closer look, then flipped to the next picture, the way I rifled through albums at a used record store.

I sank into the couch beside her, wondered what to do with

my arms. It felt good to sit next to her. I watched her look over a sultry model with full, pursed lips.

"Wait," I said, as she began to turn a page.

"Why?" she asked. I tensed, afraid I'd made a mistake.

"Do you like that?" she asked. She didn't seem jealous or offended. She seemed curious.

"I don't know. That's some expression on her face, though."

"That?" She studied the picture again. "Debbie Harry does something like that. You know the cover of *Eat to the Beat*? That's easy."

"Yeah, right," I said.

She turned the pale oval of her face toward me. As I watched, her dark eyes filled with distant longing, and her painted red lips parted just enough to let in a swizzle stick. She held the pose, and she seemed a perfect statue, but with a heartbeat beneath her satiny blouse. A statue you could fuck. This was the girl I'd followed in the halls before I even knew her name. Now I had her on my couch. I willed myself to stay calm, not to do anything reckless. Then Tasha returned, raising her eyebrows.

"You see?" she said. She went back to flipping pages.

"That was amazing."

"It's really nothing."

"If it's so nothing, tell me how you do it."

"Fine," she said. "Fine. You look at the model's face, and you let yourself feel what she was thinking as she posed. And then you imagine the same thing."

"So what was she thinking to make that face?"

"Oh," she said, closing the magazine and tossing it back on the shaggy rug. "It's really nothing that great."

"Tell me."

"I don't want to spoil it for you," she said.

It didn't seem then that I was *making a move*. It only seemed time to kiss, and time to press together on the long leather couch. Normally the idea of makeup grossed me out, but Tasha's face still felt like skin, and her rouge, which she called blush, smelled like raspberries and cream. I thought it was great.

In the middle of a long kiss, I unbuttoned her blouse. She did the same with my shirt, and pushed first one of my sleeves and then the other down my arms. Her bare stomach burned against mine.

I reached behind her back, under her loosened top, to undo her lilac-tinted bra.

"It closes in front," she said coolly.

I pulled, twisted, fumbled.

"You don't know what you're doing!" she snapped.

It was true, I didn't. It was soft satiny purple, with the clasp right between her small breasts, making me a little dizzy. I pulled away from her, leaned against a leather pillow, my damp back sticking to the slick surface. Then, slowly, I said, "I've never seen one that closes like that."

"Huh," she said.

"So *show me*," I said, matching her impatient tone. She looked at me, and arched her back, bringing her slender fingers to the lilac-toned clasp between her breasts.

"No," she said, lowering her hands again. "If you want it so badly, you can figure it out for yourself."

I tried to fumble more suavely. Out on the street, cars were honking.

"Does it bend or twist?"

"Yes," she said.

It wasn't just that the clasp was strange. I wasn't used to feeling like I was *doing something to her, getting her clothes out of my way*. Eleanor hadn't worn a bra, and we'd acted as though we only took off our sweaters and our shirts because of the heat of the room.

"Oh," I said, finally.

"Wait . . ." Tasha said. Like a magician, she pulled her bra out one arm of her blouse, then closed the blouse like a bathrobe. She climbed on top of me, pressing me into the soft couch, and tucking her blouse between our hips. Her body was heavier than I expected, delicious along the length of me, her legs on my legs, her chest on my chest. I stacked my hands behind my head for a pillow. She lifted my glasses off my face, put them aside, then pinned my forearms with hers.

"Kiss me," she said.

I arched my neck up, but as I reached for her, she slowly pulled away, her blouse pulling tight against her. When I couldn't stretch higher, she leaned in, brushing her lips against mine with a touch no heavier than breath.

"Kiss me," she said, looking into my eyes.

"I want to," I said, straining, laughing.

"Are you sure?" she asked.

I arched my back to reach her, and she arched hers away, her thighs pressing mine. My skin stretched tight across my chest, but she kept the slight distance between us, her wide brown eyes so close to me they blurred. I had the strength to shake off her grip and wrestle her down, but as I lay pinned, straining, I felt how much I wanted to kiss her, how good wanting itself could feel. I'd had no idea.

OUT THE CASEMENT windows, the sky was darkening. My father's girlfriend didn't believe in Christmas trees for Jews, so he'd strung our colored lights along the wall.

"Look," I said, when we broke off from kissing, showing Tasha our arms dappled in colors.

"How did we meet?" she asked.

"I don't know. You were so gorgeous, I just followed you around until you noticed me."

"You did not!" she said, pushing up on her elbows to look me in the eye.

"Didn't you realize? It was practically all I did at lunch."

"No way. Really?"

"Thank God for boys!" I blurted. Out of my mouth, the words sounded radical, too risky to say to a girl.

"Someone has to get things started," I blundered on, not sure if I was joking or arguing. "Otherwise the whole race would die out!"

Tasha wasn't laughing. I could imagine the way the conversation would go now—did I think I was hunting an animal? Was that all I thought of her?

"Really?" she asked. "You followed me? You picked me out and followed me?"

I didn't know what to say.

"So what did you think of me, before you knew me?" she asked.

When I was near her, words leapt out of my mouth. "I thought you were some bitch dancer," I heard myself say. What was I thinking? *Bitch* was a fighting word at Hunter, second in seriousness only to *cunt*. Tears were shed over these words, friendships ended, grudges held for months.

Tasha laughed. "It's true, I can be a real bitch," she said, sounding pleased.

My body moved almost on its own. I turned her onto her back, pinned her elbows with my forearms. Then I froze inside, afraid I'd gone too far, that this time she'd be angry. I sat up beside her outstretched legs, sipped lukewarm black tea.

"You're strong," she said, sitting up beside me.

"I'm not strong," I said, embarrassed.

"You're stronger than me. I like it."

"It's not really something I've thought about," I lied.

"Push," she said.

She held her palms up in front of her shoulders. I put my hands flat against hers and pushed. For a moment, our hands held still, then her arms began to bend back. She smiled.

"I want to watch you shave," she said.

"Now?" I asked. I was afraid I was blushing.

"Not now, but sometime. Please? I'll sit on the edge of the bathtub. I won't get in the way. What do you wear when you shave?"

Now as she sat beside me, I took her wrists, and held them behind her waist. With the other hand I grabbed her hair and pulled, slow and hard, opening her mouth for my tongue. I'd never handled a girl this way.

"Aren't we lucky I'm so limber?" she asked.

I let go of her wrists and pressed her back down onto the couch until I lay on top of her. The cushions sighed.

"Kiss me," I said.

"You're driving me crazy . . . ," she said. "Do you know that?"

"Kiss me," I said again, slowly pulling away, as she'd done to me.

"You're *enjoying* this," she said, stretching toward me again. "You must like to torture me."

"Maybe I do," I said, leaning in as if to finally kiss her, then pulling away.

"I hate you," she said.

"Poor baby," I said, struggling to keep my eagerness out of my voice. "You suffer so, don't you."

"Kiss me?" she asked. "Please?"

I did, and Eno the cat jumped up beside us, purring furiously. Ears and whiskers flattened to his face, he burrowed insistently between us, the wedge of his head surprisingly hard, his orange fur warm and silky. He purred in a rolling rhythm, and we all three thrummed to it.

"Well, this is certainly a new experience," Tasha joked.

"How do you think we top it?" I asked.

I didn't mean anything by the question, or rather, I didn't know what I meant until I said it. I didn't want to feel I was the sort of guy who followed a girl around, took her to his place, and made her comply with his desires.

Tasha freed one arm, and I turned to see what she'd do next. She checked her watch. Then she pulled away from me and Eno, who squawked in displeasure.

"Sorry, cat," she said, standing up. "I've got a train to catch."

"Shut your mouth," said a voice in my head.

She turned toward the wall, to put on her bra. I retrieved my glasses, too late for a look.

"Take that off," I wanted to tell her, "before I tear it off."

"I had a really great time," she said, looking around for her shoulder bag. "But my mom'll be expecting me. The bathroom's through here, right?"

I stared out the window. The cat was in the kitchen, crying. After listening for a few minutes, I rattled dry food into his metal bowl. At the sound, he ran from his food as though it frightened him.

Finally Tasha came out, neatly brushed and touched up, zippering clear plastic makeup bags. There was no sign of me on her anywhere.

"Your mom's expecting you on a specific train?" I asked. "Why didn't you tell me?"

"It's just better if I go now."

"I didn't say you could leave," said the voice in my head. "Take off your clothes and do as you're told. If I need your opinion, I'll ask for it."

"Can I come back soon?" she asked, heading for the door, her voice now all good-girl politeness.

JOEY DISCOVERED ME. He was the day-shift doorman, and now that Tasha checked in with him after rehearsal to find out whether I was home, and charmed him into letting her do her homework on the lobby love seat if I wasn't, I was worth talking to. Mr. McLeod, the guidance counselor, who'd never seemed to notice me before, started pointing me out to other male teachers, loudly.

"Have you seen this guy?" he asked. "Every time I walk down the hall, he's got a girl in his arms." He made boxer fists, faked with his left, and chucked me one fondly on the shoulder. "I want to bottle this guy," he said. "We're going to call it Brut Lichtenberg." I'd never been chucked on the shoulder before, didn't think of myself as a boy men took interest in. I felt like I'd learned the secret handshake.

My uncle called from out of town and made a rare request to talk to me. He wanted to hear for himself about this redhead— "fifteen going on twenty-five, your father says"—and to warn me about the foolishness of overattachment.

"It's a high school, right? The place is probably crawling with beautiful girls. Don't let this one try to get serious on you. You just enjoy. That's the best time there is. You should be like a kid in a candy store."

Maybe there really was a script for this, as women said, passed from man to man at secret meetings. *A kid in a candy store. The best years of your life.* "You know how you know you're old?" three different men asked me. "When you realize you're older than the girls in *Playboy.*"

"*That* is no Manhattan girl," my father said, after he first met Tasha.

"You make that sound like a good thing."

"Manhattan girls are too complex. Everything gets too complicated. This is much better." He turned toward a wall, smiling, pleased at his visions of me.

"That's hours of work," Ronna said, suddenly fierce. "The makeup and the clothes, keeping up with the magazines . . . that doesn't come easy."

"How many hours?" I asked.

My father went into the bedroom to change out of his work clothes.

"I'd say two," Ronna said. "A couple of hours a day, to look like that."

"That's like fifteen hours a week! That's more than I put in at Cake Masters."

"It's an extra part-time job," Ronna said. She was short and curvy and younger than my father. She wore a tailored red suit with coordinating pumps, and a blouse with a high, lace collar.

"Men don't realize," she said.

"SEX SCARES ME," Tasha wrote. Turquoise ink. "I like to think it doesn't, but it does. I mean, it's not something you should just jump into. Do you understand? If you don't, tell me."

There was a word for what we were, *virgins,* but it was not one my friends and I used much. I pictured ritual sacrifices, stone altars, hearts cut out and offered to the gods. I thought of Susie on the subject: "Could someone *please* explain what's so great about fucking a virgin? The girl's going to be inexperienced, and scared, and it's going to *hurt* her. She's going to *bleed.* What is good about that? What is with you guys?"

205

The truth was, I wished Tasha'd had some experience—maybe not a whole lot, but some. That way, at least we wouldn't both be in the dark.

I brought Tasha's note home and called her. The December rain tapped on the little panes of the window.

"I'm sorry," she said. "I don't *want* to be afraid. I just am."

"It's okay," I said. "You're right. You're totally right. We shouldn't rush into anything."

This wasn't the conversation I'd expected, but it felt strangely comfortable, almost a relief.

"You must be getting so impatient!" she said.

It was true, I was, though I wouldn't have named the feeling if she hadn't. I thought about her, I masturbated, I thought about her, I masturbated—but I didn't like the sound of *impatient*. Too demanding. If I was going to admit to impatience to fuck, what would come next? That I was sick of her tears, her family crises, her million and one reasons not to get over here and put out? Lately I was having a problem with perspective. I wasn't always sure whose eyes I looked through, couldn't always remember why we let women out-of-doors, say. Why we didn't just keep them chained to our beds.

To keep sounding reasonable, I found, it was easier to talk as though sex was a problem of hers, separate from me, like her fights with her mother, or her parents' screaming arguments. "I have felt you hesitate sometimes," I observed. "You jump up to leave, or you hold back like you're uncomfortable."

"I'm not uncomfortable," she said. "I'm not uncomfortable with you. I just don't want to give you the wrong signal. . . ."

". . . about making love?"

"Yeah."

"So, what if we say we never will without talking about it first?"

"Really? Could we do that?"

"If we say so," I said, finding the jocular, reassuring role, the voice. "I mean, why not? Aren't we the ones in charge?"

Tasha laughed, sounding like herself again. "So you're saying I can do anything I want to you, anything at all, as much as

I want"—she laughed—"and as long as I want, and it doesn't mean I've changed my mind about sex?"

"I guess I just agreed to that," I said.

"This is going to be very interesting," she said. "This is going to be a lot of fun."

That night in bed I wrote in my journal:

> *Sex? I'm eager, I'm interested, but I don't want to do any-thing* to *her so much as* with *her. . . . I'd like to talk our way through it, like a learner's game of cards, with the hands left faceup on the table.*

I WAS SURPRISED Aaron had called me, until I realized he wanted the details of my news.

"Your dad's getting remarried," he prompted.

"Yeah," I said. "It's kind of weird."

"Naah, they usually do. I suppose your mom's a mess?"

"She's okay. She says she's happy for him."

"Thrilled," Aaron said. "Right."

The truth was, the Barry Manilow records were out again. When I came for dinner, my mother kept telling me what a shock it was, that she couldn't get over the power my father still had to hurt her. Amanda hovered like a nurse, sensitive, helpful, devoted, though I knew that when my mother was at work, Amanda was getting interested in pot and the kids who could supply it. After dinner, when I left for my father's, the two of them watched me open the front door as if they couldn't believe I'd really walk out on them.

"So where'd your dad tell you the big news?" Aaron asked.

I described the place, a noisy café in the East Village.

"You'll never go there again," he said.

"Hey. I *like* Ronna."

"I'm just saying you'll never go there again."

I didn't answer. It was true, I was in no rush to go back.

"How bad was it? Did he get mushy on you?"

"Not really," I said, not wanting to add that part to the

story, not wanting it to make the rounds. My father had put on a faraway voice, part businessman and part professor. Over our steaming mugs he'd told Amanda and me, "I've come to the realization that Ronna is a core and essential part of my life."

" 'Core and essential'? " Ronna repeated, voice breaking into giggles.

From beneath her bangs, Amanda flashed the wronged-little-sister look that meant she didn't understand. The whole thing felt like a play rehearsal where the actors hadn't bothered to learn their lines.

But it did seem natural for the two of them to get married. They held hands like teenagers, called each other "honey lamb," made out on the couch. After they came to my play performance, girls at school told me, "Your parents are so cute!" And Ronna was generous with us—she made us oatmeal in the mornings, asked if our winter coats were warm enough. She earned what seemed like a whole lot of money. Living with them both was better than living with him alone—he got angry less, and she had some good Motown records. But in the overheated café, as she'd giggled and he'd acted hurt and Amanda looked at me to translate, I'd had the helpless feeling that no one was actually in charge.

"I just hope it works," I told Aaron.

"What's that supposed to mean?"

"You know, that it's the right thing to do. That it's not some big mistake."

"They'll stay together awhile," Aaron said.

"What makes you the big expert?"

"Just look at her. She's your mom again, right? Short, brown hair, Jewish, lots of energy. Isn't she?"

"I don't know."

"Sure, she's your mom again, except fewer miles, a better job, and bigger tits. They'll make it till you're in college. I'm sure of it."

"Thanks," I said. "Thanks a lot."

I could have told him he was full of shit, that he couldn't say who she was or what was going to happen, but that was the problem. He couldn't say. I couldn't say. We had no idea.

I'd studied other parents for clues. At the stroke of midnight on New Year's Eve, Tasha's had been screaming about whether or not to watch a movie. She said she didn't know what kept them together. Aaron's had divorced when he was young. He gave out two phone numbers, Thursday-through-Saturday and Sunday-through-Wednesday. His father had a girlfriend Aaron called "the live-in"; before I realized they didn't have the money, I'd thought he meant a maid. Tom claimed that his parents drew a line down the middle of their apartment after fights, the father staying on his side, the mother on hers.

Of course plenty of parents were still together. Tucson's, for instance, though I couldn't see why. His mom always sounded pained, and his father's mind seemed elsewhere. I was looking for inspiration, but my standards were tough. I ruled out as unjust all mothers who didn't work full-time for money, and all fathers who indulged themselves in bellowing. Most of the ones still together had naive disease; they required a near-constant stream of lies about sex or drugs or alcohol. The most clued-in parents, who looked you in the eye when you spoke to them, were single. It frightened me more than I could say.

IT TOOK TASHA a few weeks of negotiating, but she got permission to go out to dinner with me. We wanted the same thing—a *real* date, a glass of wine, a long conversation. My father had ideas for suitable spots. We ate Italian by candlelight on Columbus Avenue, and came home early to his apartment.

"Oh, good!" Ronna called, as we came in. "We were hoping we'd get to see you."

They were on the floor in sweatpants and T-shirts, leaning against the couch and watching television. The cats licked the last of the ice cream from glass bowls forgotten on the rug. There were hugs and kisses all around.

"So dinner was good?" Ronna asked.

"It was really nice. . . ." Tasha said.

"We're watching this awful miniseries," Ronna said. "It's wonderful. We could fill you in if you wanted—"

My father gave her a look.

"Oh, but you'd probably hate it," she said.

Tasha started laughing.

"Yeah," Ronna went on, "you'd hate it. Terrible idea."

I grinned in gratitude at my father, and he gave me his "Hey—no problem" look.

I closed the bedroom door behind Tasha and me, and then the door of the bookshelf-and-plywood wall that divided the room into my sister's half and mine. Amanda was downtown, tending to my mother.

"Your dad and Ronna seem so happy . . . ," Tasha said wistfully. "They really don't mind?"

"That we're here? No way. Having us here strikes a blow against repressive parents everywhere."

Tasha laughed, stepped out of her low boots. I took her hands, cold from the walk home.

"When they visited Ronna's parents," I said, "in Missouri the first time? They had to sleep in separate beds."

"No *way*."

"Of course. They were living in sin, right?"

"But they're adults!"

"Her parents were just being practical," I said, mock-seriously. "Why would he buy the cow when he could get the milk for free?"

"Oh, fine," Tasha said. "Just fine. How about, Because he needs the cow."

"Moo," I said.

"Shut up."

"Make me."

It must have been about an hour later that I heard my father yelling my name.

"Great," I said. "Perfect."

Tasha giggled from under the covers. I fell out of her mouth, again. She'd been having some trouble.

I climbed out of bed, looked around for my jeans.

"What?" I called to my father, pissed.

"That was Tasha's mother calling on the phone," he yelled through the two doors. When he was tense, he put on a tight, formal voice, as though he didn't know the person he spoke to. "She wanted to make sure Tasha had the train schedule. They don't want her to have to take the late train."

"So is she on the phone?"

"I told her you were still out to dinner."

"Wow!" I yelled. "Great! That's great. Thanks!"

"She sounded serious about that train," he warned.

I climbed back on the bed.

"I can't believe my mom!" Tasha said. "I'll still remember that damned train schedule when I'm a hundred."

"Amazing timing, huh?"

Tasha had worn a new cardigan for our date, in coffee-and-milk tones with big, easy buttons. She'd covered herself with it again while I was out of bed, and sat up on her folded white legs.

"Look at you," I said, unbuttoning her sweater.

"Do you have to?"

"You're shy?" I asked.

"Of this," she said. "I'm trying not to be."

I opened her soft sweater, pushed the sleeves slowly down her long arms. She hadn't let me look at her this way before, bare except for the creamy gleam of satin below her waist.

Her hips were broad, and more squared off than the hips on models in pictures. Her waist did not tuck in sharply below her ribs.

"What?" she asked. "What is it?"

Somehow I knew words for these flaws. *Thick waist. Boxy hips.* Under my gaze, she hunched her shoulders forward self-consciously. The ovals of her breasts, pale and pink-tipped and vulnerable looking, didn't remind me of any kind of fruit. For a moment, I thought I must have been mistaken, that this dizzying attraction was an error, that I should have double-checked her measurements before I fell for her.

"*Kiss* me," Tasha said.

211

I leaned into her, pressing her back onto the bed and pushing her fragrant hair out of her face. She fit her mouth to mine, and her body.

"You feel so warm," I said.

"Mmmm," she said.

"So good."

"What do you want me to do?" she asked, smiling, as though the question was amusing.

I sighed. "I guess you better make that train."

"I can handle the damned train," she said. "Tell me what you want me to do."

"Really?" I asked, embarrassed.

"You're keeping me waiting," she said.

"I'm thinking," I said, but I knew what I wanted. She'd started to do it, just before her mom had called. I hadn't needed to use words, hadn't felt I was giving orders. Now in my embarrassment I kissed her wet mouth and dragged myself against her body, moving as slowly as I could stand.

"Mmmm," she said. "Now tell me."

"I guess I'd like, I mean, I'd like you to finish."

"Finish?" she repeated.

"Go down on me again."

"What?"

I froze. It was the wrong thing to say, selfish, Neanderthal. The wrong thing to want.

"What did you say?"

I rolled away from her, sat up. I felt the dry heat from the radiator against my leg.

"What did you say?" she asked again, sitting up beside me.

"I said, I mean—"

"I never heard of that," she said. "Not that way of saying it."

"Yeah?" I said. In my nervousness her words seemed another language.

"I like it," she said. "Let's use it."

"Okay."

"So . . . tell me again what you want me to do."

"I'd like you to go down on me, please."

"*No,*" Tasha said.

"What?" I said.

"No '*please,*' " she said.

She took a long time making her way down my chest, and I wasn't sure if she was teasing me or if she'd gotten frightened, changed her mind. Finally she put her mouth around me, the feeling amazingly direct, but after a little while I felt—not that I'd had any experience—that she didn't really know what she was doing. I fell out of her mouth again.

"Sorry," she said.

I wondered if this was going to work. But she kept touching me, determined. She touched me with her hair and her lips and her tongue, with her throat and her fingers.

In the usual noise of my mind I began to hear an unfamiliar voice. Gradually this voice pushed aside the others, taking the lead. *She was doing it wrong.*

It felt surprisingly good to think the words. If she was doing it wrong, then I could reach down and make her do it right. I could say what I wanted. I palmed the warm, round bone of her head, felt the sweat on her scalp. I pushed her where I wanted her, and the crowd in my head was drowned out. I'd tried to be patient with her, thoughtful, kind. Now I was through with all that. I knew exactly what I wanted, and I wanted it now, my way, no complications.

She was doing fine, doing great. I didn't even know if she was doing anything differently, but I'd never felt anything like this in my life. Still I kept pushing her—it felt good to push, good to know what I wanted, good to take it. By the end it was all I could do not to pound her head like a drum.

Afterward, I sat smiling in a tangle of sheets.

"Wow . . ." I said.

"Look at that smile," she said. "I'm glad it made you happy."

"Wow! Wow. Did *you* like that?"

She pulled on her jeans, leaned down to zip the short zippers that pegged each calf. I heard her sniffle. Her answer was quiet and shy. "Yeah," she said.

"Really? You did?"

"I don't think I liked it as much as you did . . . ," she joked. "But, yeah." She leaned over, kissed the top of my head. Then she checked her watch. "We need to get going."

I wanted her to talk about it, wanted to hear again that she'd liked it, that it wasn't some depressing chore. Because I didn't know. At the end, I'd been nothing but demand and feeling. I'd left her alone with that; had I been doing her harm, I wouldn't have noticed.

"How did you learn?" I asked, to keep her talking. I ran my hands through my pillow-flattened hair.

"I don't know."

"You must have learned *somehow*."

"Fine!" she snapped. "Be that way. *Fast Times at Ridgemont High*. The scene with the carrot. Okay?"

She grabbed her shoulder bag, glared at me.

"Okay, okay. I was just curious. Hey—I owe you one."

As soon as I let the words out of my mouth, I wished I could yank them back. The whole bright evening seemed to dim down to everyday. Of course oral sex would be a chore, I thought. Bodily housework. She wouldn't say so now, but in time we would probably fight about it. I could take advantage, and maybe she'd let me. Or we could keep track, fair and square, her turn and my turn, and even when the math was right, we'd feel cheated. Wasn't that what couples did?

"You don't owe me," Tasha said. "I owe *you*."

What she said seemed wrong, but I couldn't answer, couldn't even ask what she meant—her words were so exactly, so alarmingly what I wanted to hear.

"Greg!" my father yelled through the door. "You really need to get going. I mean it." He sounded terrible.

"We're leaving now," I called.

"I really mean it," he warned.

I got dressed fast, to the sound of water running in the bathroom sink. Tasha came out in her cardigan and jeans, her head tipped sideways, pulling a brush down through her hair. With the hand that wasn't brushing, she set up a little makeup mirror on a bookshelf in my sister's side of the divided room.

"What's *he* so worried about?" she asked. "He's not the one who's going to get grounded."

She stopped talking to put on what looked like cream-colored lipstick.

"What's that for?"

"Moisturizer."

"Do you really need to do all that now?"

"Yes."

"Well, okay, but maybe you could do it on the train, if you think your mom—"

"You sound like *him*," she said coldly, tipping her head in my father's direction.

I watched her trace the outline of her lips with a skinny brown pencil, then paint in lipstick. I tried not to look at my sister's digital clock.

As she worked around her eyes, she asked, "Do you remember how you told me once that at the start of a test, when the teacher says, 'You may begin,' you never do? How you said you leave the test on the desk, and stretch your arms, and look around the room, until you remember that it's their test, but it's still your life?"

"Yeah?" I said.

"Well?" she asked.

I watched her hold a tiny brush to her eyelashes with her thumb and forefinger. Her hand was perfectly steady. For a moment I saw my father through her eyes, a well-meaning, middle-aged man out of his depth, wanting to play the hip and understanding 1980's dad but panicking.

In the bathroom I looked into the wavy old mirror. I wet down my fingers under the faucet and combed my hair with them, to fix what got flattened in bed. I rubbed the lipstick off my face, washed the smears off my glasses, yanked out and re-tucked my shirt. When I came back out, Tasha was pulling the zipper on her makeup case.

"Ready?" I asked.

I grabbed the doorknob with one hand, and took her hand with the other. She shouldered her bag. Whatever my father and Ronna expected to see, I doubted it was fresh, poised, presentable us. Tasha kissed him good-bye, and he brightened some.

"Take a cab!" he instructed.

In the elevator, Tasha checked her watch and said, "The theater's letting out. The forties'll be a zoo."

"The subway'll be faster," I said.

At the station, the train came as we walked down the steps.

"I think we'll make it!" I yelled over the noise, as the subway pulled into Penn Station.

"If we don't, was it still worth it?"

I kissed her until the doors slid open.

Heads turned as we ran through the drab tunnel to the commuter trains. We heard the last call for the Port Washington line. Tasha's red hair flew back behind her as she ran, and the station seemed transfigured—this couldn't be the dingy Long Island Rail Road, I thought; we had to be in Paris, Rome, Istanbul, racing to our sleeper on the Orient Express.

"I feel like James Bond!" I called, panting.

Veering left at the information kiosk, she called back, "So do I!"

Tasha sprinted to the train's open doorway. She dropped her shoulder bag inside, then turned to the conductor leaning out his little window. She smiled at him full on until she had him, and then she walked away from the train, back to me, slow and nonchalant, for one last good-night kiss.

I WATCHED THE lights of Tasha's train disappear around a curve, and walked slowly through the dirty old station. My first impulse was to hurry home, so my father wouldn't have to wonder if she'd missed the train, but then I heard her voice in my head, asking, "What's *he* so worried about?"

The night was cold and clear, and I walked up Eighth Avenue, past the run-down bus terminal and the flashing peep show theaters and the prostitutes, up through Hell's Kitchen. I felt on edge but I was relishing it, kicking at the gray metal amyl nitrate canisters in the gutter, singing love songs out loud for her to the rhythm of my walking.

Farther, at the dark, intimidating silence of Central Park, I picked up Broadway. Now with my mental Beatles I was trying to sing that I was *this boy*, who only wanted to love her, not *that boy*, who would make her cry. But like John Lennon on the live bootlegs, I kept mixing the two boys up.

The fountain at Lincoln Center stood gleaming in its circle of lights, the water in three white tiers, like a wedding cake. I sat on the flecked black marble base, feeling the cold stone through my jeans. Ahead was Avery Fisher Hall, where Tasha and I had seen Ultravox. They weren't my favorite band, but for one song the lead singer had stood alone, stage front before a silver tree of syndrums, pounding gloriously away while the light show filled the stage behind him. *I'd wanted to beat her head like a drum.* My teeth still ached from clenching, and the tip of my cock sweetly burned. The thought made me smile, and I got up to walk around the mostly empty plaza, looking up at the opera house and the theater with all their passions and murders. No harm done. Still singing to myself, I wandered to the dark, winter-drained reflecting pool. Up above I could see Orion's belt, and the Big Dipper, and all the stars they say you can't see in New York City. In the radiance of the winter night, I trusted myself to imagine.

"TASHA'S MOTHER CALLED," my father told me. "To discuss my commitment to Tasha's virginity."

It was a word I couldn't remember my father saying before—so judgmental, so square. Suddenly proud, I grinned. He didn't grin back. Just home, still in his suit, he smelled of winter air and something animal, acrid. He addressed his remarks to the scruffy, off-white rug.

"She asked if I would agree to act as chaperon when the two of you were in my home."

Light snared the thick rectangular lenses of his glasses.

"So what did you say?"

"I told her I'd always trusted you, that I trusted you now, and that I was sure she trusted Tasha."

"That's great!" I said. "That's perfect." How could her mother possibly answer that? But as he turned to me, I could see he had no enthusiasm for it. His lips were pursed, his face pale. He smelled like worry. He turned back to the rug.

I wanted to make a joke, something with a manly swagger—what a wolf she must think I was, preying on her helpless daughter. Something to make him laugh at the outdated fears of an uptight Catholic housewife.

"You've got a problem here," he said, in a voice at once gravelly and loud, as though he'd removed himself from where I was, and now needed to yell to be heard.

"What's going on?" I asked.

"What's *going on*," he said, "is that you've got yourself a problem, and I'm not going to be the one to solve it for you."

I tried to think of a law Tasha and I were in danger of breaking, some catastrophe we needed his help to avert. Marriage? Pregnancy? I'd been coached to avoid those twin disasters for years.

He hurried back to his bedroom as though I'd been wasting his time, and pulled the door tightly shut. Even with it closed, I could feel his doubt in me radiating with the heat of accusation. Despite myself, I put words to his silence. I was blind, reckless, a lousy bet. When this unnamed disaster struck, he sure as hell wouldn't be there with me.

TASHA AND I had certain wishes, certain fantasies we wanted to live out. She wanted us to dress together for a fancy evening, the two of us in the same room, so she could watch me put on my suit, lace my dress shoes. I wanted to wake up with her, not as we had at Marci Glotzer's party, on a hallway floor at six A.M. with a dozen other bedraggled teenagers, but late in the morning, alone with each other in a wide bed. We wanted to make French toast together, a leisurely brunch at home.

One day, for some reason, morning classes were canceled. Tasha came over to my father's to make the French toast. She asked to hear my new copy of "Sex (I'm A . . .)," and as Terri Nunn sang her list of all the roles she lived when she made love, Tasha cracked eggs one-handed into a Pyrex bowl. The little closet-kitchen had no counter space, so we worked together on the brown stovetop. I measured salt and vanilla. Tasha poured milk from the carton.

"Why is this so great?" I asked.

Tasha smiled, kissed me. "Where do you keep the sugar?" she asked.

I said we didn't need sugar, since we were going to have maple syrup. I was heating the bottle in a pan of hot water.

"It needs the *sugar* so it will *brown* properly, okay?"

"What are you talking about?" I said, rising to the occasion. "This is food. It's to eat. It doesn't have to be *browned* properly."

"God!" she said. "That is so like a boy! You're just going to stuff it in your face anyway, so who cares what it looks like going in!"

I lost my deadpan, laughed.

"I am totally serious," she said, smiling.

It was another thing on our private list: to disagree, and fight, and get through, and stay together.

After we ate, we sat on the leather couch without music or talk. It was the middle of winter, the overcast sky yellow and the wind raw, but our indoors smelled of butter and cinnamon. The leftover Christmas bulbs still hadn't come down, and the little colored lights flickered off the white walls and the window glass. I felt we could call a locksmith, change the locks, and start a new life together.

"I'll always remember this morning," Tasha said quietly. "It was perfect. I'll never forget it."

These moments of hers embarrassed me. She'd said the

same thing about a couple of notes I'd written her, which she'd memorized and recited for me, and about the night we raced for the train. It seemed too much to talk that way, to act as though we'd remember these events years later, that they'd continue to live in us and to matter. When the phone rang, I was relieved to break the moment.

"Greg," said the voice in the receiver, "this is Tasha's mother. I know she's there. Put her on the phone."

"God!" Tasha said, when she'd hung up. "Be that way! I can't believe her."

"You didn't tell her you were coming over?"

"Why should I ever tell her anything? She's just going to say no."

WHEN TASHA WAS grounded, as she often was, my only chance to see her was at rehearsals for *Anything Goes*—song rehearsals, dance rehearsals, acting rehearsals, they seemed to go on endlessly. The musical director was Eunice, the same Eunice I'd ridden to day camp with years ago. At Hunter I'd avoided her. She walked through the halls hunkered down, as though she wished she could pull her head turtle-style into the baggy shell of her clothes. Most of us treated her as though she brought her awkwardness and isolation on herself, as though she looked and acted the way she did purely out of spite.

Still, Eunice was useful. Alarmingly eager to please, she kept track of other people's messages for cast members they cared about, a virtual secretary at a piano. Sometimes when I came into the theater she would tip her turtle head, still playing, to point me in the direction Tasha had gone. When Tasha was busy and Eunice was free, she wanted to talk.

"You can pick Tasha out of any singing group," she told me. "It's that timbre, that look. There's nothing hidden about her. Nothing ashamed."

One afternoon, as I stood by the piano bench watching Tasha rehearse, Eunice said, "You really like her."

"Yes!" I said, surprised, grateful. From Eunice, it didn't seem like an accusation.

"You're in love with her," she said. She smiled hard, eyes slits, and checked her square, black digital watch. "Well," she said, "who isn't?"

I turned to stare at her, but she'd stood up, resting her muscled hands on the battered black piano.

"All right, people!" she yelled. She was met with scattered groans and curses, as though all the long effort of putting on a musical was her fault. We'd switched places, I realized, since we'd competed for the love of Ann Horowitz. She was the outsider now, the one who had to watch and wait and plot, dreaming of lukewarm tolerance.

MY MOTHER MET Tasha only once. She cooked us dinner, but she barely gave Tasha a second look. Most of the meal she spent talking about her new job in marketing, and asking me about my classes. About Tasha she said only one thing, when she called me privately into the kitchen: "Let's just not get anybody pregnant."

The next time I saw my mother, she told me that there had been nothing about my father, no flaw or threat, that wasn't obvious before they were married. She just hadn't been willing to read the signs, she said. I didn't know why she would tell me this now, but I had a feeling. With him, she ought to have known better—after all, he'd been raised in the Dark Ages. It was my betrayals, my painted younger girlfriend, my cruel absences that were the shocks. I'd broken the divorce agreement and chosen to live with my father, and now that I was gone, Amanda was following me, splitting her time between them, leaving my mother alone every other week in the apartment she had kept unchanged for our sakes. I was the one who had gutted her family.

•   •   •

"YOU WILL NOT believe what Eunice did at the cast preparty," Tasha told me. "You will not *believe* it."

We were standing just outside of school, the cold February wind slipping into our big wool overcoats.

"That girl took over the bedroom. The *master bedroom*. With her girlfriend."

"She has a girlfriend? A *girlfriend* girlfriend?"

"I'd have to say she does now!"

"Whoa," I said. "I feel so dumb. I mean, I didn't—"

"Now you do!" Tasha said. "Now everyone does." She laughed and took my gloved hand in hers. The cast was rehearsing a number that Bonnie, Tasha's character, wasn't in. We walked past the scaffolded construction site on Ninety-fourth Street, and turned down Madison.

"I can't believe Eunice," Tasha said. "She just went ahead and *did* it. Some of the guys will barely speak to her."

"You don't sound very upset," I said.

Tasha lifted my arm and put it over her shoulders. In the wind, her hair fluttered against my face.

"I want you to talk to me now," she said. "I want you to talk to me about sex."

"You do?"

"Is there somewhere we could sit?" she asked.

The Sweet Suite had gone out of business, and I didn't know where else to go. I led us to a bench on the street in front of a children's bookstore. My mother had been a salesclerk there during one rough patch after an "impossible" male boss had fired her.

"I told my dad that you liked James Bond," Tasha said, wrapping her green coat around her and pressing beside me for warmth. "He wanted to know, Connery, Lazenby, or Moore."

"Oh, please."

"I told him. Then he asked, the movies or the Fleming books."

"Come on, the books."

"That's what I told him!" Tasha said. "You know, I think he approves."

I gave her a look.

"No, really, I think he does. If it weren't for my mom, I don't think he'd mind me . . . you know."

I started to tell her again that she didn't have to talk this way, that I really hadn't been impatient or angry when she'd said she was scared, that there was no need to rush.

"I'm not scared anymore," she said. Her breath felt warm in my ear. The wind turned it cold.

"You don't have to say that."

"Really, I'm not," she said. "I think it would be nice. I think it would be nice with you."

An empty yellow taxi was passing. Tasha laughed and kissed my earlobe.

A thought flashed through my mind, faster than I could stop it. *I'm a fucking genius.* All this time, telling her there was no rush for sex, that she didn't have to do anything she didn't want to, acting like such a nice guy, caring, sensitive, reasonable. But what strategy! She was practically eating out of my hand.

"I trust you," she said. "Don't you trust me?"

"Of course I trust *you*," I said. Maybe, I thought, there was only one thing on my mind after all, and the rest was cover, deep enough to fool even me. A gender double agent—out of the world's two billion Don Juans, merely one of the more thorough liars. Who knew what I would do, given the chance?

"This is a whole conversation," I said, pushing her away from me, standing up. She grabbed the iron arm of the bench to keep from falling. "And you need to get back to rehearsal. You're probably late already."

"Why do you sound like my mom?" she asked.

I steered her back to school, talking nonstop—how few days there were left to study for each midterm; whether the Barron's book was actually good preparation for the SAT's. Tasha stared.

"Will you think about what I told you?" she asked.

"I think about everything you tell me."

"Oh, fine. Fine. Be that way."

Tasha walked back toward the doors of the redbrick school building, boot heels knocking on the cold cement. Alone, I walked among the bare trees of wind-whipped Central Park, my arms flexed like a weight lifter's, bare hands fisted for warmth in the holey pockets of my coat. This must be nerves, I told myself. A virgin's jitters. I found some protection from the wind in the hills and trees of the Ramble, but there the sound of my footsteps grew loud. I passed a tilted lamppost with a smashed lamp, realized I'd passed it before, maybe more than once. My head pounded, and I told myself I should go home, but I kept walking. *She trusted me.* What kind of fool was she?

Around a shadowed twist of the concrete path I heard a sound like a barked laugh. I thought of my father, and I began to imagine that he was off ahead of me, in the deepening shadows. It felt safe to stay out in the night, to refuse to come home. Out in the cold, I wasn't going to do any harm. I clenched my teeth to keep them from chattering, stiffened my arms so I wouldn't shiver. This was my trick. I could refuse. Hours after I finally let myself into my father's apartment, my head still pounded and my red hands burned and itched.

IN THE NEAR dark, I picked up the phone and dialed a number I hadn't tried in weeks.

"Aaron," I said.

"Greg," he answered. No pause. He never seemed to be in the middle of something. It was as though the chance for good conversation was more important than anything—food, sleep, schoolwork certainly. He was always ready, if you had something interesting to say. That was my favorite thing about him.

"Everyone is so pissed about you and that sophomore," Aaron said. "I think it's great."

"It doesn't feel so great," I said. "I feel like some kind of outcast."

"Look," he said. "The girls are just jealous. So what? You've got a chance with a really sexy sophomore. Who cares what anybody thinks?"

"How am I supposed to figure out what *I* think if I don't have anyone to talk to? Tasha's mom won't even let her use the *phone* these days."

"Fuck it!" he said. "You sound so *guilty.*"

In his impatience I heard a rallying cry. Why shouldn't we be Don Juans if the sophomores were willing? I sat on my bed with the receiver hard in my ear, listening to his protest-singer voice as he told me how unconcerned he'd be. But I felt no thrill. *Not this,* I thought.

"I'm just not sure what to do," I said.

"Do whatever you want! The girls had their own private little Judy Chicago hen party, whatever that was. . . . Just do whatever the hell you want."

For a moment, I thought I could see me his way, a nice Jewish boy from hyperliberal Greenwich Village, who made a federal case out of nothing because he carried a bone for some redhead.

"When Bob Dylan went electric," Aaron intoned, as one of our great-grandfathers might have invoked Torah, "he didn't care what the folkies thought. Even when he came out with a new single, if a friend didn't like it, game over. End of friendship. You can't worry about what anyone else says or thinks. Just do what you want."

Off the phone, I still heard it in my head. *Just do what you want.* Tasha had said almost the same thing. *Won't you tell me what you want?* Just to remember her saying it got me going.

In a small brown bag behind a row of paperbacks by my bed, I had a box of three condoms. My father had explained the options to me, sheepskin or latex, lubricated or dry, the function of the reservoir tip. About the equipment he'd been patient, encouraging, enthusiastic, as he'd been back when the girls we talked about were only hypothetical. After our talk, riding a wave of grinning confidence, I'd bought myself the little box, feeling more proud than embarrassed as I waited in line for the cash register. But as I paid the pharmacist, the wave broke. At home I'd stuck the box in its hiding place.

Now I dug it out again, pulled out a crinkly square packet,

tore it open. I'd never seen one except in a gutter. The smell was something between garage and hospital, and the color was dull, lifeless yellow. I thought I'd practice, so at least this part wouldn't be new. I rolled it on, damp and clammy like the inside of a slicker when you sweat.

Tell me what you want. Tasha's breathy voice, her hair falling across her face. I lay on my side on my narrow bed. My penis felt foreign in my hand, plastic-wrapped, and mixed in with desire I felt a kind of hopelessness. Tasha was nowhere near, and I was afraid I knew exactly what I wanted: to pin her hands above her head, to tie her to the bed and fuck her, for hours, for days, until the police came for the missing person. I jerked off alone now, as though I'd already lost her, trying to fill my mind with Tasha in twins, Tasha in triplets, Tashas coming off an assembly line like redheaded Outerborough Barbies. The fantasies escalated like an argument—was this what I wanted? To tie her down so she couldn't refuse me, to break her legs so she couldn't run away? How bad would it have to get? My own private prison camp?

Yank on my dick and you could find all this. It was all strung through me, the valentines tangled with the horror movies. I didn't know how to sort it out, didn't know where one left off and another began. It wasn't even sexy anymore—I was still pumping my hand on my softening dick, but it wasn't doing anything for me. I pulled the condom off by the tip, and it snapped like a rubber band. I wadded it in tissues, climbed down off my bed, leaving myself with the inner jitter of unsatisfaction, and medicine smells on my fingers—latex and chemical ointment, not really garage. Hospital.

WEEKEND NIGHTS, I held out until the last minute, waiting to see if Tasha would get permission to come into the city. When my plans fell through, I came out into the living room, crestfallen, to see if I could tag along with my father and Ronna. They went to the movies and to romantic dessert spots—gelato and cookies at snobby Sant Ambroeus, gleaming pots of hot chocolate at Rumpelmayer's, truffles from the chocolatier at the Plaza Hotel. My father and Ronna seemed to like having me along, to get to be a family out together. Sometimes I'd hang out with them at home and watch a movie on TV, or we'd talk about kids at school, or their coworkers.

"This guy comes into my office," Ronna said one night. "I see him every day, right? He comes in and he says, 'Hey, Ronna! Have you heard about this new douche, S-S-Y?' And I look at him, and I say why no, now that you mention it, I have not. And he says, 'It takes the pee-yew! out of pussy!' "

She looked from me to my father. He was shaking his head, lips pursed tight, though how much out of disapproval and how much to keep from laughing, I couldn't tell.

"He's a colleague of mine, right? We work together. Why doesn't he just say, 'Hey, Ronna? Guess what? I hate women! I can't even stand the smell of them!' "

Again she looked from my father to me. We had no explanations.

I was feeling so cut off from my friends that I told my father and Ronna almost everything. I repeated the things Tasha's mother said she wanted from her—that she attend school, get her homework done. I told them her parents might be calming down, getting used to the idea of me—when Tasha had told her mother about the hours the cast had wasted at the weekend-long technical run-through for *Anything Goes*, her mother had said, "You could have been off somewhere with Greg." It seemed a new sign of her taking us seriously as a couple.

"You can't be worrying about Tasha's mother and Tasha's father and all these other people and factors," he told me. "You have to play your own side of the net."

We were sitting at the round table in front of clear glass bowls. Ronna was scooping out chocolate chocolate chip Häagen-Dazs.

"What net?" I asked.

"The tennis net," Ronna explained.

My father had been captain of his high school tennis team,

but he'd never talked about it. I'd only found out about it recently.

"You hit Tasha your best serve," he said, "and after that it's up to her. She has to return it. You can't go running over to her side of the net and hitting it back for her."

I thought about this.

"What kind of game would that be?" my father asked.

"*Mmmmm*," Ronna said to her ice cream.

"But it's not a competitive sport," I said.

"Tennis is not a competitive sport?"

Ronna giggled, then covered her mouth.

"*Love*," I said, encouraged.

My father glared at Ronna beside him at the little table. When the blood left his face, he looked almost yellow. The short black brush of his mustache bristled beneath his nose.

"A relationship isn't a competitive sport!" I went on. "I mean, what am I trying to do, beat her?"

Ronna looked from me to him to her chocolate-smudged bowl.

"Now look," my father said to me. "These parents can say anything they want, but they will never, never be civilized about this. Never."

He leaned back in his chair and threw his hands up between us, so his palms faced out, showing the shiny scar from when he'd smashed open the apple juice bottle. I'd never felt certain what this palms-out gesture meant. No tricks up his sleeves? Back off or he'd shove?

"I'm helping you," he told me. "If you're saying you don't want my help, if you're saying you can cut out all this moping and waiting around for us to cheer you up and dragging your little cloud around the apartment *without* my help—"

"Jimmy, stop . . . ," Ronna said softly.

"—then cut it out."

I could have yelled at him then, like any normal teenager. I could have screamed, smacked the table, slammed doors. Once, my father tore the seat off the toilet and threw it into the bathtub—I knew how these things were done. I could have screamed that he was being a coward and a bully, that he was useless to me now, worse than useless.

I sat at the round table with my father and his future wife, making the third point in the triangle of our would-be family. I kept my eyes on the grain of the wood in the table. I swallowed hard. I finished my ice cream.

ALONE AGAIN IN the locker-lined hall, cutting class. Trying to calm myself down. Tom standing with his fingers in the front pockets of his corduroys, tapping one boat shoe on the tiled floor, nodding his head to the rhythm of mental music.

I said his name like a greeting, and he jerked his foxlike head backward in cool acknowledgment. I walked up to him, put my fingers in my front pockets.

"You still with that redhead?" he asked.

"Tasha," I said.

"That's her given name?" Tom blurted, and then turned away, showing me his profile as he fought a smile. He made a show of getting himself under control.

"Yeah. . . ."

"She's from, like, Long Island somewhere?"

"Queens," I said. Tom knew as well as I did that Hunter only took kids from the five boroughs. There wasn't anyone from Long Island.

"So our girl's a New Yorker," he said. "Technically."

"What the hell's that supposed to mean?"

"It doesn't mean anything," he said. "It doesn't mean anything at all. I'm just trying to get everything straight."

Tom loved this pose, I knew, the Only Sane Guy in a Crazy World, too classy even to complain. He was loving this little chat, eating it up. The other Click guys had given him such a hard time about Amy, about the way he talked about her, as though he only wanted her for how hot she was. But my redhead wasn't even our age, had no obvious legitimizing virtues. She was just some perfume-and-eye-shadow girl from nowhere, a pretty wanna-be with a porn-star name.

Tom fixed his dark eyes on me. I started to walk away.

"She's a good-looking girl," he said suddenly. I could feel his manner soften, hear the cold relish melt from his voice. "I mean, I wouldn't know, but she seems like she likes you, and she's good-looking enough. . . ."

His voice had turned approving, brotherly.

"We don't talk anymore," Tom said. "Why don't we talk? You should come over some time."

Gratitude rose up in me, hot in the corners of my eyes. I grinned, ashamed.

"Call me sometime," Tom said, ambling down the hall away from me. "The number's the same. She can't keep you busy *every* night of the week, right?"

This is how he'd felt to me when we'd been closer— brusquely charming, as though we were two men of the world. A shared understanding. We'd talked on the phone, and once in the direst time after my parents separated, he'd come to din- ner with my father and me and acted as though everything— the lousy little apartment, the dirt-cheap Chinese food, the desperate way we kept making jokes—was okay.

Now he seemed ready to take me back. We could talk about girls, he'd seemed to promise. We could brag and lie and laugh. First, I suspected, there would be certain things I'd need to say. I'd show him I hadn't really minded the way he'd talked about Amy, that I'd only been faking outrage, seeming to go along with the girls and their attitude just to get on their good side. We'd steal some of his parents' liquor and stay up late.

And all I had to do was declare the truth. Was that so hard? A clean confession, that I'd always known what really mat- tered in a girl: looks, pleasing habits, compliance. There were no moral questions here, no politics—hell, we were just guys, young guys, *kids in a candy store*. All of that wrong think- ing was just a phase I'd gone through, a childish mistake to outgrow.

Tom never asked me to say any of these things. Yet I imag- ined that precisely by knowing without being told, I could prove I'd finally come to my senses. Crazy, maybe, but I could picture a floodlight sharp in my eyes, and stark on a table in front of me a microphone and a prepared statement, to be read and signed for the TV camera. My public confession. I'd renounce my traitorous ways, wash clean my wrong thoughts. And Tom would come unlock the door and let me out of solitary.

"TALK TO ME about sex," Tasha wrote in a note.

I didn't respond.

She wrote again a couple weeks later, when her parents let her out for Durba Ghosh's birthday party. I stalled.

When I sidestepped the issue, Tasha didn't push, didn't get upset. She acted as trusting as the Click girls were full of doubt. I knew this trust was supposed to be a dream come true, but I was waiting for her to get angry, to remind me that she was a person too, a full person with needs. Once, when we were fooling around, I leaned down without thinking and planted a kiss on the front of her panties. The curly hairs underneath the soft satin felt springy against my lips. Tasha froze. I don't even think she breathed. We stayed like that for what seemed a long time, my face above her parted white thighs, and I thought to myself that after her blow jobs, I owed her. It was possible she had orgasms when we fooled around—I wasn't sure, I got so lost in feeling—but even so, it was unfair. I had that thought, and then I went back to kissing her face, and we pretended I'd never had the other impulse.

Sometimes after she went down on me, I made up excuses for not reciprocating.

It would spoil it to be even-steven.

It would only embarrass her.

I didn't know how—guys I knew didn't talk about it, and there was no mango scene in *Fast Times at Ridgemont High*.

She never asked.

Instead of objecting, she told me about her favorite Italian restaurant, on Minetta Lane, where she'd thought for a long time that she'd like to go with a boyfriend, a special boyfriend, after a special night.

But though Tasha didn't complain, her life grew thick with obstacles. *Anything Goes* went up, and her church show after it, but as the weeks passed getting time alone grew more complicated, not less. She never said I'd disappointed her, only that her parents had made plans. One week she said her parents had changed their minds about letting her out. The next week, when I pushed her to get permission early, she told me she'd already asked, then revealed the night before our date that she hadn't. She wouldn't give me reasons, or take any more of my advice. On the phone she sounded distant, resigned. We made dates every weekend, but when I called to pin her to a time, or to make sure she had her parents' permission, she'd say offhandedly that she couldn't go.

Until now I'd always talked out my relationships with other girls, friends. But the Click girls were out. My neighbor Anne was always ready to come over after aerobics and tell me what great boyfriend material I was, how Tasha didn't appreciate me, but Tasha had beaten her out for a lead in *Anything Goes*, and I worried she was looking for revenge. At the Model United Nations weekend, I stopped by Susie's hotel room and told her that the relationship was complicated. She lifted her skirt to pull up her panty hose and asked if I wanted to fool around. I fled. Kerry and Wendy, my makeup-crew friends, liked to quiz me on my views about serious relationships, but by definition that ruled Tasha out. I was so naive, they told me. No one could be serious about Tasha— just *look* at her.

My last chance, I thought, was Amanda. But she was busy being the caring, responsible child my mother had failed to raise in me, and I was ashamed to burden her more.

THROUGH MY PARENTS' separation, their divorce, the hidden panics about money, Granny Fran's death, the frustration of schoolbooks and clean clothes misplaced in two different apartments, and my estrangement from my mother, I'd kept my A average. Now I couldn't work. When I thought I would get time alone with Tasha, I panicked, my mind wild like the day I wandered Central Park in the wind and cold. When she canceled, I raged in my head. Sometimes I couldn't even concentrate enough to rant in my journal.

In physics, the trouble was vectors. Hapless objects were launched with a clear goal, then blocked and blindsided, made to fight gravity and wind resistance, pushed in three or four directions at once; they never arrived where they were aimed. I'd start to work on a problem and then it was gone from my mind, and I had to read the question again. And again. On one unit test, while Mr. Guarracino stood with one foot out the classroom door, Jonathan, Tasha's director, reached over with his pen and changed a few of my multiple choice answers.

"What are you doing?" I whispered, appalled and relieved.

The curls hanging down to his eyebrows swayed as he shook his head. "No lab partner of mine is going to get those wrong," he said.

"Those were all wrong?"

"Don't worry." He laughed. "I'm only fixing the really dumb mistakes."

MY FATHER SAID it was time for an ultimatum. This relationship with Tasha was too stressful for me, he said, and he wanted me happy again for his wedding in May. Either she made a plan for a weekend night date and kept it, or I should break up with her. Ronna agreed. Harold, the butcher at Nevada Meats, agreed. Even my mother said it was a good idea.

I was hoping for different advice from my guitar teacher, Ken. I was like him at my age, he liked to tell me. Serious about my axe, my practicing. But he hadn't taken himself seriously enough, he said. He'd given up playing in college, and wasted five good years of building his chops. It all counted, he said. It didn't matter what age you were.

I told him I didn't know what to do about Tasha.

"Do you have fun?" he asked.

"Yeah—I mean, sometimes. We did, but it's complicated now."

"It shouldn't be complicated," Ken said. "At your age, you shouldn't be doing anything with her but having fun. When it's no fun, it's time for the next girl."

I listened to the buzzing from the amplifier. Music was something to be serious about, like your schoolwork and your work for money. But it seemed it was different with girls.

"Got that?" Ken joked. I didn't smile, and he looked away. I had the feeling that he was holding back laughter, and I thought I knew what was funny. Me. The overserious kid. Seriousness was a man's suit I wore all wrong, flopping around in it like playing dress-up.

"This ought to be a great time for you," he said. "You're almost seventeen, right? Next year, senior in high school . . . You're gonna feel like a kid in a candy store."

I CALLED TASHA and told her to get back to me that night with a day and a time she would keep, or consider us broken up.

"You just can't go on this way," I told her.

"You sound like my *mother*," she said.

"Maybe your mother is right."

"Oh, fine," she said. "Fine."

"So you'll call me back tonight?"

"I'll call you," she said.

It was a Saturday, and I stayed home waiting, playing "Something in the Way She Moves" on the guitar, not even using the phone, just to be sure. In the morning I told my father and Ronna it was over. They praised my courage, and sang a duet chorus of "Breaking Up Is Hard to Do," standing with their coffee and their white bag of croissants and sticky buns, warbling the harmony in morning voices.

Later Ronna took me aside and said there was something

she needed to talk to me about. She didn't mean to embarrass me, she said, but she thought it was important.

"Now that you're on your own, I think you should start masturbating."

I didn't answer.

"It's something you could do in the shower in the morning," she explained, as though it was a logistical question. I was afraid for a moment she might offer to describe the mechanics.

"You have to be careful of backed-up sperm," she went on, speeding nervously through my silence.

I looked at her.

"Half the violence in New York City is due to backed-up sperm."

She laughed as though this was a joke. I laughed as though I shared it. I wondered who in the world she thought she was talking to, what world it could be, and how I'd gotten myself marooned there.

That evening, sitting with my physics problem set, feeling empty and hopeless and totally unable to concentrate, I got a call from Tasha. She'd talked to her parents, she said. She was going to work on "straightening out her life" and taking responsibility for her schoolwork. Her parents had agreed to trust her when she was out of the house.

F O R   O U R   D A T E , I picked a restaurant where my parents had taken me when they were still together, a cozy, narrow room with a collection of carved elephants on the wall. No matter how long it had been since we'd had private time together, once we got a few minutes to talk, everything I felt for her came rushing back. My mother's apartment was waiting for us, empty while she was at a sales conference.

After dinner, we fooled around and talked and fooled around again, working each other down to one piece of underwear. The lamp with the railroad-train shade gave a straw yellow light.

"It could feel like this," Tasha said. We lay on our sides,

moving against each other. The old springs of my childhood bed creaked in protest.

"This feels. Really. Really good," I said.

"I mean *it*," Tasha murmured. "It could feel just like this. The two of us together." She took my bicep in her warm hand, and looked into my eyes as though she could look straight into me. All that kept our bodies apart were wisps of fabric and inexperience, and I could feel how ready these things were to be lost. I heard the clicking of the baseboard heater.

"Just like this, only more," she said.

It was the *more* that scared me. Even if I didn't bungle the moves too badly, shoot off in two seconds like they said, she would still look into me, know me—not just the nice guy, patient when she cried, but the whole frustrated mess. At least with a blow job, my body was her blindfold. I didn't want to take that blindfold off her, didn't want her to see inside.

And yet, at the same time, I did. I wanted her to look straight into my eyes, in through the slit in the prison door. I wanted her to see it all, and to like what she saw, what we could make of it. Maybe, I felt, she already did.

Tasha lay beside me, not even pulling the sheet around to hide herself. *She trusted me.* In her last note she'd written, "You are my religion."

She lifted her hand toward me, hesitated, pushed a strand of hair out of her face.

"What is it?" she asked. "What's wrong?"

For a moment, I'd believed a man could be trusted this far, and no harm done. But who believed that? Just hoping it, I could almost hear the laughter. Up within me welled a rage. How could she be so dumb? *Why did she tempt me?*

"Won't you tell me what you want?" she asked.

"Go down on me," I said.

"What?"

"You heard me. I want you to go down on me."

"Now?"

"Yes, of course now."

She hesitated, cast her eyes down. Slowly she bent over, her falling hair hiding her face. She didn't tell me that what I said I wanted was wrong for her now, that I was hurting her. She only slid down my unhairy chest, and as she did I found I could despise her a little. I leaned back on the bed, then propped myself up on my elbows, to look down at her on her knees.

After she swallowed, I heard her sniffling. I caught my breath, eyes still closed, and smiled to myself, drawing out the moment, imagining laughing about this with an invented guy friend. What is it about girls? I imagined saying. How it's like your dick gets all the way in their heads, up in their sinuses or something—the weird noises they make? I laughed with the guy in my head, and felt the mattress shift as Tasha sat up. On her face I saw the shiny streaks of tears. She stumbled out of bed, her feet thumping hard on the wooden floor. She steadied herself for a moment against the tall bookshelf, then half ran, half fell to the bathroom.

Soon I'd feel what had happened was simple. It does not seem simple to me now, but then it seemed perfectly clear. Tasha had glimpsed the hidden part of me after all, the part most hidden and most true. Now we could end this charade.

ON MY OWN again, "single," I found I could do the things that other people—teachers, parents, friends—asked me to do, with only a feeling of sluggishness. I could maintain myself as far as feeding and hygiene went. I could even flirt. But when I had time to myself, my will vanished. There was nothing in me to do. I played records I didn't really hear, ate to keep from having to feel hungry. Tasha called now and then, sent me notes. I was the one who made sure she was never alone with me again. Refusing to inflict myself on her anymore made me proud.

Tasha chopped off her hair at the neck. She painted her fingernails black and filed them to points. From across the brick courtyard at lunch I watched her, puncturing empty soda cans with her bare white hands.

.   .   .

A SATURDAY AFTERNOON in late spring, a warm cheerful day I was avoiding by procrastinating on a paper for
Modern Drama. Tasha telephoned. On the line I heard street
noise—cars droning by, chatter of passing conversations.
    "Where are you?" I said.
    "Here," she said. "Downstairs. I was just in the neighbor-
hood."
    I pulled the receiver to the window and tried to see the
phone booth at the corner of Columbus, but the angle was impossible. The sun was bright on the cars and the people in the
wide street.
    "I don't see you," I said.
    My father walked out of his bedroom and shuffled loudly
through a pile of junk mail. He had teased me, back when
Tasha and I were together, for having a different phone voice
with her than with anyone else.
    "Can you come down?" she asked.
    "I don't know if that's such a good idea."
    She didn't answer.
    "Maybe another time," I said, and then nonsensically, "I'm
sorry you had to come all this way."
    I wondered whose officious little voice had just spoken. The
phone was at my ear like a seashell, and in it I heard a great
churning ocean of human life, far away. I felt a proud, momen-
tary thrill, as though I'd forced back tears and no one suspected.
    "I think I'd better go," Tasha said. The last word faded into
street noise as she hurried the receiver to the hook. I listened to
the dial tone.
    The old casement window had an iron latch. I swiveled the
window open, leaned out over the wide street. Tasha was
gone. I hung out the window as though roped in place. My
mother was out of sight, to the west and downtown, and my
father was the one behind me now, waiting for me to join him.
    "Is she there?" he asked. "Did she see you?"

Epilogue

■ ▮ ■

I HATE THE WAY that story ends. For years I hated it so much I refused it. Into my twenties, when I visited New York and walked through Penn Station, I still imagined that any minute Tasha would appear from out of the crowd, laughing at my surprise, ready to pick up where we'd left off.

My dark moods returned, often just as I settled into a new relationship. They came and went for years, checking up on me like prison guards. At worst, I felt drawn to convenient nearby threats—oncoming trucks and trains, roofs one might fall off almost without trying. But I didn't want to die: I didn't want to want anything. Wanting—to be a man, wanting— seemed exactly the problem. There were days a hard-on in my pants disgusted me.

I told myself my story in the worst possible way, that I'd grown up in a failed experiment, that our dreams of equality set to rock and roll had made us no more than freaks, that all I'd gained playing catch with my mother was this crippling confusion. At times I could almost believe it would be best to go back to the old ways of men and women, the ways I'd barely known before they exploded. There seemed nothing left from the wreck of our new life but a dusty record collection, some outdated books and clothes, and these stories.

TWO MONTHS BEFORE I turned thirty, I got engaged. When I told my sister I was getting married, she said, "No, you're not." My college roommate had recorded a song about his nonbelief in matrimony; he said, "I can't believe you're doing this to me." Now the supposed gender traitor had a fiancée with a diamond ring, an appointment to talk with a rabbi, an old-fashioned engagement, long and hectic with planning. Thads, who'd known me since Hunter, said, "Well, this is something. *Greg Lichtenberg* getting married"—as though it might only be a rumor, as though I wasn't standing right next to him. A friend in Los Angeles kept me on the phone for two hours, insisting he wouldn't come to the wedding until I'd explained why marriage was necessary.

It was all so *traditional*, my mother objected, and as I heard that word from others, as well, I began to imagine one of my ancestors, some severe, responsible forefather in a black coat and hat, watching me. I felt his eyes when Meredith and I were planning our wedding, sitting in T-shirts and shorts on a sidewalk bench. He might have recognized these old Greenwich Village streets, but not this unkempt couple, out for breakfast, unshowered on a Sunday morning, tossing ideas back and forth, laughing, drafting versions of marriage vows on the back of a used envelope. In the heat of the August morning we passed the pen between us, working from notes about traditional marriage contracts and recently jotted-down hunches. I felt the old man glare as I listened to this outspoken, outgoing, unchaste woman I so loved, this woman who in a few weeks would put on a suit, lift a briefcase, and go to her office while her husband stayed home to do his work. She was a skeptic in many ways, attuned to tactics and angles, but in the matter of our vows she was as sincere as any five-year-old. We read aloud to each other, improvising for our times around lines from the Bible, rearranging, blending, imagining choices beyond the cruelties of tradition and the shortsightedness of rebellion.

Only after revolution could this seem *traditional*.

When we'd read the drafts aloud and made all our changes, I put my arms around Mer. She pulled close, and her kisses tasted like iced coffee. Maybe every young couple in love thinks they have the answers their parents lacked, but it wasn't answers I felt we had—only something like a habit, a particular way of listening to each other.

AT THE START of a traditional Jewish wedding ceremony, the bride walks seven circles around the groom, to show that from now on her world revolves around him. Of all the wedding rituals Mer and I had seen or read about, we hated this one most. Our mothers and grandmothers before them had refused it, and hardly anyone at our wedding could have remembered the last time a bride in our families had performed that ritual.

And yet, at the start of our ceremony, in the crowded, hushed room, Mer stepped in slow, careful circles around me, the knocking of her heels on the floor muffled by her rustling white dress. The circles she made were for protection and care, which we agreed were worth not giving up—but they meant more to me than that. I wanted the old ritual. I wanted her world to revolve around me. It was a dangerous desire, but I had no interest anymore in an equality that kept my wife at a safe distance, off in her own cold corner of space while I hung righteously alone in mine.

I no longer believed that the highest form of responsibility was self-restraint. It seemed possible there was good to be made from all of our desires, that we could imagine a life as satisfying as it was just. After Mer walked her circles around me, I walked my circles around her, to show our two worlds revolving around each other—swinging past, double-time, I imagined, to a backbeat you couldn't lose. I stepped around the lace train of her dress, and looked up to see my father and stepmother standing together, my mother with the good man in her life, Mer's beaming parents, our sisters, friends, the room full of people who apparently did not think we had lost our integrity or our minds. Out the windows stretched Manhattan, long streets below, tall buildings gathered near, helicopters crossing in the air above. As I completed my last circle, Mer took my arm, and we stepped onto the platform to begin.

Acknowledgments

■ ▌ ■

I would like to express my gratitude to the late James Michener and the Copernicus Society of America for support during the writing of this book.

I would also like to acknowledge several individuals whose contributions went beyond professionalism. Beth Vesel recognized early what I was up to, and stuck by the project straight through. Toni Burbank thoroughly disproved the current doomsaying about editors. Robin Michaelson also provided insight and support.

A number of people provided valuable readings of chapters in progress. These include: Peter Bergman, Michael Gabriel Farella, Yance Ford, Amanda Lichtenberg, Jennifer Litt, Susan Lohafer, Will Provost, Karen Schlossberg, and Jane Shapiro. Particular thanks go to Amity Gaige, Erik Huber, Lowry Pei, and Emilie White, for their extensive responses. Finally, my wife, Mer, critiqued drafts at every stage, for which I am especially grateful.

My father and mother each provided me with copies of their

freelance writings and related correspondence from the time of my early childhood. These materials and our various conversations helped me to place my childhood memories on an adult time line. I must stress however that this is a work of my memory, and that memoirists navigate by the light of questions no one knew how to ask at the time.